D0258850

the THIRD edition

New Headway

Intermediate
Student's Book

Liz and John Soars

OXFORD
UNIVERSITY PRESS

CONTENTS

LANGUAGE INPUT

SKILLS DEVELOPMENT

READING	SPEAKING	LISTENING	WRITING p102
'Wonders of the modern world' – amazing technological and scientific achievements p10	Information gap – a UN Goodwill Ambassador p9 Discussion – what's the most important invention? p12	My wonders – three generations give their ideas about the wonders of the modern world p12	Correcting mistakes (1) – finding and correcting language mistakes in an informal letter p103
'The clown doctor' – a woman describes the job she loves p18	Discussion – what makes people happy? p14	Sports – three people talk about their free time activities p21	Letters and emails p104
'The painter and the writer' – the lives of Pablo Picasso and Ernest Hemingway (jigsaw) p26	Information gap – 'An amazing thing happened!' p25 Describing a book or a film you like p28	Books and films – people talk about their favourite books and films p28	A narrative (1) p106
'A world guide to good manners' – how to behave abroad p34	Talking about rules and regulations p32 Roleplay – starting a new job p33 Discussion – what advice would you give a foreign visitor? p34	Come round to my place! – entertaining friends in three different countries p36	For and against p108
'My kind of holiday' – a travel agent talks about her holidays p42	Arranging to meet p41 Discussion – your ideal holiday p42	A weather forecast p44	Making a reservation p109
'Global pizza' – the history of the world's favourite food p50	Talking about popular food and popular places to eat p50 Discussion – restaurants, cities and people you know p52	New York and London – An English couple talks about living in New York; an American gives his impressions of living in London (jigsaw) p52	A description (1) p110

LANGUAGE INPUT

SKILLS DEVELOPMENT

1 It's a wonderful world!

Tenses · Auxiliary verbs · Short answers · What's in a word? · Social expressions

TEST YOUR GRAMMAR

1 Make questions with *you* from the sentences.

1 I come from Scotland. *(Where?)*

> *Where do you come from?*

2 I was born in London in 1984. *(Where? When?)*
3 I live in Milan. *(Where?)*
4 I've got two brothers and a sister. *(How many?)*
5 I'm studying English because I need it for my job. *(Why?)*
6 I've been studying English for three years. *(How long?)*
7 I've been to the United States, Canada, Japan, and Australia. *(Which countries?)*
8 I went to Canada three years ago. *(When?)*

2 Ask and answer the questions with a partner.

> *Where do you come from?*

> *From Mexico.*

> *Where were you born?*

> *In Puebla, a city near Mexico City.*

3 Tell the class about your partner.

Enrique comes from Mexico. He was born in Puebla in 1985, but now he lives in Mexico City.

WHAT DO YOU KNOW?

Tenses and auxiliary verbs

1 Answer the questions in the quiz.

T 1.1 Listen and check.

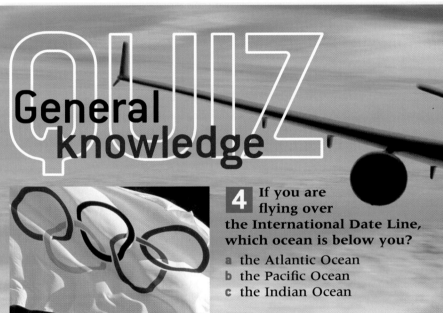

QUIZ

General knowledge

1 When did the modern Olympic Games start?

a 1806 b 1896 c 1922

2 How long does it take for the sun's rays to reach the Earth?

a 8 minutes
b 8 hours
c 8 days

3 What was Neil Armstrong doing when he said in 1969, 'That's one small step for a man, one giant leap for mankind'?

4 If you are flying over the International Date Line, which ocean is below you?

a the Atlantic Ocean
b the Pacific Ocean
c the Indian Ocean

5 What doesn't a vegetarian eat?

6 What does www. stand for?

7 Where were glasses invented?

a Mexico
b Italy
c China

8 How many times has Brazil won the World Cup?

GRAMMAR SPOT

1 Which questions in the quiz contain the following tenses?

Present Simple	Past Simple	Present Perfect Simple
Present Continuous	Past Continuous	Present Perfect Continuous
Present Simple passive	Past Simple passive	

2 Which tenses use the auxiliary verbs *do/does/did* to make the negative and question?
Which tenses use the auxiliary verb *have*?
Which tenses use the auxiliary verb *be*?

▶▶ **Grammar Reference 1.1–1.3 pp134–135**

2 In groups, write some general knowledge questions. Ask the other groups.

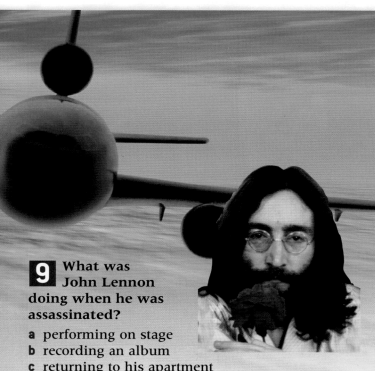

9 **What was John Lennon doing when he was assassinated?**

a performing on stage
b recording an album
c returning to his apartment

10 **Which language is spoken by the most people in the world?**

a Spanish b Chinese c English

11 **Why didn't Nelson Mandela become President of South Africa until he was 76 years old?**

12 **How long have people been sending emails?**

a since the 1960s
b since the 1970s
c since the 1990s

PRACTICE

Negatives and pronunciation

1 Correct the information in the sentences.

1 The sun rises in the west.
2 Cows eat meat.
3 Mercedes-Benz cars are made in Canada.
4 Neil Armstrong landed on the moon in 1989.
5 John Lennon was performing on stage when he was assassinated.
6 The Pyramids were built by the Chinese.
7 We've been in class for five hours.
8 We're studying Italian.

> *The sun doesn't rise in the west! It rises in the east!*

T 1.2 Listen and compare. Notice the stress and intonation. Practise saying the sentences.

Talking about you

2 Complete the questions.

1 **A** What _____ do last night?
  B I stayed at home and watched television.
2 **A** What kind of books _____ like reading?
  B Horror stories and science fiction.
3 **A** _____ ever been to the United States?
  B Yes, I have. I went there last year.
  A _____ like it?
  B Yes, I really enjoyed it.
4 **A** What _____ the teacher _____?
  B He's helping Maria with this exercise.
5 **A** _____ your mother do?
  B She works in a bank.
6 **A** Why _____ do your homework last night?
  B Because I didn't feel well.
7 **A** What _____ doing next weekend?
  B I'm going to a party.
8 **A** _____ you _____ a TV in your bedroom?
  B No, I haven't. Just a CD player.

T 1.3 Listen and check. With a partner, ask and answer the questions about you.

is or *has*?

3 **T 1.4** Listen to the sentences. They all contain *'s*. Write *is* or *has*.

1 _is_	3 _____	5 _____	7 _____
2 _____	4 _____	6 _____	8 _____

MAKING CONVERSATION
Short answers

1 `T 1.5` Listen to the breakfast conversation. How does Emma feel?

Dad Good morning! Did you have a nice time last night?
Emma Yes.
Dad Do you want breakfast?
Emma No.
Dad Have you had any coffee?
Emma Yes.
Dad Is Bill coming round tonight?
Emma No.
Dad OK. Are you leaving for school soon?
Emma Yes. Bye!

2 `T 1.6` Listen to a similar conversation. What are the differences?

3 Complete the conversation.

Dad Good morning! Did you have a nice time last night?
Emma Yes, _____. I went round to Bill's house.
Dad Do you want breakfast?
Emma No, _____, thanks. I'm not hungry.
Dad Have you had any coffee?
Emma Yes, _____. I don't want any more, thanks.
Dad Is Bill coming round tonight?
Emma No, _____. He's going out for dinner with his family.
Dad OK. Are you leaving for school soon?
Emma Yes, _____. I'm going right now. Bye!

`T 1.6` Listen again and check.

4 Close your books. Try to remember the conversation.

GRAMMAR SPOT

1 We use short answers in English conversation because *yes* or *no* on its own can sound impolite. It helps if you can add some information.

> *Did you watch the match last night?*

> *Yes, I did. It was great!*

2 Reply to these questions using a short answer. Add some information.

Do you like cooking?   **No, I don't. But I like eating!**
Have you got any brothers or sisters?
Is it cold out today?
Are you working hard?
Did you go out last night?
Have you ever been to Singapore?

 **Grammar Reference 1.4 p135**

5 `T 1.7` Listen to the questions. Answer using a short answer, and add some information.

PRACTICE

Conversations

1 Match a question in **A** with a short answer in **B** and a line in **C**.

	A	B	C
1	Do you like studying English?	No, I haven't.	It's freezing.
2	Is it a nice day today?	Yes, I am.	It's my favourite subject.
3	Have you seen my pen?	Yes, I do.	I couldn't afford to.
4	Are you staying at home this evening?	No, I didn't.	Do you want to come round?
5	Did you go on holiday last summer?	No, it isn't.	You can borrow mine if you want.

T 1.8 Listen and check. Practise the conversations with a partner.

2 Read the class survey and add two questions of your own. Stand up! Ask three students the questions and complete the chart. Remember to add some information in your reply.

Class Survey

		S1	S2	S3
1	Have you got a computer at home?	○	○	○
2	Are you going out tonight?	○	○	○
3	Do you play a musical instrument?	○	○	○
4	Did you watch TV last night?	○	○	○
5	Have you seen any good films lately?	○	○	○
6	Are you going to have a coffee after the lesson?	○	○	○
7	_____	○	○	○
8	_____	○	○	○

Getting information

3 The United Nations invites celebrities from all over the world to be Goodwill Ambassadors. Work with a partner. You each have different information about Kaori Sato, who works for the UN. Ask and answer questions.

Student A Look at p151.
Student B Look at p152.

1 Match each topic in **A** with two items in **B**.

A	B
International travel	solar system
	airlines
Medical science	competition
	online
The Internet	corn
	health care
Agriculture	drug abuse
	penicillin
Space travel	famine
	galaxies
The Olympic Games	abroad
	website

2 Read the text about the wonders of the world. Write a topic from **A** in the paragraph headings 1–6.

3 Answer the questions.
1 What has changed because of the Internet? What will happen with the Internet?
2 What has happened in space exploration since 1969?
3 What is the most noticeable result of better health care?
4 **✗** = the number of people who travelled abroad in the nineteenth century. What does **✗** also equal?
5 What are the good and bad things about the Olympics?
6 What point was Jonathan Swift making about farmers and politicians?
7 'We are still here!' Why is this a wonder?
8 What do these numbers refer to?

100 million	a few hundred	1969		
millions of people	47	four	1709	50

Talking about you

4 In groups, discuss one of these questions.
- What are your favourite websites?
- When did you last travel by plane? Where were you going?
- Are there any stories about health care in the news at the moment?
- What sporting events are taking place now or in the near future?

WONDERS OF

I don't believe **that today's wonders are similar in kind to the wonders of the Ancient World. They were all buildings, such as the Pyramids in Egypt, or other architectural structures. Over the past 100 years, we have seen amazing technological and scientific achievements. These are surely our modern wonders.**

1

It is everywhere. More than half a billion people use it, and the number of people who are online increases by 100 million every year. In 1994 there were only a few hundred web pages. Today there are billions.

It has revolutionized the way we live and work. But we are still in the early days. Soon there will be more and more interactivity between the user and the website, and we will be able to give instructions using speech.

2

In 1969, Neil Armstrong stepped out of his space capsule onto the surface of the moon and made his famous statement: 'That's one small step for a man, one giant leap for mankind'. Since then, there have been space probes to Mars, Jupiter, Saturn, and even to the sun. One day, a space observatory will study how the first stars and galaxies began.

So far, it seems that we are alone in the universe. There are no signs yet that there is intelligent life outside our own solar system. But who knows what the future holds?

THE MODERN WORLD

by
Ann
Halliday

3

Surely nothing has done more for the comfort and happiness of the human race than the advances in health care! How many millions of people have benefited from the humble aspirin? How many lives has penicillin saved? Average life expectancy worldwide has risen dramatically over the past 100 years, from about 47 years in 1900 to about 77 years today.

4

We are a world on the move. Airlines carry more than 1.5 billion people to their destinations every year. It is estimated that, at any one time these days, there are as many people travelling in aeroplanes as the total number of people who travelled abroad in the whole of the nineteenth century (but I have no idea how they worked this out!).

5

It is true that they are now commercialized, and there is greed and drug abuse. However, it is a competition in which almost every country in the world takes part. Every four years, for a brief moment, we see the world come together in peace and friendship. We feel hope again for the future of mankind.

6

In 1724, Jonathan Swift wrote, 'Whoever makes two blades of grass or two ears of corn grow where only one grew before serves mankind better than the whole race of politicians'. In Europe our farmers have done this. In 1709, whole villages in France died of hunger. Now in Europe, we can't eat all the food we produce. If only politicians could find a way to share it with those parts of the world where there is famine.

7 We are still here!

The last wonder of the modern world is simply that we are still here. We have had nuclear weapons for over 50 years that could destroy the world, but we haven't used them to do it. This is surely the greatest wonder of all.

LISTENING AND SPEAKING
My wonders

1 **T 1.9** Listen to three people from the same family saying what they think are the wonders of the modern world. Complete the chart.

Sam
Kelly
Peter

	What is the wonder?	What's good about it?	Are there any problems?
Sam	*dishwasher*		
Kelly			
Peter			

2 Work with a partner. Which of these inventions do you think is the most important? Mark them ☐1 for the most important to ☐8 for the least important.

☐ the computer   ☐ nuclear weapons
☐ the car   ☐ the space rocket
☐ the television   ☐ the mobile phone
☐ the aeroplane   ☐ the space satellite

3 Work in groups of four. Work together to agree on the three most important inventions. Which has changed the world the most?

4 Talk together as a class. What other machines, inventions, or discoveries would you add to the list?

VOCABULARY
What's in a word?

These exercises will help you with your vocabulary learning.

Parts of speech and meaning

1 These sentences all contain the nonsense word *uggy*. Is *uggy* used as a verb, an adjective, a noun, or an adverb? How do you know?

  1 I couldn't hear the film because the man next to me was eating his *uggy* so loudly.
  2 There was a lot of snow on the road. Unfortunately, I *uggied* on some ice and crashed into a tree.
  3 When Pierre and Madeleine met, they fell *uggily* in love and got married one month later.
  4 After an *uggy* day at work, with meetings and phone calls all day, I was ready for a quiet evening.

Can you guess what *uggy* means in the four sentences?

Which real English word goes in each sentence?

• passionately   • skidded   • hectic   • popcorn

Spelling and pronunciation

2 In these groups three words rhyme, but one is different. Work with a partner and read them aloud. <u>Underline</u> the word in each group which has a different vowel sound.

▶▶ **Phonetic symbols p159**

1 /ʊ/ or /uː/?   good   food   wood   stood
2 /iː/ or /e/?   bread   head   read (*present*)   read (*past*)
3 /eɪ/ or /e/?   paid   made   played   said
4 /ʌ/ or /əʊ/?   done   phone   sun   won
5 /eə/ or /ɪə/?   dear   hear   bear   near
6 /ɜː/ or /ɔː/?   work   fork   walk   pork

T 1.10 Listen and check. What do you notice about English spelling?

3 Here are some of the words from exercise 2 in phonetic symbols. Read them aloud, then write them.

1 /fuːd/ _____   5 /riːd/ _____
2 /nɪə/ _____   6 /wɜːk/ _____
3 /stʊd/ _____   7 /fəʊn/ _____
4 /peɪd/ _____   8 /wɔːk/ _____

T 1.11 Listen and check.

Word formation

4 Write different forms of the word *act* using the suffixes from the box.

-or	-ion	-ing	-ive	-ivities

1 My brother's an act_____.
   He's making an advert now.
2 My grandmother is 89, but she's
   still very act_____ .
3 This is not a time to do nothing.
   It is a time for act_____.
4 Act_____ is not usually a
   well-paid job.
5 We do a lot of act_____ in class to
   learn English.

Words that go together

5 Match a word in **A** with a word in **B**.

A	B
strong	carefully
full-time	**coffee**
film	in love
drive	**a jumper**
fall	**star**
try on	job

Keeping vocabulary records

6 Do you have a vocabulary notebook?
Discuss with your teacher and other
students how you record new
vocabulary. Which of these do you use?

- the translation
- the part of speech (verb, noun, etc.)
- the meaning (using other words)
- the pronunciation
- an example sentence

hectic (adj) /ˈhektɪk/ = very busy
   I had a hectic day at the office.

WRITING: Correcting mistakes (1)
▶▶ Go to p103

EVERYDAY ENGLISH
Social expressions

1 When we're talking with friends we use a lot of idiomatic expressions.

Hurry up, we're late.

*Hang on a sec!
I need to go the loo!*

Match a line in **A** with a line in **B**.

A	B
1 Sorry I'm late. I got stuck in traffic.	That sounds like a good idea. The break will do you good.
2 Bye, Mum! I'm off to school now.	So am I. I can't stand all this rain.
3 Have you heard that Jenny's going out with Pete?	Never mind. You're here now. Come in and sit down.
4 How long did it take you to do the homework?	Ages! How about you?
5 I don't know about you, but I'm sick and tired of this weather.	Yes, it cost a fortune!
6 Who was that I saw you with last night?	Really? I don't know what she sees in him!
7 I'm tired. I'm taking next week off.	I'm sorry. I can't make it then. What about a bit later?
8 Let's go for a run in the park!	Take care, my love. Have a nice day!
9 Can we get together this afternoon at 3.00?	Me? Run? You must be joking!
10 What a gorgeous coat! Was it expensive?	Mind your own business!

T 1.12 Listen and check. Practise the conversations with a partner.

2 **T 1.13** Listen to the sentences. Reply using a line from **B** in exercise 1. Make any necessary changes.

3 Choose some of the conversations from exercise 1 and continue them.

A What a gorgeous coat! Was it expensive?
B Yes, it cost a fortune. But the material's beautiful, don't you think?
A Wow! Where did you get it?
B I saw it in the window of that new shop in the High Street, you know, it's called 'Chic'.
A Yes, I know it. They have some really nice stuff.

Get happy!

Present tenses · Simple or continuous? · Passive · Sport · Numbers and dates

TEST YOUR GRAMMAR

Look at the pairs of sentences.
Which one is correct? Why?

1 They have a teenage son.
They're having a teenage son.

2 She speaks five languages.
She's speaking five languages.

3 Don't turn off the TV! I watch it.
Don't turn off the TV! I'm watching it.

4 Oh no! It rains.
Oh no! It's raining.

5 We're thinking opera is boring.
We think opera is boring.

6 English speaks all over the world.
English is spoken all over the world.

WHAT MAKES PEOPLE HAPPY?
Present tenses

1 Look at the ingredients for happiness. How important is each one
to you? **1** = very important; **5** = not important.

☐ good health in mind and body   ☐ a big house
☐ job satisfaction   ☐ regular holidays
☐ a loving marriage   ☐ a supportive family
☐ hobbies and leisure activities   ☐ lots of friends
☐ no money worries

Compare your answers with a partner.

2 What do you think is the happiest time of a person's life –
when they are young or when they are old? Why?

3 **T 2.1** Read and listen to the text about Sidney Fisk. Answer the questions.

1 What do you think are the good and bad things about Sidney's life?
2 Do you think his life is exciting or boring? Would you like to have a life like Sidney's?
3 Do you know any people with similar lives? Are they happy?

'I don't know if I'm happy.'

Sidney Fisk, 45

Work

Sidney Fisk is a lawyer. He's paid very well, but he usually has to work long hours. He works for an international company in Dallas, Texas, so he travels a lot in his job. At the moment he's working in Mexico, and next week he's travelling to France.

Home life

Sidney is married and he's got two children, aged 11 and 14. He rarely sees his children because so much of his time is spent away from home. He's got a beautiful house in a suburb of Dallas. It's very big, with eight bedrooms. His wife is an interior designer.

Free time

If he's at home at the weekend, he and his wife sometimes play golf, but that doesn't happen very often. They never have much time to relax together.

Is he happy?

He says he doesn't know if he's happy. He's too busy to think about it.

GRAMMAR SPOT

1 Find these words in the text about Sidney Fisk: *usually, often, rarely, never.* What kind of words are they?

2 What tense are most of the verbs in the text? Why?

3 Find two examples each in the text of the Present Continuous and the Present Simple passive. Which auxiliary verb is used to form these?

4 Complete the questions and answers with the correct auxiliary verbs.

   a _____ he travel a lot?   Yes, he _____.
   b _____ she work in a bank?   No, she _____.
   c _____ they play golf?   Yes, they _____.
   d _____ you play tennis?   No, I _____.
   e _____ he paid a lot?   Yes, he _____.
   f _____ he working in France at the moment?   No, he _____.

▶▶ **Grammar Reference 2.1 and 2.2 pp135–136**

4 Complete the questions about Sidney. Then ask and answer them with a partner.

- . . . married?
- What . . . do?
- Where . . . live?
- Has . . . any children?
- What . . . his wife do?
- Which sports . . . play?
- Where . . . working at the moment?
- . . . paid very well?

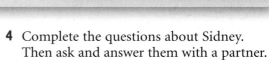

Is he married?

Yes, he is.

T 2.2 Listen and check.

5 Ask and answer similar questions with your partner.

Are you married?

No, I'm not.

Have you got any brothers or sisters?

PRACTICE

Listening and speaking

1 **T 2.3** Look at the photos and listen to Jeff Norman. What's unusual about his lifestyle? What does he like about it?

Extra! Extra! Read all about it! 45-year-old college graduate makes $60,000 a year as a paperboy!

JEFF NORMAN from Iowa City, Iowa

---

2 What did Jeff say? Complete the sentences.

1 I __'m__ __paid__ good money – $60,000 a year. And I often _____ $50 a week in tips.

2 I _____ _____ at 2.00 a.m. The first newspaper _____ _____ at 2.30 a.m.

3 I _____ a red Chevy Blazer and the newspapers _____ _____ into the back.

4 I _____ the peace and quiet.

5 Occasionally, I _____ a jogger.

6 I usually _____ _____ home by 7.00 a.m.

7 My wife _____ at the University of Iowa.

8 Some days I _____ my kids' baseball team, other days I _____ golf.

9 I _____ also _____ for my master's degree at the moment. I _____ _____ be a marriage counsellor.

10 Some people _____ it's not much of a job, but, hey, when they _____ _____ in an office, I _____ _____ golf.

T 2.4 Listen and check.

3 Write notes about Sidney and Jeff in the chart.

	Sidney Fisk	Jeff Norman
Work		
Home and family		
Free time		

Work with a partner. Compare Sidney's life with Jeff's. How old are they? How many things do they have in common? Who do you think is happier? Why?

WHAT DO YOU DO?
Simple or continuous?

1 **T 2.5** Read and listen to the conversation.

A What do you do?
B I'm an interior designer. I decorate people's homes and give them ideas for furniture and lighting.
A And what are you working on these days?
B Well, I'm not working on a home at the moment. I'm working on a hotel. I'm designing a new lobby for the Plaza.
A Do you like your job?
B Yes, I love it.

Memorize the conversation and practise it with a partner.

2 Work with a partner. Have similar conversations with some of these jobs.

an architect	a research scientist	an artist	an actor
a rock musician	a web page designer	a journalist	
a film director	a football player	a zookeeper	

3 Ask each other about your own jobs or studies.

GRAMMAR SPOT

1 Some verbs are used in both simple and continuous forms. These are called **action verbs**.

She usually **drives** to work, but today she **isn't driving**. She's **walking**.

2 Some verbs are almost never used in the continuous form. These are called **state verbs**.

I **like** black coffee. (NOT ~~I'm liking~~ black coffee.)

3 Seven of these verbs are *not* usually used in the Present Continuous. Underline them.

like	know	understand	work	enjoy	think (= opinion)
come	play	have (= possession)		love	want

▶▶ **Grammar Reference 2.3 p136**

PRACTICE
Discussing grammar

1 Are these sentences correct (✓) or incorrect (✗)? Correct the mistakes.

1 What do you want to drink? ✓
2 I'm not understanding this word. ✗
   I don't understand this word.
3 I'm loving you a lot.
4 Do you think Michiko plays golf well?
5 I'm sorry. I'm not knowing the answer.
6 We're enjoying the lesson very much. We're working hard.
7 I'm thinking you speak English very well.
8 The lions are fed once a day. They're being fed at the moment.

2 Complete the pairs of sentences using the verb in the Present Simple or the Present Continuous.

1 come
   Alec and Marie are French. They _____ from Paris.
   They'll be here very soon. They _____ by car.

2 have
   Lisa can't come to the phone. She _____ dinner now.
   She _____ a beautiful new car.

3 think
   I _____ that all politicians tell lies.
   I _____ about my girlfriend at the moment. She's in Australia.

4 not enjoy
   We _____ this party at all. The music is too loud.
   We _____ big parties.

5 watch
   Be quiet! I _____ my favourite programme.
   I always _____ it on Thursday evenings.

6 see
   Joe isn't here. He _____ the doctor at the moment.
   I _____ your problem, but I can't help you. I'm sorry.

7 use (Careful!)
   This room _____ usually _____ for big meetings.
   But today it _____ being _____ for a party.

READING AND SPEAKING
I'm a clown doctor!

1 What does a doctor do? What does a clown do? Write down three things for each. Tell the class your ideas.

2 Which of these things did you think of? Which do clowns do? Which do doctors do? Which do both do?

wear funny clothes	wear white coats
make children feel better	do magic tricks
perform operations	give injections
wear red rubber noses	make funny faces
tell jokes	give medicine

3 Look at the pictures. Lucy Cheetham is a clown doctor working for *Theodora Children's Trust* – a charitable organization. What do you think a clown doctor does?

4 Read the introduction. What is the new kind of medicine?

5 Read the rest of the article. Answer the questions.
   1 Who is Dr LooLoo? Who is Dr Chequers?
   2 In what ways is their job 'extremely silly'? Give examples.
   3 How did Lucy become a Theodora clown doctor?
   4 Why does she like her job?
   5 What does she wear?
   6 What would be useless?
   7 Why is it useful to eat in the hospital cafeteria?
   8 What does she do after work?
   9 Where does the money for Lucy's salary come from?
   10 Describe a typical working day for Lucy.

   She arrives in the hospital with …
   Then she goes into the wards and …

GRAMMAR SPOT

1 Complete these sentences from the text.
   All over the world, children in hospital _____ _____ _____ with a new kind of medicine.
   It's a charity; so we _____ _____ with the money people give.
   What tenses are they?

2 Complete these passive sentences.
   1 People of all ages love clowns.
      Clowns _____ _____ by people of all ages.
   2 He is giving her an injection.
      She's _____ given an injection.

▶▶ **Grammar Reference 2.4 p137**

THE CLOWN DOCTOR

All over the world, children in hospital are being treated with a new kind of medicine: laughter. LUCY is 23 and works for *Theodora Children's Trust*. She is one of many clown doctors who bring a smile to the faces of sick children.

"I'm a Theodora clown doctor, I call myself Dr LooLoo. I spend two days a week in children's hospitals being extremely silly with my friend and colleague Dr Chequers. We make funny faces, tell jokes, and do magic tricks. As I walk into the wards I blow bubbles, shake hands with the kids, and make up nonsense songs for those children well enough to sing. We take special balloons to make 'balloon animals' and tell funny stories about them. We often meet kids who one week look really sick, then we go back the next week and they're racing about yelling 'Hi there, Dr LooLoo! Hi Dr Chequers!'

I'm naturally a very cheerful person. I've always been a clown. In fact my father's a clown and I started working with him when I was eight years old. I knew it was just the job for me and I became a clown doctor because I think it's a great way to cheer up sick, frightened children in hospital. I wear a fancy coat, a yellow shirt, and tights with big stripes. Also, I have a red rubber nose and wear my hair in crazy plaits.

Being a clown in a hospital is very tiring both physically and emotionally. We have to learn not to show our feelings, otherwise we'd be useless. Clown doctors are sensitive but this is not a side most people see. To the children we're happy all the time. I'm still learning to allow myself to feel sad occasionally. There are special kids you get really close to. At the

moment I'm working with a very sick little girl from Bosnia who speaks no English, so our only common language is laughter. She's been in and out of hospital for operations so many times and she's always on my mind.

At lunchtime we eat in the hospital cafeteria and that's really useful because we meet the nurses and doctors. They tell us about particular kids who they think will benefit from a clown doctor visit. If a child is frightened, perhaps they're being given an injection or some nasty medicine – we can distract them so the nurses can do their job.

About six o'clock Dr Chequers and I take off our make-up and change our clothes. We're totally exhausted. Sometimes I have a night out with friends, it helps me unwind. When I finally fall into bed, I crash out. At weekends we are often asked to participate in events to raise money for *Theodora Children's Trust*. It's a charity; so we are paid with the money people give. Being a clown doctor makes the worries of everyday life seem small. All in all, I feel privileged to do this job.

Language work

6 Find lines in the text which mean the same as the following.

1. They're running about shouting.
2. I have a happy personality.
3. We would be no help at all.
4. I'm always thinking about her.
5. I go out for the evening with friends.
6. It helps me relax.
7. I go to bed and immediately fall into a deep sleep.
8. I am lucky to have this job.

7 Read the interview with Lucy (L). Complete the interviewer's (I) questions.

I _____ ?

L Oh yes, I do. I enjoy my job very much.

I _____ ?

L Because I love working with children and making them laugh.

I _____ ?

L I wear crazy clothes. A fancy coat and stripy tights.

I _____ ?

L Well, at the moment I'm working with a very sick little girl from Bosnia. She's had so many operations. She's very special to me.

I _____ ?

L No, she doesn't. We communicate through laughter.

I _____ ?

L Yes, it is. It's very tiring indeed. I'm exhausted at the end of each day.

I _____ ?

L No, I don't. I often go out with friends. I have the best friends and the best job in the world.

T 2.6 Listen and compare your answers. Are your questions exactly the same? What are the differences?

What do you think?

Discuss the questions in groups.

- What are some of the good and bad points about being a clown doctor?
- What kind of jobs make people happiest?
- When are you happiest? At work? At home? With friends?
- What were your happiest times last year?
- It's often said 'laughter is the best medicine'. Do you agree?

VOCABULARY AND LISTENING
Sport and leisure

1 Make a list of as many sports and leisure activities as you can think of. Use the pictures to help you.

2 Write *play*, *go*, or *do*.

_____ snowboarding _____ aerobics _____ volleyball _____ fishing _____ golf

_____ jogging _____ basketball _____ football _____ yoga _____ mountain biking

3 Choose some of the sports or leisure activities from your list and complete the chart. Use a dictionary to look up any new words that you need.

Sport / Activity	People	Place	Equipment and clothes
go snowboarding	snowboarder	ski resort / dry ski slope	snowboard / boots / helmet / goggles / waterproof jacket and trousers

4 **T 2.7** Listen to three people talking about a sport or activity they enjoy and take notes.

	Mary	Jenny	Thomas
Which sport / activity are they talking about?			
How often do they do it?			
Where do they do it?			
What equipment and clothes do they need?			
Are they good at it?			

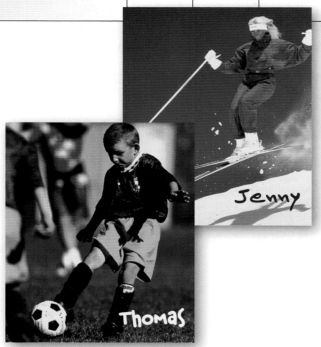

5 Ask and answer questions with a partner.
- What sports do you play?
- How often . . . ?
- Where . . . ?
- What equipment . . . ?
- Are you good at . . . ?

WRITING: Letters and emails
▶▶ Go to p104

EVERYDAY ENGLISH
Numbers and dates

1 Say the numbers.

15 50 **406** 72 128

90 **19** **850** 36 1,520

247 **5,000** 100,000 **2,000,000**

T 2.8 Listen and practise.

2 Say the numbers.

Money
£400 **50p** €9.40 €47.99 ¥5,000 **$100**

Fractions
¼ ¾ ⅔ ⅞ **12½**

Decimals and percentages
6.2 17.25 50% **75.7%** 100%

Dates
1995 **2020** 1789 **15/7/94** 30/10/02

Phone numbers
01865-556890 **800 451-7545** 919 677-1303

T 2.9 Listen and practise.

3 **T 2.10** Listen to the conversations. Write the numbers you hear.

1 ___fifteenth___ _____
2 _____ _____
3 _____ _____
  ▯▯▯▯ ▯▯▯▯ ▯▯▯▯ ▯▯▯▯
4 _____ _____
5 _____

Discuss what each number refers to with a partner.
The 15th is a date.

4 Work with a partner. Write five numbers that are important in your life and explain why.

3 Telling tales

Past tenses · Passive · Art and literature · Giving opinions

TEST YOUR GRAMMAR

Match the sentences and pictures.

1 When Carol arrived home, Mark cooked dinner.
2 When Carol arrived home, Mark was cooking dinner.
3 When Carol arrived home, Mark had cooked dinner.

What is the difference in meaning?

a

b

c

A NATIVE AMERICAN FOLK TALE
Past tenses

1 Look at the pictures. They tell the story of Gluskap, a warrior from the Algonquian tribe of North America. What can you see? What do you think the story is about?

2 Read the story on p23 and the phrases below. Complete the story with the phrases.
   a had run a few miles
   b had fought and won so many battles
   c was still screaming
   d had never heard such a terrible noise
   e was sitting and sucking a piece of sugar
   f had never heard of Wasis

   T 3.1 Listen and check. What do you think is the moral of the story?

GRAMMAR SPOT

1 Which tense is used in these two sentences? Which verbs are regular? Which are irregular?

He **laughed** and **went** up to the baby.
He **danced** and **sang**.

Find more examples in the story and <u>underline</u> them.

2 What are the tenses in these sentences? What is the difference in meaning?

He **laughed** when he **saw** the baby.
He **was laughing** when he **saw** the baby.
He **laughed** when he**'d seen** the baby. (he'd = he had)

3 Find two examples of the Past Simple passive in the story.

▶▶ **Grammar Reference 3.1–3.4 pp137–139**

Pronunciation

3 Work with a partner. Write the verbs from the box in the chart according to the pronunciation of the -ed ending.

~~laughed~~	covered	wanted	stopped	shouted	listened
opened	boasted	looked	danced	screamed	pointed

/t/	/d/	/ɪd/
laughed		

T 3.2 Listen, check, and practise.

THE TALE OF GLUSKAP AND THE BABY

Gluskap the warrior was very pleased with himself because he (1)___. He boasted to a woman friend: 'Nobody can beat me!'

'Really?' said the woman. 'I know someone who can beat you. His name is Wasis.' Gluskap (2)___. He immediately wanted to meet him and fight him. So he was taken to the woman's village. The woman pointed to a baby who (3)___ on the floor of a teepee.

'There,' she said. 'That is Wasis. He is little, but he is very strong.' Gluskap laughed and went up to the baby. 'I am Gluskap. Fight me!' he shouted. Little Wasis looked at him for a moment, then he opened his mouth. 'Waaah! Waaah!' he screamed. Gluskap (4)___. He danced a war dance and sang some war songs. Wasis screamed louder. 'Waaah! Waaah! Waaah!' Gluskap covered his ears and ran out of the teepee. After he (5)___, he stopped and listened. The baby (6)___. Gluskap the fearless was terrified. He ran on and was never seen again in the woman's village.

PRACTICE

What was she doing?

1 Judy works for MicroSmart Computers in London. Read about what she did yesterday.

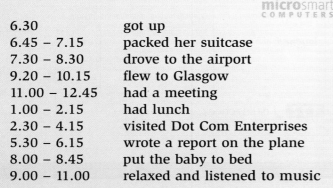

6.30	got up
6.45 – 7.15	packed her suitcase
7.30 – 8.30	drove to the airport
9.20 – 10.15	flew to Glasgow
11.00 – 12.45	had a meeting
1.00 – 2.15	had lunch
2.30 – 4.15	visited Dot Com Enterprises
5.30 – 6.15	wrote a report on the plane
8.00 – 8.45	put the baby to bed
9.00 – 11.00	relaxed and listened to music

2 Work with a partner. Ask and answer questions about what Judy was doing at these times.

7.00 a.m.	8.00 a.m.	10.00 a.m.	11.30 a.m.	
1.30 p.m.	3.00 p.m.	6.00 p.m.	8.30 p.m.	10.00 p.m.

T 3.3 Listen and check.

> *What was she doing at 7 o'clock yesterday morning?*

> *She was packing her suitcase.*

3 Write a similar list about what you did yesterday. Ask and answer questions with your partner.

> *What were you doing at 7 o'clock yesterday morning?*

> *I was having a shower.*

Had you heard it before?

4 Work with a partner.

Student A Read a statement from your box.
Student B Answer with the correct response from your box.

STUDENT A
1 I didn't laugh at his joke.
2 Were you surprised by the ending of the film?
3 I went to the airport, but I couldn't get on the plane.
4 I was homesick the whole time I was living in France.
5 The hotel where we stayed on holiday was awful!
6 I met my girlfriend's parents for the first time last Sunday.
7 My grandfather had two sons from his first marriage.

STUDENT B
Why? Had you left your passport at home?
Why? Had you heard it before?
That's a pity. Hadn't you stayed there before?
Really? I didn't know he'd been married before.
Really? I thought you'd met them before.
No, I'd read the book, so I already knew the story.
That's really sad! Had you never lived abroad before?

T 3.4 Listen and check, then listen and repeat.

5 Choose two of the conversations and continue them.

> *I didn't laugh at his joke.*

> *Why? Had you heard it before?*

> *No, I hadn't. I just didn't think it was very funny, that's all.*

> *Really? I thought it was hilarious!*

An amazing thing happened!

6 Wanda and Roy had an amazing story to tell about their holiday. Work with a partner.
Student A Look at p151.
Student B Look at p152.

7 Wanda is telling a friend, Nicola, what happened. Work with a partner. One of you is Wanda and the other is Nicola. Continue their conversation.

> **N** Hi, Wanda. Did you have a good holiday?
> **W** Oh, yeah, we had a great time. But I have to tell you – the most *amazing* thing happened!
> **N** Really? What was that?
> **W** Well, Roy and I were at the beach …

T 3.5 Listen and compare.

Discussing grammar

8 Complete the sentences. Check your answers with a partner. Discuss the differences in meaning.

1 When I arrived at the barbecue, they _____ eating sausages.

When I arrived at the barbecue, they _____ eaten all the sausages.

2 We thanked our teacher for everything she _____ doing to help us pass the test.
We thanked our teacher for everything she _____ done to help us pass the test.

3 He told me that they _____ staying at the Carlton Hotel.

He told me that they _____ stayed at the Carlton Hotel before.

4 _____ you learn Italian when you went to Italy?
_____ you already learned Italian when you went to Italy?

5 _____ Shakespeare write *Hamlet*?
_____ *Hamlet* written by Shakespeare?

> **WRITING:** A narrative (1)
> ▶▶ Go to p106

VOCABULARY
Art and literature

1 Write these nouns in the correct column. Which noun goes in both columns?

> painter author poet poem sculpture novel
> picture brush palette chapter biography
> exhibition fairy tale portrait play art gallery
> masterpiece novelist sketch act

ART	LITERATURE

2 Which of these verbs can go with the nouns in exercise 1?

> read write paint draw go to

Read a poem, read a novel …

3 Complete the sentences.

1 Shakespeare _____ many famous _____ and poems.
2 I couldn't put the book down until I'd _____ the last _____.
3 I love _____ about the lives of famous people so I always buy _____.
4 _____ often begin with the words 'Once upon a time'.
5 My friend's a great artist. He _____ my _____ and it looked just like me.
6 He _____ a quick _____ of the trees.
7 We _____ an _____ of Picasso's paintings and sculptures.

READING AND SPEAKING
The painter and the writer

1 Who are or were the most famous painters and writers in your country?

2 You are going to read about the lives of Pablo Picasso and Ernest Hemingway. Discuss these questions.

- Why are they famous?
- What nationality were they?
- Which century were they born in?
- Do you know the names of any of their works?
- Do you know anything about their lives?

3 The sentences below appear in the texts. Try to guess which sentences go with which man. Write **P** (Picasso) or **H** (Hemingway).

1 ☐ His first word was *lápiz* (Spanish for *pencil*) and he could draw before he could talk.

2 ☐ He had wanted to become a soldier, but couldn't because he had poor eyesight.

3 ☐ His portraits of people were often made up of triangles and squares with their features in the wrong places.

4 ☐ In the 1930s, he became a war correspondent in the Spanish Civil War and World War II.

5 ☐ He was awarded the Nobel Prize for literature, but he was too ill to receive it in person.

6 ☐ At the age of 90 he was honoured by an exhibition in the Louvre in Paris.

4 Work in two groups.

Group A Read about Pablo Picasso.
Group B Read about Ernest Hemingway.

Check your answers to exercises 2 and 3.

PABLOPICASSO
The painter

HIS EARLY LIFE

On 25 October, 1881, a baby boy was born in Málaga, Spain. It was a difficult birth and to help him breathe, cigar smoke was blown into his nose! This baby grew up to be one of the twentieth century's greatest painters – **PABLO PICASSO**.

Picasso showed his genius from a very young age. His first word was *lápiz* (Spanish for *pencil*) and he could draw before he could talk. He was the only son in the family, so he was thoroughly spoiled. He hated school and often refused to go unless he was allowed to take one of his father's pet pigeons with him!

Apart from pigeons, his great love was art. When in 1891 his father got a job as an art teacher, Pablo went with him to work and watched him paint. Sometimes he was allowed to help. One evening, his father was painting a picture of their pigeons when he had to leave the room. When he returned, Pablo had completed the picture. It was so beautiful and lifelike that he gave his son his palette and brushes and never painted again. Pablo was just thirteen.

HIS LIFE AS AN ARTIST

His genius as an artist was soon recognized by many people, but others were shocked by his strange and powerful paintings. He is probably best known for his Cubist pictures. His portraits of people were often made up of triangles and squares with their features in the wrong places. One of his most famous portraits was of the American writer Gertrude Stein, who he met after he'd moved to Paris in 1904.

His work changed ideas about art around the world, and to millions of people, modern art means the work of Picasso. *Guernica* [below], which he painted in 1937, records the bombing of that small Basque town during the Spanish Civil War, and is undoubtedly one of the masterpieces of modern painting.

HIS FINAL YEARS

Picasso married twice and also had many mistresses. He had four children. The last, Paloma, was born in 1949 when he was 68 years old. At the age of 90 he was honoured by an exhibition in the Louvre in Paris. He was the first living artist to be shown there.

Picasso created over 6,000 paintings, drawings, and sculptures. Today, a Picasso costs millions of pounds. Once, when the French Minister of Culture was visiting Picasso, the artist accidentally spilled some paint on the Minister's trousers. Picasso apologized and wanted to pay for them to be cleaned, but the Minister said, 'Non! Please, Monsieur Picasso, just sign my trousers!'

Picasso died of heart failure during an attack of influenza in 1973.

Guernica

ERNESTHEMINGWAY
The writer

HIS EARLY LIFE

ERNEST HEMINGWAY was one of the great American writers of the twentieth century. He was born on 21 July 1899, in Oak Park, Illinois, the second of six children. His family was strict and very religious. His father taught his children a love of nature and the outdoor life. Ernest caught his first fish at the age of three, and was given a shotgun for his twelfth birthday. His mother taught him a love of music and art. At school, he was good at English and wrote for the school newspaper. He graduated in 1917, but he didn't go to college. He went to Kansas City and worked as a journalist for the *Star* newspaper. He learned a lot, but left after only six months to go to war.

HEMINGWAY AND WAR

Hemingway was fascinated by war. He had wanted to become a soldier, but couldn't because he had poor eyesight. Instead, in the First World War, he became an ambulance driver and was sent to Italy, where he was wounded in 1918. After the war, he went to live in Paris, where he was encouraged in his work by the American writer Gertrude Stein. In the 1930s, he became a war correspondent in the Spanish Civil War and World War II. Many of his books were about war. His most successful book, *For Whom the Bell Tolls*, was written in 1940 and is about the Spanish Civil War. Another novel, *A Farewell to Arms*, is about the futility of war.

HIS PERSONAL LIFE

Hemingway's success in writing was not mirrored by similar success in his personal life. He married four times. His first wife divorced him in 1927. He immediately married again and moved to Key West, Florida, where he enjoyed hunting, fishing, and drinking, but he also suffered from depression. This wasn't helped when, in 1928, his father committed suicide. Hemingway's health was not good and he had many accidents. Two more marriages failed and he began to drink heavily. In 1954, he survived two plane crashes. In October of the same year he was awarded the Nobel Prize for literature, but he was too ill to receive it in person.

HIS FINAL YEARS

His final years were taken up with health problems and alcohol. He began to lose his memory and he couldn't write any more. On Sunday, 2 July 1961, Hemingway killed himself with a shotgun, just as his father had done before him.

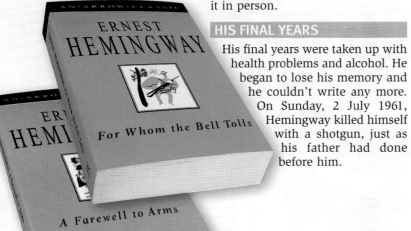

5 Answer the questions about your person.
   1 Where and when was he born? When and how did he die?
   2 Did he have a happy family life?
   3 How did his parents play a part in his career?
   4 What do you think were the most important events in his early life?
   5 When did he move to Paris? Who did he meet there?
   6 How did war play a part in his life?
   7 How many times was he married?
   8 Which of these dates relate to your person? What do they refer to?

1891	1917	1918	1927	1928
1937	1940	1949	1954	

6 Find a partner from the other group and go through the questions in exercise 5. What similarities and differences can you find between the two men?

They were both born in the nineteenth century. Picasso was spoiled, but Hemingway's parents were strict.

GRAMMAR SPOT

1 What tense are these verbs?
   Guernica **was painted** by Pablo Picasso.

   A Farewell to Arms and *For Whom the Bell Tolls* **were written** by Ernest Hemingway.

   Find more examples in the texts and underline them.

2 Complete the sentences with the auxiliaries *was*, *were*, or *had*.
   a Pablo's father left the room. When he returned, Pablo ____ completed the picture.
   b Picasso ____ given his father's palette and brushes.
   c Both Hemingway and Picasso ____ living in Paris when they met Gertrude Stein.
   d Both men ____ honoured in their lifetime.

▶▶ **Grammar Reference 3.5 p139**

LISTENING AND WRITING
Books and films

1 Work in groups. Do you have a favourite book or film? Why do you like it? Tell your group.

2 Look at the list of books and films. Which do you know? Which are both book *and* film?

- ☐ Dracula
- ☐ Frankenstein
- ☐ Spiderman
- ☐ Harry Potter and the Philosopher's Stone
- ☐ The Silence of the Lambs
- ☐ Titanic
- ☐ Captain Corelli's Mandolin
- ☐ The Godfather
- ☐ Star Wars
- ☐ The Lord of the Rings
- ☐ The Sun Also Rises

3 **T 3.6** Listen to four friends chatting about their favourite books and films. Tick (✓) the titles they mention in exercise 2. What do they say about them? Discuss with your group, then with the class.

4 Write some notes about a book or film that you know and like. Use these questions to help you. Discuss your notes with a partner.

- What's it called?
- Who wrote it?
- Who directed it?
- Who starred in it?
- Who are the main characters?
- Where does it take place?
- What's it about?
- Why do you like it?

5 Use your notes to write a paragraph about the book or film that you chose.

Vinnie

Maeve

Sue

Will

EVERYDAY ENGLISH
Giving opinions

1 What do the <u>underlined</u> words refer to in these sentences?

a <u>It</u> was really boring! I fell asleep during the first act.
a play

b I didn't like his first <u>one</u>, but I couldn't put his latest one down until the last page.

c <u>It</u> was excellent. Have you seen it yet? It stars Julia Kershaw and Antonio Bellini.

d <u>She</u>'s usually good, but I don't think she was right for this part.

e I think they spoil <u>them</u>. They always give them whatever they want.

f <u>It</u> was a nice break, but the weather wasn't very good.

g <u>They</u> were delicious. John had tomato and mozzarella and I had tuna and sweetcorn.

h <u>It</u> was really exciting, especially when David Stuart scored in the closing minutes.

2 Match questions 1–8 with the opinions in exercise 1.

1 Did you like the film? `c`
2 What did you think of the play? ☐
3 Did you like your pizzas? ☐
4 Do you like Malcolm Baker's novels? ☐
5 What do you think of their children? ☐
6 What was your holiday like? ☐
7 What did you think of Sally Cotter? ☐
8 What was the match like? ☐

T 3.7 Listen and check. Practise the questions and answers with a partner.

3 Write down some things you did, places you went to, and people you met last week. Work with a partner and ask for and give opinions about them.

I went to a party.

Really? What was it like?

Great! I really enjoyed it.

I met Maria's sister.

What did you think of her?

She's really nice. I liked her a lot.

4 Doing the right thing

Modal verbs 1 – obligation and permission • Nationality words • Requests and offers

 TEST YOUR GRAMMAR

Look at the sentences.

I	can should must have to	go.

1 Write the negatives.
2 Write the questions.
3 Write the third person singular.
4 Which verb is different?

I'm sorry, but I have to go now.

TEENAGERS AND PARENTS
have (got) to, can, and be allowed to

1 **T 4.1** Listen to Sarah and Lindsay, aged 14 and 15. What are some of the things they like and don't like about being a teenager?

2 Complete the sentences.

1 You _____ go to work.
2 You _____ pay bills.
3 You _____ go out with your friends.
4 I always _____ tell my mum and dad where I'm going.
5 What time _____ get back home?
6 You _____ buy whatever you want.
7 Adults _____ worry about paying the bills.
8 They _____ always do what they want.
9 We _____ bring mobile phones to class.
10 I _____ go. I _____ do my homework.

T 4.2 Listen and check. Practise saying the sentences.

3 Lindsay talks about her parents. What are some of the things they *have to* do and *don't have to* do?

Her mother has to ...

Her father ...

1 Which two sentences mean the same?

I	am allowed to can have to	stay at my friend's house tonight.

Which sentence expresses obligation? Which sentences express permission?

2 Complete the sentences with *have to* or *don't have to*.

Children _____ go to school.

Millionaires _____ work.

You _____ go to England if you want to learn English.

In England, you _____ drive on the left.

3 *Have got to* and *have to* both express obligation. *Have got to* refers to an obligation now or soon. It's often reduced to *gotta* /ˈɡɒtə/ when we speak, especially in American English.

I've got to go now. Bye!

▶▶ **Grammar Reference 4.1 p140**

PRACTICE

Discussing grammar

1 Put these sentences into the negative, the question, and the past.

1 Henry can swim.
   Henry can't swim.   Can Henry swim?   Henry could swim.
2 I have to wear a uniform.
3 She has to work hard.
4 He can do what he likes.
5 We're allowed to wear jeans.

Talking about you

2 Look at the chart. Make true sentences about you and your family.

I don't have to do the cooking.

A	B	C
I My parents My mother My father My sister My brother My grandparents My husband/wife	have to has to don't have to doesn't have to had to didn't have to	go to work. get up early. go shopping. clean my room. do the cooking. take out the rubbish. do the washing. do the washing-up.

Compare your sentences with a partner.

3 Complete the sentences with *'ve got to/'s got to* and a line from **C** in exercise 2.

1 Where's my briefcase? I _____.
2 Look at those dirty plates! We _____.
3 Pamela and Charles don't have any food in their house. They _____.
4 John needs to get an alarm clock. He _____ tomorrow.
5 I haven't got any clean socks. I _____.
6 The chef's ill, so the waiter _____.

T 4.3 Listen and check. Practise saying the sentences.

4 Work in groups. Talk about your school.

• Are/Were your teachers strict?
• What are/were you allowed to do?
• What aren't/weren't you allowed to do?

Signs

5 What do these signs mean? Use *have to/don't have to*, *can/can't*, or *(not) be allowed to*.

 1

 2 **Admission** Summer Exhibition / Adults €10.00 / Children free

 3 **No parking** 8am-6pm Mon-Fri

 4 **50**

 5

 6 **passport**

 7 *Fresh* Use by June 16

 8 **fasten seatbelts**

 9 **No skateboarding**

What do you think?

Is it the same in your country?

In Britain ...
- you can get married when you're 16.
- you can't drink alcohol until you're 18.
- you have to wear a seat-belt in a car.
- you can vote when you're 18.
- young people don't have to do military service.
- there are lots of public places where you aren't allowed to smoke.

PLANNING A TRIP
should and *must*

1 **T 4.4** Antony and his friend George are going to travel around Asia. Listen to them talking about their trip. What two decisions do they make?

2 Practise the conversation.

A I can't stop thinking about this trip.

G Same here. I spend all my time just looking at maps.

A What do you think? Should we take cash or traveller's cheques?

G I think we should take traveller's cheques. It'll be safer.

A Yeah, I think you're right.

G When should we go to Thailand?

A Well, I don't think we should go during the rainy season. I'd rather go in February or March, when it's drier.

G Sounds like a good idea to me. I can't wait to get going!

3 Match a line in **A** with a sentence in **B** to make more suggestions. Use *I think/don't think we should …*

I think we should buy some guidebooks. They'll give us a lot of information.

A	B
1 … buy some guidebooks.	Our bags will be too heavy to carry.
2 … take plenty of suncream.	I have some friends there.
3 … pack too many clothes.	We don't want to get ill.
4 … take anything valuable.	It'll be really hot.
5 … go to Japan first.	That would be really stupid.
6 … go anywhere dangerous.	They'll give us a lot of information.
7 … have some vaccinations.	We might lose it.

4 **T 4.5** Listen to Antony and his grandmother. She is worried about the boys' trip.

Grandmother	You must write to us every week!
Antony	Yes, I will.
Grandmother	You mustn't lose your passport!
Antony	No, I won't.

Work with a partner. Make similar conversations between Antony and his grandmother. Use the prompts and *must /mustn't*.

- look after your money
- talk to strangers
- go out when it's dark
- drink too much beer
- make sure you eat well
- have a bath regularly
- phone us if you're in trouble
- go anywhere that's dangerous

T 4.6 Listen and check.

GRAMMAR SPOT

1 Look at the sentences below.

   We **should** take traveller's cheques.
   You **must** look after your money.

   Which sentence expresses strong obligation?
   Which sentence expresses a suggestion?

2 What type of verb are *should* and *must*?

▶▶ **Grammar Reference 4.2 p140**

PRACTICE

Suggestions and rules

1 Make suggestions. Use *I think/don't think … should.*

1 Peter's got the flu.
   I think he should go to bed. I don't think he should go to work.
2 I've lost my cheque book and credit cards.
3 Tony got his driving licence last week, and now he wants to drive from London to Edinburgh.
4 My teenage daughter doesn't get out of bed until noon.
5 I never have any money!
6 Jane and Paul are only 16, but they want to get married.
7 I'm really fed up with my job.
8 My grandparents complain they don't go out enough.

Do you have any problems? Ask the class for advice.

2 Write some rules for your school.

Students must arrive for lessons on time.

A new job

3 **T 4.7** Dave is about to start a new job. Listen to him talking to the manager. What's the job?

4 Work with a partner. Choose a job. Then ask and answer questions about the responsibilities, hours, breaks, etc.

Student A You are going to start the job next week.

Student B You are the boss.

What time do I have to start?

Do I have to wear a uniform?

When can I take a break?

Check it

5 Correct these sentences.
1 Do you can help me?
2 What time have you to start work?
3 We no allowed to wear jeans at school.
4 We no can do what we want.
5 My mother have to work very hard six days a week.
6 You no should smoke. It's bad for your health.
7 Passengers must to have a ticket.

WRITING: For and against
▶▶ Go to p108

READING AND SPEAKING
How to behave abroad

1 Are these statements true (✓) or false (✗) for people in your country?

1 ☐ When we meet someone for the first time, we shake hands.
2 ☐ Friends kiss on both cheeks when they meet or when they say goodbye.
3 ☐ We often invite people to our home for a meal.
4 ☐ If you have arranged to do something with friends, it's OK to be a little late.
5 ☐ You shouldn't yawn in public.
6 ☐ We call most people by their first names.

2 Read the text *A World Guide to Good Manners*. These lines have been taken out of the text. Where do they go?

a many people prefer not to discuss business while eating
b some businesses close in the early afternoon for a couple of hours
c for greeting, eating, or drinking
d the deeper you should bow
e should wear long-sleeved blouses and skirts below the knee

3 Answer the questions.

1 What nationality do you think the people in the pictures are?
2 What are the two differences between the American and the Japanese greeting?
3 List some of the clothes you think women *shouldn't* wear in Asian and Muslim countries.
4 Is your main meal of the day the same as in Italy or Spain?
5 In which countries do they prefer *not* to discuss business during meals?
6 What are some of the rules about business cards?
7 Why is it *not* a good idea to say to your Japanese business colleagues, 'I don't feel like staying out late tonight.'?
8 Which *Extra Tips* are about food and drink? Which ones are about general behaviour?

What do you think?

Discuss these questions in groups.

• There is a saying in English: 'When in Rome, do as the Romans do.' What does it mean? Do you agree? Do you have a similar saying in your language?

• Think of one or two examples of bad manners in your country. For example, in Britain it is considered impolite to ask people how much they earn.

• What advice would you give somebody coming to live and work in your country?

A WORLD GUIDE TO
Good Manners
How not to behave badly abroad

by Norman Ramshaw

Travelling to all corners of the world gets easier and easier. We live in a global village, but this doesn't mean that we all behave in the same way.

• Greetings

How should you behave when you meet someone for the first time? An American or Canadian shakes your hand firmly while looking you straight in the eyes. In many parts of Asia, there is no physical contact at all. In Japan, you should bow, and the more respect you want to show, (1)___. In Thailand, the greeting is made by pressing both hands together at the chest, as if you are praying, and bowing your head slightly. In both countries, eye contact is avoided as a sign of respect.

• Clothes

Many countries have rules about what you should and shouldn't wear. In Asian and Muslim countries, you shouldn't reveal the body, especially women, who (2)___.
In Japan, you should take off your shoes when entering a house or a restaurant. Remember to place them neatly together facing the door you came in. This is also true in China, Korea, Thailand, and Iran.

• Food and drink

In Italy, Spain, and Latin America, lunch is often the biggest meal of the day, and can last two or three hours. For this reason many people eat a light breakfast and a late dinner. In Britain, you might have a business lunch and do business as you eat. In Mexico and Japan, (3)___. Lunch is a time to relax and socialize, and the Japanese rarely drink alcohol at lunchtime. In Britain and the United States, it's not unusual to have a business meeting over breakfast, and in China it's common to have business banquets, but you shouldn't discuss business during the meal.

• Doing business

In most countries, an exchange of business cards is essential for all introductions. You should include your company name and your position. If you are going to a country where your language is not widely spoken, you can get the reverse side of your card printed in the local language. In Japan, you must present your card with both hands, with the writing facing the person you are giving it to.

In many countries, business hours are from 9.00 or 10.00 to 5.00 or 6.00. However in some countries, such as Greece, Italy, and Spain, (4)___ then remain open until the evening.

Japanese business people consider it their professional duty to go out after work with colleagues to restaurants, bars, or nightclubs. If you are invited, you shouldn't refuse, even if you don't feel like staying out late.

EXTRA TIPS

HERE ARE SOME EXTRA TIPS BEFORE YOU TRAVEL:

1 In many Asian cultures, it is acceptable to smack your lips when you eat. It means that the food is good.

2 In France, you shouldn't sit down in a café until you've shaken hands with everyone you know.

3 In India and the Middle East, you must never use the left hand (5)___.

4 In China, your host will keep refilling your dish unless you lay your chopsticks across your bowl.

5 Most South Americans and Mexicans like to stand very close to the person they're talking to. You shouldn't back away.

6 In Russia, you must match your hosts drink for drink or they will think you unfriendly.

7 In Ireland, social events sometimes end with singing and dancing. You may be asked to sing.

8 In America, you should eat your hamburger with both hands and as quickly as possible. You shouldn't try to have a conversation until it is eaten.

VOCABULARY
Nationality words

1 Match a line in **A** with a line in **B**.
Notice the stress.

A	B
The I'talians	cook lots of noodles and rice.
The Chi'nese	wear kilts on special occasions.
The 'British	produce champagne.
The Ca'nadians	eat raw fish.
The French	invented football.
The Japa'nese	eat a lot of pasta.
The Scots	often watch ice hockey on TV.

T 4.8 Listen and check.

> **!** 1 All nationality words have capital letters in English.
>
> the French   the Italians   the British
>
> 2 If the adjective ends in /s/, /z/, /ʃ/, or /tʃ/ there is no -s at the end of the word for the people.
>
> Japanese   the Japanese
> Spanish   the Spanish
>
> 3 Sometimes the word for the people is different from the adjective.
>
> Scottish   the Scots
> Finnish   the Finns

2 Complete the chart and mark the stress.
Add some more countries.

Country	Adjective	A sentence about the people
'Italy	I'talian	The Italians love pasta.
'Germany		
Aus'tralia		
'Scotland		
'Russia		
'Mexico		
the U'nited 'States		
'Greece		
'England		
'Sweden		

LISTENING AND SPEAKING
Come round to my place!

1 Have you ever been a guest in someone's home in a foreign country? When? Why? What was different?

2 **T 4.9** You will hear three people talking about inviting guests home for a meal. Listen and complete the chart.

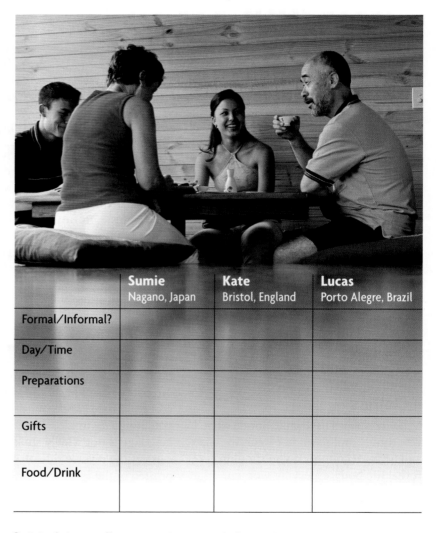

	Sumie Nagano, Japan	Kate Bristol, England	Lucas Porto Alegre, Brazil
Formal/Informal?			
Day/Time			
Preparations			
Gifts			
Food/Drink			

3 Work in small groups. Compare information.

4 What happens in your country? Is it usual to invite people to your home for a meal? What are such occasions like in your home?

EVERYDAY ENGLISH
Requests and offers

1 Match a line in **A** with a line in **B**. Who is talking? Where do you think the conversations are taking place?

A	B
1 Could you bring us the bill, please?	White or black?
2 Would you give me your work number, please?	No problem. It's stuffy in here.
3 Can I help you?	Of course. Oh, shall I give you my mobile number, too?
4 Two large coffees, please.	That line's engaged. Would you like to hold?
5 Can you tell me the code for Paris, please?	Yes, sir. I'll bring it right away.
6 I'll give you a lift if you like.	One moment. I'll look it up.
7 Would you mind opening the window?	Just looking, thanks.
8 Could I have extension 238, please?	That would be great! Could you drop me off at the library?

2 **T 4.10** Listen and check. Which are offers? Which are requests? Practise the conversations, paying particular attention to intonation and stress.

▶▶ **Grammar Reference 4.3 and 4.4 p141**

3 **T 4.11** Listen to the conversations. Complete the chart.

	Who are they?	What are they talking about?
1		
2		
3		
4		

T 4.11 Listen again. What are the words used to make the requests?

1 _____   3 _____

2 _____   4 _____

Roleplay

Work with a partner. Choose one of the situations and make up a conversation using the words.

Situation 1	**Situation 2**	**Situation 3**
Student A You are a customer in a restaurant. **Student B** You are a waiter/waitress.	**Student A** You are moving flat next week. **Student B** Offer to help.	**Student A** You are cooking a meal for 20 people. **Student B** Offer to help.
Use these words: • table near the window • menu • order • clean fork • dessert • bring the bill	**Use these words:** • pack boxes • load the van • clean • look after the plants • phone the gas board • unload the van	**Use these words:** • prepare the vegetables • make the salad • stir the sauce • check the meat • lay the table

5 On the move

TEST YOUR GRAMMAR

1 Match a sentence in **A** with a sentence in **B**. <u>Underline</u> the verb forms that refer to the future. What is the difference between them?

A	B
1 The phone's ringing.	I think it's going to rain.
2 Look at those black clouds!	Don't worry! It'll be spring soon.
3 What are you doing tonight?	We might go to Prague, or we might go to Budapest.
4 I'm sick and tired of winter!	I'll get it!
5 Where are you going on your holiday?	I'm staying at home. I'm going to watch a video.

2 Answer the questions about you.

• What are you doing after class today? • What's the weather forecast for tomorrow? • Where are you going on your next holiday?

BEN'S LIST
Future forms

1 Ben always writes a list at the beginning of the day.
Read his list. Where's he going today?
What's he going to do?

He's going to the hairdresser's.
He's going to buy some sugar.

Things to do
haircut
petrol
electricity bill — bank
tickets — travel agent
library
visit Nick?

Things to buy
sugar
yoghurt
milk
tennis balls

2 **T 5.1** Listen and complete the conversation between Ben and Alice.

B I'm going shopping. Do we need anything?

A I don't think so. … Oh, hang on. We haven't got any sugar.

B It's OK. It's on my list. I _____ some.

A What about bread?

B Good idea! I _____ a loaf.

A What time will you be back?

B I don't know. I might stop at Nick's. It depends on how much time I've got.

A Don't forget we _____ tennis with Dave and Donna this afternoon.

B Don't worry. I _____ forget. I _____ back before then.

A OK.

Memorize the conversation. Close your books and practise with a partner.

3 Alice also asks Ben to get these things.

- stamps
- two steaks
- some shampoo
- some film for the camera
- a newspaper
- a tin of white paint
- a video
- a CD

Which shops will Ben go to? Work with a partner to make conversations.

Can you get some stamps, please, honey?

OK. I'll go to the post office.

*And we need some …
Don't forget …*

GRAMMAR SPOT

1 Look at the future forms in these sentences from the conversation:

It's on my list. I**'m going to buy** some.
Good idea! I**'ll get** a loaf.

In each sentence when did Ben make his decision? Before speaking, or at the moment of speaking?

2 Which of these sentences expresses a future possibility, which a prediction, and which a future arrangement?

We**'re playing** tennis this afternoon.
I **might stop** at Nick's.
I**'ll be** back before then.

▶▶ **Grammar Reference 5.1 p141**

PRACTICE

Discussing grammar

1 Work with a partner. <u>Underline</u> the correct verb form.

1 'Why are you putting on your coat?'
  'Because *I'll take / I'm going to take* the dog for a walk.'

2 'Would you like to go out for a drink tonight?'
  'How about tomorrow night? *I'll call / I'm calling* you.'

3 'What's the score?'
  '6–0. *They're going to lose / They'll lose.*'

4 'It's Tony's birthday next week.'
  'Is it? I didn't know. *I'll send / I'm going to send* him a card.'

5 'Are you and Alan still going out together?'
  'Oh yes, *we'll get / we're getting* married in June.'

6 'Where are you going on holiday this year?'
  'We haven't decided. *We might go / We're going* to Italy.'

What's going to happen?

2 **T 5.2** Listen to three short conversations. Say what is going to happen.

They're going to catch a plane.

What do you think will happen?

3 Make sentences using *I think … will* and the prompts in **A**. Match them with a sentence in **B**.

I think Jerry will win the tennis match. He's been playing really well lately.

A	B
1 Jerry/win the tennis match	But we'd better get going.
2 it/be a nice day tomorrow	He's been playing really well lately.
3 I/pass my exam on Friday	The forecast is for warm and dry weather.
4 you/like the film	You have the right qualifications and plenty of experience.
5 we/get to the airport in time	It's a wonderful story, and the acting is excellent.
6 you/get the job	I've been studying for weeks.

T 5.3 Listen and check. Practise saying them.

4 Make sentences using *I don't think … will* and the prompts in **A** in exercise 3. Match them with a sentence in **C**.

I don't think Jerry will win the tennis match. He hasn't practised for weeks.

C
There's too much traffic.
I haven't studied at all.
The forecast said rainy and windy.
He hasn't practised for weeks.
They're looking for someone with more experience.
It's a bit boring.

T 5.4 Listen and check. Practise saying them.

Talking about you

5 Make true sentences about you starting with *I think …* or *I don't think … .*

1 I/bath tonight
2 the teacher/give us a lot of homework
3 I/eat out tonight
4 it/rain tomorrow
5 I/go shopping this afternoon
6 my partner/be a millionaire one day
7 we/have an exam this week

Arranging to meet

6 **T 5.5** Liz and Min Young are arranging to meet over the weekend. What plans do they already have? Listen and complete the chart. Where and what time do they arrange to meet?

Liz

	Liz	Min Young
FRIDAY		
morning		
afternoon		
evening		
SATURDAY		
morning		
afternoon		
evening		

Min Young

7 It is Friday morning. Fill in your diary for this weekend. What are you doing? When are you free?

Friday

morning

afternoon

evening

Saturday

morning

afternoon

evening

Sunday

morning

afternoon

evening

8 With a partner, think of a reason to get together this weekend. Arrange a day, time, and place to meet.

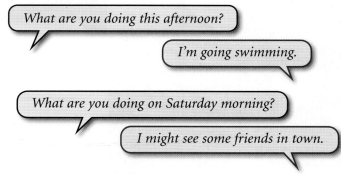

What are you doing this afternoon?

I'm going swimming.

What are you doing on Saturday morning?

I might see some friends in town.

When you have finished, tell the class when and where you're meeting.

We're meeting on Sunday morning at my flat. We're going to . . .

READING AND SPEAKING
Hotels with a difference

1 Look at the photos of the three hotels and answer these questions.
  - Which countries do you think they are in?
  - What do you think people can do on holiday there?

2 Write another question about each hotel.

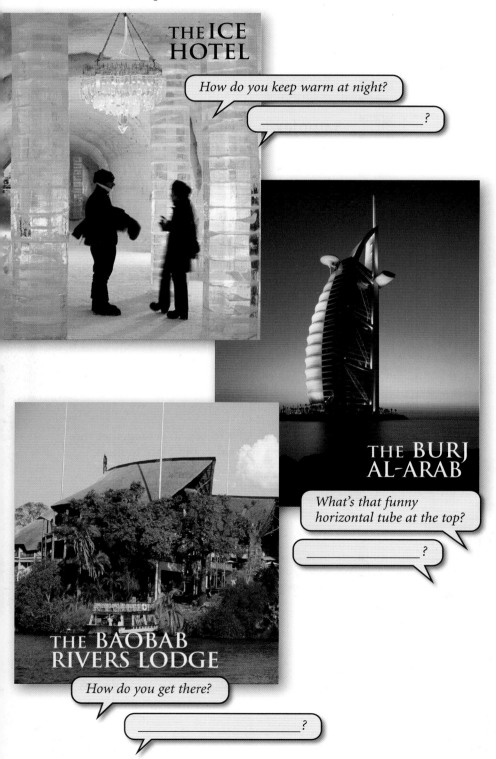

THE ICE HOTEL

How do you keep warm at night?

_____?

THE BURJ AL-ARAB

What's that funny horizontal tube at the top?

_____?

THE BAOBAB RIVERS LODGE

How do you get there?

_____?

3 Read the article and the brochure on p43. Which questions from exercise 2 can you answer? With a partner, answer these questions.
  - What is Karen's job?
  - Why does she take working holidays?
  - What is her idea of a perfect holiday?
  - Why does she spend her holidays at home?
  - Animals are mentioned. Which ones, and why?

4 Complete the chart about Karen's trips to Canada and Dubai.

	Canada	Dubai
Which hotel is she staying at?		
How long is she staying there?		
What's special about the hotel and her room?		
What's she going to do there?		

5 Work with a partner. Look again at the brochure for the Baobab Rivers Lodge. Ask and answer questions about Karen's trip there.

Language work

Find words or expressions in the text with similar meanings.

My ideal holiday
1 doing nothing *lazing*
2 stopping to look around in
3 I'm very interested in
4 move around without any hurry

My business holidays
5 in an exciting and impressive way
6 things that should not be missed

What do you think?
- Do you know any unusual holiday destinations?
- In your opinion, what is *the* ideal holiday?
- Where are you going for your next holiday?

> **WRITING:** Making a reservation
> ▶▶ Go to p109

My kind of **holiday**

She travels for her job, but when it's her own holiday, Karen Saunders stays at home.

Karen Saunders has her own travel agency in Mayfair, London that sends people all over the world on their dream holidays. She needs to know where she's sending them, so she goes on working holidays four or five times a year.

" My ideal holiday

My ideal holiday has a little bit of everything. I like lazing on a beach with a pile of books, but then I get bored and I need to do something. I love exploring new places, especially on foot, and nosing around in churches, shops, museums, and restaurants. I'm very into cooking, so I love going around markets and food stores.

However, I must confess that my favourite 'holiday resort' is home. I travel so much in my job that just waking up in my own bed is heaven. I potter around the house in my pyjamas, read the paper, do some gardening, shop for some food, then make a delicious meal in the evening.

My business holidays

I have three trips coming up. I'm looking forward to going to Canada soon, where I'm staying for four nights at the Ice Hotel. This is a giant igloo situated in Montmorency Fall Park, just 20 minutes from downtown Quebec. It is made from 4,500 tons of snow and 250 tons of ice, and it takes 5 weeks to build. It will stay open for three months. When the spring arrives, it will melt. Then it will be built again for next year – maybe in a different place! Each room is supplied with a sleeping bag made from deer skins. The hotel has two art galleries featuring ice sculptures, and an ice cinema. It also has a bar where all the drinks come in glasses made of ice. Of course I'll visit them all!

In complete contrast to the Ice Hotel, I'm going to Dubai the following month, to stay a few days at the spectacular Burj al-Arab, which means the Arabian Tower. It's shaped like a giant sail, and it rises dramatically out of the beautiful blue water. Each room has sea views. I really want to try the restaurant in the tube at the top next to the helipad. Other must-dos include shopping in the markets, called *souks*. (You can buy designer clothes, perfumes, and spices, but what I want is some gold jewellery.) I'm also going to visit the camel races.

The next trip, different again, is to Baobab Rivers, in Selous, Tanzania, for a seven-day safari and I'm looking forward to a few days in

THE BAOBAB RIVERS LODGE
IN SELOUS, TANZANIA

– so remote, you arrive by boat!

WHAT TO SEE	Each tree-top room has views over the vast forested banks of the Rufiji River, which runs through one of the largest game reserves in Africa
WHAT TO DO	Safari by Land Rover in search of elephants, rhinos, and lions; or by boat along the Rufiji River in search of crocodiles, hippos, and rare birds

LISTENING AND VOCABULARY
A weather forecast

1 Complete the chart with words from the box.

~~sunny~~	snowing
windy	fog
snowy	stormy
ice	blowing
wind	icy
cloud	rain
snow	cloudy
shining	raining
foggy	rainy
sunshine	
(thunder)storm	

	Adjective	Noun	Verb
	It's _sunny._	_____	The sun's _____
	It's _____	_____	It's _____
	It's _____	_____	It's _____
30 →	It's _____		The wind's _____

	Adjective	Noun
	It's _____	_____
	It's _____	_____
FOG	It's _____	
ICE	It's _____	_____

2 Look at the map of Western Europe. Can you name the countries 1–10?

1 _____ 3 _____ 5 _____ 7 _____ 9 _____
2 _____ 4 _____ 6 _____ 8 _____ 10 _____

Which countries make up Scandinavia? Find them on the map.

In pairs, choose two of the countries and talk about:

- the climate • the capital city • geographical features

3 **T 5.6** Work in four groups A–D. Listen to the weather forecast and make notes about your part. When you have finished, swap information.

4 Work with a partner. What's the weather like where you are today? What do you think it will be like tomorrow? Write a forecast and read it to the class.

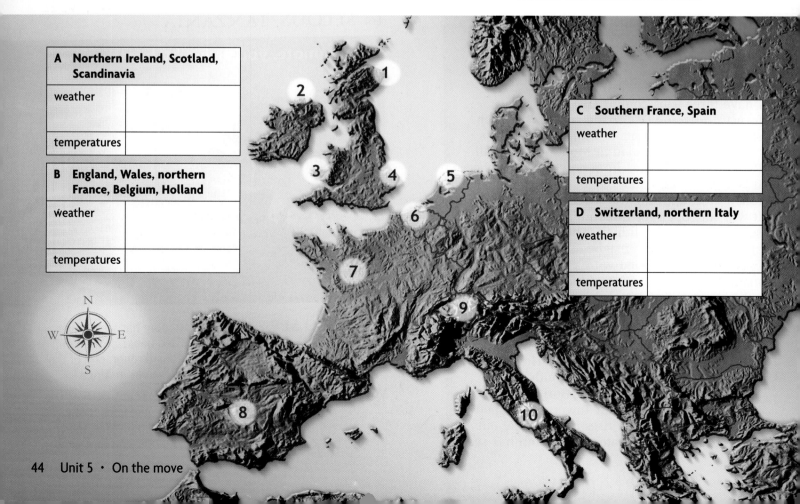

A Northern Ireland, Scotland, Scandinavia	
weather	
temperatures	

B England, Wales, northern France, Belgium, Holland	
weather	
temperatures	

C Southern France, Spain	
weather	
temperatures	

D Switzerland, northern Italy	
weather	
temperatures	

EVERYDAY ENGLISH
Travelling around

1 Here are some lines from conversations on different kinds of transport. Where does each conversation take place? Choose from the box.

car bus taxi underground
train plane ferry

1 Do you think it'll be a rough crossing?
2 Excuse me, I think those seats facing the front are ours.
3 We're going to Market Street. Could you tell us when it's our stop?
4 Can you take us to the airport?
5 Can I take these bags on with me?
6 That's all right. You can keep the change.
7 Excuse me, are we landing on time?
8 No, no! He said turn *left* at the lights, not right!
9 How do I get to Oxford Circus?

2 Match a line from exercise 1 with a reply.
a ☐ Look! *You* drive and *I'll* give directions from now on! Right?
b ☐ Of course. Hop in!
c ☐ I'm sorry. Only one item of hand luggage per passenger.
d ☐ Oh, I'm sorry. We didn't know they were reserved.
e ☐ Yes. We're beginning our descent soon.
f ☐ Well, the forecast is good, so it should be pretty smooth.
g ☐ Just sit near the front and I'll call it out.
h ☐ Take the Piccadilly Line, eastbound, and change at Green Park.
i ☐ Thanks a lot. Do you want a hand with those bags?

T 5.7 Listen and check. Practise the conversations with a partner.

Roleplay

Work with a partner. You are in a hotel.

Student A You are the receptionist.
Student B You are a guest.

The guest has several requests, and calls the front desk from his/her room. Use these situations. Change roles after three conversations.

- There are no towels in the room.
- You'd like some coffee and a sandwich in your room.
- You want the telephone number of the railway station.
- You want the front desk to recommend a good place to eat.
- You can't get the television to work.
- You want a wake-up call at 7.00 in the morning.
- You want to order a taxi to take you to the airport.

Can I help you?

Yes, there are no towels in my room. Could you send some up, please?

Certainly. I'll take care of it right away.

Thanks. Bye.

6 I just love it!

like • Verb patterns • Describing food, towns, and people • Signs and sounds

TEST YOUR GRAMMAR

1 Complete these sentences about you.

1 I look just like my . . .
2 I like my coffee . . .
3 On Sundays, I like . . .
4 After this class, I'd like to . . .
5 When I'm on holiday, I enjoy . . .
6 Yesterday evening, I decided to . . .

2 Tell the class some of the things you wrote.

I look just like my dog.

A STUDENT VISITOR
Questions with *like*

1 Many students go to study in a foreign country. Do you know anyone who has studied abroad?

2 Sandy and her friend Nina in Melbourne, Australia, are talking about a student visitor from South Korea. Complete the conversation using these questions.

What does she like doing?	How is she now?	What's she like?
What does she look like?	What would she like to do?	

Sandy Our student from Seoul arrived on Monday.
Nina What's her name?
Sandy Soon-hee.
Nina That's a pretty name!
    (1)_____
Sandy She's really nice. I'm sure we'll get on well. We seem to have a lot in common.
Nina How do you know that already?
    (2)_____
Sandy Well, she likes dancing, and so do I. And we both like listening to the same kind of music.
Nina (3)_____
Sandy Oh, she's really pretty. She has big, brown eyes and long, dark hair.

Nina Why don't we do something with Soon-hee this weekend? What should we do? Get a pizza? Go clubbing? (4)_____
Sandy I'll ask her tonight. She was a bit homesick at first, so I'm pretty sure she'll want to go out and make some friends.
Nina (5)_____
Sandy Oh, she's OK. She called her parents and she felt much better after she'd spoken to them.
Nina Oh, that's good. I can't wait to meet her.

T 6.1 Listen and check. Practise the conversation with a partner.

GRAMMAR SPOT

1 Write a question from exercise 2 next to the correct definition.

Question		Definition
a _____	=	Tell me about her because I don't know anything about her.
b _____	=	Tell me about her physical appearance.
c _____	=	Tell me about her interests and hobbies.
d _____	=	Tell me about her preferences for tomorrow evening.
e _____	=	Tell me about her health or happiness.

2 Which questions use *like* as a verb? Which questions use *like* as a preposition?

▶▶ **Grammar Reference 6.1–6.3 pp142–143**

PRACTICE

Talking about you

1 Ask and answer with a partner.
- What do you like doing at the weekend?
- Who do you look like in your family?
- How are your parents and grandparents?
- What is your best friend like?
- What's your school like?
- What does your teacher look like?

Listening and asking questions

2 **T 6.2** Listen and tick (✓) the question each person is answering.

1 ☐ Do you like Thai food?
   ☐ What's Thai food like?

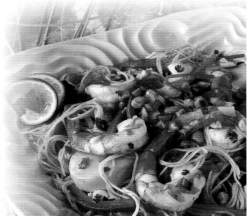

2 ☐ Who does Bridget look like?
   ☐ What's Bridget like?
3 ☐ How's your brother?
   ☐ What's your brother like?
4 ☐ What does she like?
   ☐ What does she look like?
5 ☐ What's the weather like there?
   ☐ Do you like the weather there?
6 ☐ What does he look like?
   ☐ What's he like?
7 ☐ What do you like doing on holiday?
   ☐ What was your holiday like?
8 ☐ What kind of books do you like?
   ☐ What kind of books would you like?

A THANK-YOU LETTER
Verb patterns

Soon-hee has returned home to Seoul. Read her letter and choose the correct verb form.

Sang-chul and me

SOON-HEE

Seoul
December 15

Dear Sandy and family,
    I just wanted (1) to say / saying
thank you for (2) to have / having me
as your guest in your beautiful home. I had a great
time. I really enjoyed (3) meeting / to meet your
friends. You all made me (4) feel / to feel so welcome.
You know how much I missed my family at first,
but you were so kind that I soon stopped
(5) to feel / feeling homesick. I can't find the words
to tell you how grateful I am. I'd like
(6) to call / calling you. What's a good time to call?
    You know that on my way home I stopped
(7) to visit / visiting my aunt in Perth. It was
so hot! It was over 35 degrees all the time
but I absolutely loved it. My aunt wanted
(8) that I stay / me to stay longer, but I wanted
(9) to see / seeing my parents and my brother, Sang-chul.
But she's invited me (10) to go / going back and I'd love
(11) to do / to doing that. I'm thinking of (12) go / going
next year.
    Anyway, I'm looking forward to (13) hear / hearing from
you very soon. Let me (14) to know / know if you ever want
to visit Seoul. My brother and I could take you to a
'norebang' (a singing room). It's a bit like karaoke!
Love to you all,

    Soon-hee

p.s. Do you like the picture of Sang-chul and me?

RSON
A DRIVE
URNE 8100
RALIA

T 6.3 Listen and check.

GRAMMAR SPOT

Verb patterns

1 Complete these examples from Soon-hee's letter.

a I really **enjoyed** _____ your friends.

b I just **wanted** _____ _____ thank you.

c My aunt **wanted** _____ _____ _____ longer.

d You all **made** _____ _____ so welcome.

e **Thank you** _____ _____ me as your guest.

2 Match a sentence with a picture.

1 They **stopped to talk** to each other.

2 They **stopped talking** to each other.

What's the difference in meaning between sentences 1 and 2?

3 Complete these examples from the letter.

I soon stopped _____ homesick.

I stopped _____ my aunt.

▶▶ **Verb patterns p158**

PRACTICE

What's the pattern?

1 Write the examples from Soon-hee's letter on the chart.

verb + -ing	verb + to + infinitive	verb + sb + to + infinitive	verb + sb + infinitive (no to)	preposition + -ing
enjoyed meeting				

2 **T 6.4** Listen to the sentences. Write each verb in the correct column in exercise 1.

promise   succeed in   **let**

tell   **ask**   help

finish   need   **hate**

forget   don't mind   look forward to

Check your answers on p158.

Discussing grammar

3 In these sentences, two verbs are correct and one is not. Tick (✓) the correct verbs.

1 My father _____ to mend my bike.

  a ☑ promised b ☐ couldn't c ☑ tried

2 She _____ her son to turn down his music.

  a ☐ asked b ☐ wanted c ☐ made

3 I _____ going on long walks.

  a ☐ refuse b ☐ can't stand c ☐ love

4 We _____ to go shopping.

  a ☐ need b ☐ 'd love c ☐ enjoy

5 She _____ me do the cooking.

  a ☐ wanted b ☐ made c ☐ helped

6 I _____ working for the bank 20 years ago.

  a ☐ started b ☐ stopped c ☐ decided

4 Make correct sentences using the other verbs in exercise 3.

My father couldn't mend my bike.

READING AND SPEAKING
The world's favourite food

1 Do you know any typical dishes from these countries? Discuss with the class.

• Spain	• Japan	• Mexico
• Italy	• Hungary	• the United States
• Germany	• China	• England

Can you think of any foods that might be popular in all of the countries above?

2 Which of these are fish or seafood?

> oil garlic anchovies eel squid herring salmon
> peas shrimp pineapple bacon tuna sweetcorn

T 6.5 Listen and repeat.

3 Work in groups. Read the text quickly and find the foods in exercise 2. How many other foods can you find?

4 Read the text again and answer the questions.
1 What does *McDonald's Golden Arches span the globe* mean?
2 What are the similarities and differences between the hamburger and the pizza?
3 What year was pizza invented?
4 Which came first, *picea* or *plakuntos*? How are they different from pizza?
5 Why are Mexico and Peru important in the development of pizza?
6 What do the Italian flag and a Pizza Margherita have in common?
7 When and how did pizza become really popular in the United States?

5 Work in groups. Read *Pizza Trivia* again and make questions.

How many . . . ?	How much . . . ?	Which month . . . ?
Where and when . . . ?	Which toppings . . . ?	

Close your books. Ask and answer questions.

What do you think?
• Which facts in Pizza Trivia do you find most interesting? Why?
• Why do different countries prefer such different toppings?
• Do you like pizza? What are your favourite toppings?
• What are the most popular places to eat in your country? Why?
• What is your favourite place to eat?

Language work

Study the text and find an example of:
• *like* used as a verb
• *like* used as a preposition
• verb + *-ing* form
• verb + infinitive
• adjective + infinitive

NAPLES, ITALY, ON VALENTINE'S DAY

PIZZA IN SPACE

GLOBAL PIZZA

BY CONNIE ODONE

So you thought the hamburger was the world's most popular fast food? After all, McDonald's Golden Arches span the globe. But no, there is another truly universal fast food, the ultimate fast food. It's easy to make, easy to serve, much more varied than the hamburger, can be eaten with the hands, and it's delivered to your front door or served in fancy restaurants. It's been one of America's favourite foods for over 50 years. It is, of course, the pizza.

A BRIEF HISTORY OF PIZZA

It's kind of silly to talk about the moment when pizza was 'invented'. It gradually evolved over the years, but one thing's for certain – it's been around for a very long time. The idea of using pieces of flat, round bread as plates came from the Greeks. They called them 'plakuntos' and ate them with various simple toppings such as oil, garlic, onions, and herbs. The Romans enjoyed eating something similar and called it 'picea'. By about 1000 AD in the city of Naples, 'picea' had become 'pizza' and people were experimenting with more toppings: cheese, ham, anchovies, and finally the tomato, brought to Italy from Mexico and Peru in the sixteenth century. Naples became the pizza capital of the world. In 1889, King Umberto I and Queen Margherita heard about pizza and asked to try it. They invited pizza maker, Raffaele Esposito, to make it for them. He decided to make the pizza like the Italian flag, so he used red tomatoes, white mozzarella cheese, and green basil leaves. The Queen loved it and the new pizza was named 'Pizza Margherita' in her honour.

Pizza migrated to America with the Italians at the end of the nineteenth century. The first pizzeria in the United States was opened in 1905 at 53½ Spring Street, New York City, by Gennaro Lombardi. But the popularity of pizza really exploded when American soldiers returned from Italy after World War II and raved about 'that great Italian dish'. Americans are now the greatest producers and consumers of pizza in the world.

PIZZA TRIVIA

1 Americans eat 350 slices of pizza per second.
2 There are 61,269 pizzerias in the United States.
3 Pizza is a $30 billion per year industry.
4 October is national pizza month in the United States.
5 The world's first pizzeria, the Antica Pizzeria Port'Alba, which opened in Naples in 1830, is still there.
6 Pizza Hut has over 12,000 restaurants and takeaway outlets in over 90 countries.
7 In America, pepperoni is the favourite topping. Anchovies is the least favourite.
8 In Japan, eel and squid are favourites. In Russia it's red herring, salmon, and onions.
9 In Brazil, they like green peas on their pizza. In Australia the favourites are shrimp and pineapple.
10 The French love bacon and crème fraîche on theirs. The English love tuna and sweetcorn.

51

VOCABULARY
Adjectives for food, towns, and people

1 In each group, *four* of the adjectives cannot go with the noun. Which ones?

junk fast delicious tasteless
fresh plain tasteful
disgusting ~~disgusted~~ **FOOD** vegetarian
frozen home-grown
rich wealthy starving

excited home old university
exciting young
polluted **TOWN** modern
capital busy
industrial agricultural
antique cosmopolitan historic small

young sophisticated long elderly antique
expensive shy
bored boring **PEOPLE** starving
wealthy sociable outgoing rude tall
crowded

2 Complete the conversations with adjectives from exercise 1. Where necessary, use the comparative or superlative forms.

1 **A** Nick's really quiet and _____. He never says a word.
   B Yeah, his brother is much _____ _____.

2 **A** What's Carrie's boyfriend like?
   B Well, he's _____, dark, and handsome, but he's not very polite. In fact, he's even _____ than Carrie!

3 **A** How was your lunch?
   B Ugh! It was awful. The pizza was _____. We were really _____, but we still couldn't eat it!

4 **A** Mmm! These tomatoes are really _____. Did you grow them yourselves?
   B Yes, we did. All our vegetables are _____.

5 **A** Did you have a good time in London?
   B We had a great time. There's so much to do. It's a really _____ city. And there are so many people from all over the world. I think it's nearly as _____ as New York.

T 6.6 Listen and check. Practise the conversations with a partner.

Talking about you

3 Work with a partner. Look at p153.

LISTENING AND SPEAKING
New York and London

1 Look at the pictures of New York and London. Write down what you know about these cities. Compare your lists as a class. Has anyone been to either city?

2 Work in two groups.

Group A **T 6.7** Listen to Justin and Cinda who are English but live and work in New York.

Group B **T 6.8** Listen to Alan, an American, who lives and works in London.

What do they say about these things?
- people
- work/holidays
- shops
- places
- getting around
- food

3 Find a partner from the other group. Compare your information.

WRITING: A description (1)
▶▶ Go to p110

EVERYDAY ENGLISH
Signs and sounds

1 Where would you see these things written?

1
All visitors must sign in

2
100% NYLON
DRY CLEAN ONLY
COOL IRON
DO NOT IRON TRIM
MADE IN INDIA   4493073046/2068

3
Pay and Display

4 **lso contains:** White Soft Paraffin urified Water.

FOR EXTERNAL USE ONLY

Do not use after the expiry date sl
CROOKES   Crookes Hea

5
Coats and other articles left at owner's risk.

6

PLEASE WAIT TO BE SEATED

7

IRRITANT
CONTAINS SODIUM HYPOCHLORITE
Keep out of reach of children –
do not mix with other ~~lavatory cleaner~~.
contact with acid liberates toxic gas. Irritating to eyes and skin.
Avoid contact with eyes.
In case of contact with eyes, rinse immediately with plenty of water

8
LIGHTS
SMOKING CAUSES FATAL DISEASES

9
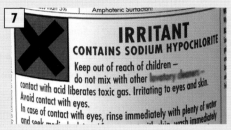
Arrivals Baggage reclaim →

10
! KEEP CLEAR

2 Where would you hear these things?

Coming up next – traffic, news, and the weather.

Please listen carefully to the following options. To purchase tickets for today's performance, press one . . .

Please place your tray tables in their fully upright and locked positions.

How would you like the money?

Just looking, thanks.

We apologize for the delay on the 18.13 service.

7 The world of work

Present Perfect active and passive · Phrasal verbs · On the phone

TEST YOUR GRAMMAR

1 Answer these questions about you.

1 What do you do?
2 How long have you had your present job?
3 What did you do before that?

4 Which foreign countries have you been to?
5 When and why did you go there?

2 Ask and answer the questions with a partner. Tell the class about your partner.

Antonio is a student. He's been at the University of Madrid for ...
Before that he was ...

3 What tenses are used in the questions?

> What do you do?

THE JOB INTERVIEW
Present Perfect

1 Read the job advertisement. Would you like this job? Do you have any of the qualifications?

Worldwatch Europe

Business Journalist

This international business magazine, with 1,000,000 readers worldwide, is seeking a journalist, based in Geneva, to cover business news in Europe.

Requirements:

- a master's degree in journalism
- at least two years' experience in business journalism
- fluent in French and German. If possible, some knowledge of Spanish
- excellent communication skills
- international travel experience is a plus

Please send CV and letter of application to:

David Benton, Worldwatch Europe IPA
56 Merritts Avenue, Overland Park, Reading RG2 6HD

Visit us on the web: **http://www.wep@ipc.co.uk**

2 **T 7.1** Listen to Nancy Mann being interviewed for the job. Do you think she will get it? Why/Why not?

3 Read the first part of Nancy's interview. Complete the sentences with *do*, *did*, or *have*.

D Who _____ you work for now, Nancy?

N I work for Intertec Publishing. We publish international business magazines.

D I see. And how long _____ you worked for them?

N I _____ worked there for nearly five years. No, *exactly* five years.

D And how long _____ you been in charge of Eastern Europe publications?

N For two years.

D And what _____ you do before you were at Intertec?

N I worked for the BBC World Service.

T 7.1 Listen again and check.

GRAMMAR SPOT

1 Does Nancy still work for Intertec? Does she still work for the BBC?

2 Nancy says:

  I **work** for Intertec Publishing.
  I**'ve worked** there for nearly five years.
  I **worked** for the BBC World Service.

What are the different tenses? Why are they used?

▶▶ **Grammar Reference 7.1 and 7.2 pp143–144**

4 Read and complete the second part of the interview.

D As you know, this job is based in Geneva. _____ you _____ lived abroad before?

N Oh yes. Yes, I _____ .

D And when _____ you _____ abroad?

N Well, in fact, I _____ born in Argentina and I _____ there until I was eleven. Also, I lived in Berlin for one year, when I _____ working for the BBC.

D That's interesting. _____ you _____ a lot?

N Oh yes, yes, absolutely. I _____ _____ to most countries in South America and many countries in Europe. I _____ also _____ to Japan a few times.

D Oh yes? And why _____ you _____ to Japan?

N It was for Intertec. I _____ there to interview some Japanese business leaders.

T 7.2 Listen and check.

WRITING: A letter of application

▶▶ Go to p112

PRACTICE

Life stories

1 Here are some more events from Nancy's life. Match a line in **A** with a time expression in **B** to tell her life story.

A	B
1 She was born	for the last five years.
2 She went to school in Buenos Aires	five years ago.
3 She studied modern languages and journalism	until she was eleven.
	while she was working for the BBC.
4 She's worked for Intertec	twice.
5 She left the BBC	yet.
6 She lived in Berlin	for three years at University
7 She's been married	College, London.
8 She's visited Japan	in Argentina in 1969.
9 She hasn't heard if she got the job at Worldwatch Europe	a few times.

T 7.3 Listen and check. Then tell Nancy's life story to a partner.

2 Make a similar chart for your own life. Ask your partner to match the events and the times to tell the story of your life.

Talking about you

3 Complete the sentences about you.
1 I've known my best friend for …
2 I've been at this school since …
3 I haven't learned to … yet.
4 I've never …
5 My mother/father has never …
6 I started … ago.
7 I've lived in … since …
8 I went to … when I was a child.

Have you ever … ?

4 These verbs are all irregular. What is the Past Simple and past participle?

> go write drive lose have read ride sleep be eat win meet

▶▶ **Irregular verbs p157**

5 Work with a partner. Choose from the list below and have conversations.

- go/California?
- drive/a lorry?
- be/on TV?
- lose/your job?
- sleep/in the open air?
- meet/anyone famous?
- have/an operation?
- eat/Indian food?
- win/an award?
- ride/a motorcycle?
- read/a book in English?
- write/a poem?

A Have you ever been to California?
B Yes, I have. / No, I haven't. I've never been there.
A When did you go there?
B Two years ago. I went there on business.

Tell the class about your partner.

IT'S IN THE NEWS
Present Perfect active and passive

1 Read the newspaper headlines. Check any new words.

Dangerous prisoner escapes

Novelists awarded Nobel Prize

Hurricane hits Caribbean

Car workers laid off

LEWIS KNOCKED OUT IN 5TH ROUND

2 **T 7.4** Read and listen to the TV news headlines of the same stories. Complete the sentences with the words you hear.

CHANNEL 1

'The News' transcript—ref:23012003jmf

Here are today's news headlines.
Convicted murderer Charles Watkins
(1) _____has escaped_____ from Belmarsh Prison in South London. Two Spanish novelists
(2) _____ the Nobel Prize for literature. Hurricane Jeffrey
(3) _____ the Caribbean, causing widespread damage in Puerto Rico. Two thousand workers from a UK car factory
(4) _____ due to a slowdown in the economy. Desmond Lewis
(5) _____ in the fifth round of his heavyweight championship fight in Las Vegas.

GRAMMAR SPOT

1 Which of these questions can you answer? Which can't you answer? Why?

  1 Who has escaped from jail?
  2 Who has awarded the novelists the Nobel Prize?
  3 What has hit the Caribbean?
  4 Who has laid off the workers?
  5 Who has knocked out Desmond Lewis?

2 Which sentences in exercise 2 are active? Which are passive?

▶▶ **Grammar Reference 7.3 p144**

PRACTICE
Writing news stories

1 Here are some more headlines from newspapers. Make them into TV news headlines.

  1 **Dangerous prisoner recaptured**
     The murderer Charles Watkins has been recaptured by police.

  2 Cruise ship sinks near Florida

  3 Famous ex-model leaves £3 million to pet cat

  4 **Priceless painting stolen from Madrid art gallery**

  5 **Floods kill 20, 200 more left homeless**

  6 **18-year-old student elected mayor**

  7 Company Director forced to resign

  8 **Runner fails drugs test**

T 7.5 Listen and compare.

2 What's in the news today? What national or international stories do you know?

Discussing grammar

3 Discuss where the words in the box can go in these sentences. There are several possibilities.

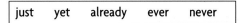

just	yet	already	ever	never

  1 I've washed my hair.
  2 Have you played basketball?
  3 He hasn't learned to drive.
  4 They've finished the exercise.
  5 She's learned a foreign language.
  6 We've met your teacher.
  7 Have they finished doing the washing-up?
  8 Has it stopped raining?

4 Work with a partner. Underline the correct verb form.

  1 The President *has resigned / has been resigned* and a new president *has elected / has been elected*.
  2 His resignation *announced / was announced* yesterday on television.
  3 'Where *did you go / have you gone* on your last holiday?' 'To Peru. It was fabulous.'
  4 '*Did* John ever *go* / *Has* John ever *been* to Paris?' 'Oh, yes. Five times.'
  5 The plane *took off / has taken off* a few minutes ago.
  6 A huge snowstorm *has hit / has been hit* Toronto. Over 40cm of snow *fell / has fallen* over the past twelve hours. Residents *have advised / have been advised* to stay at home.

READING AND SPEAKING
Dream jobs

1 What is your dream job? Close your eyes and think about it. Then answer these questions.

- Does the job require a lot of training or experience?
- Is it well-paid?
- Does it involve working with other people?
- Is it indoors or outdoors?
- Do you need to be physically strong to do it?
- Is it dangerous?
- Does it involve travel?

Work with a partner. Ask and answer the questions to guess each other's dream jobs.

2 Here are the stories of three people who believe they have found their dream job. Work in three groups.

Group A Read about Stanley Karras, the hurricane hunter.
Group B Read about Linda Spelman, the trapeze artist.
Group C Read about Michael Doyle, the cowboy in the sky.

Answer the questions in exercise 1 about your person.

3 Find a partner from the other two groups and compare information.

- Which of the jobs do you find most interesting?
- Would you like to do any of them?

4 Read the other two articles quickly. Answer the questions.

1 Who <u>gets on well with</u> the people they work with?
2 Who <u>took up</u> gymnastics?
3 Who hasn't <u>come up with</u> an experiment to do in space yet?
4 Whose job <u>was handed down</u> from father to son?
5 Who is <u>cut off from</u> his/her family?
6 Who finds it exciting <u>to end up</u> in different cities and countries?
7 Who often <u>takes off</u> at a moment's notice?
8 Who <u>came across</u> an ad?
9 Who wants to <u>carry on</u> working until they are at least 50?
10 Who <u>gave up</u> work as a lawyer?

Language work

The <u>underlined</u> words in exercise 4 are all phrasal verbs. Match them with a verb or expression from the box below.

start doing (a hobby)	separated from
leave the ground and fly	stop doing
finally find yourself	think of
have a good relationship with	find by chance
continue	pass down

Roleplay

Work with a partner. Look at p153.

The Hurricane Hunter

‘There's no such thing as an average day in my job!’

Stanley Karras works as a meteorologist in Tampa, Florida. It's his job to follow hurricanes by plane and provide information about them to scientists.

How did you get the job? I was working for the National Meteorological Office in Bracknell, near London, in the autumn of 1995, and I saw a documentary with my family called *Stormchasers*. It was about hurricane hunters and I thought, 'Wow, that's an interesting job!' As it happened, two months later I came across an ad for a meteorologist to work in Florida with the same people who had made the documentary. I applied, was interviewed over the phone, moved to the US, and started work here in Tampa in May 1996.

What do you like most about it? I love the travel. I've been all over the world chasing hurricanes. It's exciting to end up in different cities and different countries day after day. If you're a meteorologist, you have to love flying. I also love working with top scientists. I've learned so much from them. For me, it's like a classroom in the sky.

What's an average day like? There's no such thing as an average day in my job! It all depends on the weather, and you can't control that. We often take off at a moment's notice to chase storms. I'm the one who decides whether we fly low through a storm. I don't want to take us into a hurricane that could be particularly nasty.

Have you made any sacrifices to do this job? Yes, one big one. I'm away from my family. They all live in the UK. My wife's with me, of course, but her family is also in the UK, so we're pretty cut off from all of them.

What would you like to do next? I'd like to join a space programme and be the first meteorologist in space, but I haven't come up with an experiment to do in space yet. There aren't any hurricanes!

What advice would you give to someone who wanted to do your job? Study maths and science and get a degree in meteorology. I've taken the hurricane hunter path, but you could be a weather forecaster or do research. It's a fascinating subject and the pay's pretty good.

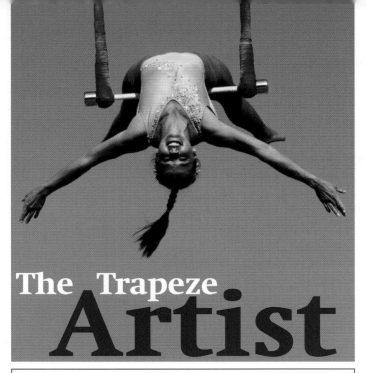

The Trapeze Artist

'You only live once so why stay in a boring job?'

Linda Spelman was a lawyer who found a new career in a circus. She now works as a trapeze artist, travelling with circuses throughout Canada, Europe, and East Asia.

How did you get the job? That's quite a long story. My father's a lawyer, so I thought I'd become one, too. Studying law was really, really hard work, so I took up gymnastics in the evenings to help me relax. When I finally passed my exams, I thought, 'I need a break. I want to travel and learn a language.' I'd heard of the École Nationale du Cirque in Montreal, so I thought, 'I'll join the circus.' I went to Canada and did a trapeze course and, amazingly, I was good at it.

What do you like most about it? The excitement and the travel. I always wanted to travel and learn languages and I've done all of that. Also, I get on really well with circus people. They're all nationalities. I've learned so much about life from them.

What's an average day like? Everyone has to help in the circus, so you begin the day in a new town handing out flyers. In the afternoon, you work in the box office and rehearse. Then you do the act in the evening. At the end of a week, I'm so tired I spend a day in bed. Last month I twisted my shoulder and couldn't work for a week.

Have you made any sacrifices to do this job? No, I haven't, not really. I gave up doing something that I hated and I'm doing something that I love. I do miss my family sometimes, but that's all. And of course I earn a lot less than a lawyer.

What would you like to do next? I'm 34 now. I'd like to carry on doing this until I'm at least 50. There are Russian trapeze artists still going strong in their fifties.

What advice would you give to someone who wanted to do your job? You need to be fit and strong and have a good head for heights. But generally, I'd say to anyone with a dream, 'Go for it! You only live once, so why stay in a boring job?'

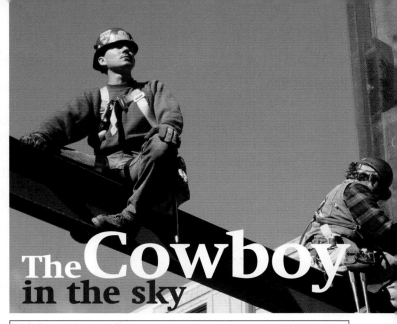

The Cowboy in the sky

'Many of today's ironworkers are descendants of the men who built New York's first skyscrapers.'

Michael Doyle is an ironworker in New York City. He's one of 100 or so ironworkers currently erecting the steel frame of a new 40-storey building in Times Square. These ironworkers are known as 'cowboys in the sky'.

How did you get the job? Ironwork is a trade that is still handed down from father to son. Many of today's ironworkers are descendants of the men who built New York's first skyscrapers. My great-grandfather came over from Ireland in 1930 to work on the construction of the Empire State Building. My father and grandfather were also ironworkers.

What do you like most about it? To me, ironworkers are the kings of construction. We make the skeleton that the other workers build on. We have real pride in our work – you look at the New York skyline and think 'I helped build that.' Also, we work hard, we play hard. We get on well together. We ironworkers depend on each other for our lives. Oh, and the pay is good!

What's an average day like? You never stop in this job. Eight hours a day, from seven in the morning until three in the afternoon. You're moving all the time. The crane lifts the iron girders and you have to move them into place. There's always danger. It's a fact of life for us.

Have you made any sacrifices to do this job? Yes, one big one – physical health. The wear and tear to the body is enormous. I've fallen three times. My father fell two storeys, lost a finger, and broke his ankles.

What would you like to do next? I'd like to work on something really important like my great-grandfather did. Or like my father did, who helped build the World Trade Center. It's weird – he helped build it and I helped take it away.

What advice would you give to someone who wanted to do your job? You need to be strong, really strong. You have to be OK with height. It usually takes about a year to get used to it. You can't work and hold on with one hand all the time. Many guys try it once, then back off and say, 'This is not for me.'

VOCABULARY
Phrasal verbs

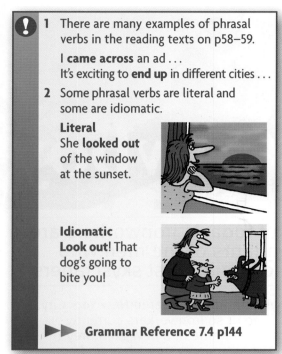

> **1** There are many examples of phrasal verbs in the reading texts on p58–59.
>
> I **came across** an ad ...
> It's exciting to **end up** in different cities ...
>
> **2** Some phrasal verbs are literal and some are idiomatic.
>
> **Literal**
> She **looked out** of the window at the sunset.
>
> **Idiomatic**
> **Look out!** That dog's going to bite you!
>
> ►► **Grammar Reference 7.4 p144**

Literal or idiomatic?

1 In these pairs of sentences, one meaning of the phrasal verb is literal and the other is idiomatic. Say which is which.

1. a The plane has just *taken off*.
   b Please *take off* your coat and sit down.
2. a Oh, no! The lights have *gone out* again.
   b If you *go out*, take an umbrella. It's going to rain.
3. a (*On the phone*) Hello? Hello? I can't hear you. I think we've been *cut off*.
   b She *cut off* a big piece of meat and gave it to the dog.
4. a She *looked up* and smiled.
   b I *looked up* the word in the dictionary.
5. a Can you *pick up* my pen for me? It's under your chair.
   b I *picked up* some Italian when I was working in Rome.

Separable or inseparable?

2 Replace the words in *italics* with a pronoun.

1. He turned on *the light*. **He turned it on.**
2. I'm looking for *my glasses*. **I'm looking for them.**
3. She's taken off *her boots*.
4. He took up *golf* when he retired.
5. I get on well with *my parents*.
6. I came across *the ad*.
7. I looked up *the words* in my dictionary.
8. The waiter took away *the dirty plates*.

Verbs with two particles

3 Complete each pair of sentences below with one of the phrasal verbs from the box.

get on with	put up with	run out of
looking forward to		come up with

1. How do you manage to ☐ the noise from your neighbours?
   Most parents won't ☐ bad behaviour from their children.

2. I'm broke. I have to ☐ an idea for making money.
   We need to ☐ a solution to this problem.

3. Has the photocopier ☐ paper again?
   The children always ☐ school as soon as the bell rings.

4. How well do you ☐ your colleagues?
   Our teacher told us to ☐ our work quietly.

5. She's ☐ going on holiday.
   We're ☐ meeting you very much.

In which pairs of sentences is the meaning of the phrasal verb different?

LISTENING AND SPEAKING
The busy life of a retired man

1 Work in groups and discuss the questions.
- Is anyone in your family retired? Who?
- What job did they do before retiring?
- How old were they when they retired? How long have they been retired?
- What do they do now?

2 **T 7.6** Look at the photo of Thomas Wilson and his granddaughter, Philippa. Listen to them talking.

Who do you think is happier, Thomas or Philippa? Why?

3 Underline the correct verb form. Then answer the questions.
1. How long *was he / has he been* retired?
2. How long *did he work / has he worked* for *Courtauld's*?
3. When *did he go / has he gone* to Wales?
4. How long *was he married / has he been married*?

4 Answer the questions.
1. Why does Thomas like playing golf?
2. Which countries has he visited since he retired? Where did he go two years ago?
3. Who are the following?
   - Rover
   - Keith
   - Kylie
   - Ted and Marjorie
   - Miriam
   - Helen
4. What are the two sad events that Thomas mentions?
5. What does Philippa complain about?

What do you think?
- What is the usual retirement age for men and women in your country?
- What do you think is the best age to retire?
- When would you like to retire?
- What would you like to do when you retire?

EVERYDAY ENGLISH
On the phone

1 Complete the conversations with phrases from the box.

> I'll give it   to hold   I'm phoning   line's busy   Speaking
> leave a message   speak to   we'll get back to you   This is
> phone back later   take a message   I'm afraid   have extension
> putting you through   take your call   at her desk

1. **A** Hello. Could I _____ Sam Jackson, please?
   B _____ Mr Jackson's in a meeting. It won't be over until 3.00. Can I _____?
   A Yes, please. Could you ask him to phone me? I think he's got my number, but _____ to you again just in case. It's 743 219186.

2. **A** Can I _____ 2173, please?
   B The _____ at the moment. Would you like _____?
   A Yes, please.
   (Five seconds later.)
   B I'm _____ now.
   A Thank you.

3. **A** Could I speak to Alison Short?
   B I'm afraid she isn't _____ at the moment. Do you want to hold?
   A No, don't worry. I'll _____.

4. **A** Can I speak to Terence Cameron, please?
   B _____.
   A Ah, Mr Cameron! _____ Holly Lucas. _____ about a letter I got this morning.

5. **A** Hello. This is Incom International. There's no one here to _____ at the moment. Please _____ and _____ as soon as we can.

T 7.7 Listen and check. Practise the conversations.

2 Your teacher will give you a role card. Prepare what you're going to say, then act it out.

8 Just imagine!

Conditionals • Time clauses • Base and strong adjectives • Making suggestions

TEST YOUR GRAMMAR

1 Match a line in **A** with a line in **B**.

A	B
1 If I had £5 million,	I'll tell her the news.
2 If you're going to the post office,	I'd give up my job and travel around the world.
3 If I see Anna,	you have to work hard.
4 If you want to do well in life,	go to bed and rest.
5 If you don't feel well,	could you post this letter for me?

What verb forms are used in the two parts of each sentence?

2 Answer these questions about you.

- If you have a problem, who do you talk to?
- If you won a lot of money, what would you do with it?
- What will you do if the weather's nice at the weekend?

A PLACE IN THE SUN
First conditional and time clauses

1 **T 8.1** Jack and Annie are tired of English weather. So they're moving to Spain to live in the sun and grow lemons. Their friend David thinks they're crazy. Listen and complete the conversation with these verbs.

> 'll only know   will you do (x2)   'll have   'll regret
> don't like (x2)   won't earn   won't need

David	You're both mad. I think you _____ it. You were earning good money here. You _____ much growing lemons.
Jack	We know that, but we _____ a lot of money to live there.
David	But what _____ if you can't find anywhere to live?
Annie	There are lots of cheap, old farms. We _____ no trouble finding somewhere.
David	But you don't even like gardening. What _____ if you _____ farming either?
Jack	We _____ if we _____ farming when we try it.
David	Well, OK. But what if you . . . ?

T 8.1 Listen again and check. Practise the conversation.

2 Have more conversations. What will you do if you . . .

- miss your family and friends
- have problems with the language
- can't stand the heat
- want to move back to the UK
- fall ill
- run out of money
- get bored
- don't like the food

What will you do if you miss your family and friends?

No problem! We'll . . . !

3 **T 8.2** Listen to the next part of the conversation. Put the verbs in the correct form.

David Will you keep in touch with friends?

Annie Of course we will. When we _____ (get) there, we _____ (give) you a call.

David And how will I contact you?

Jack Well, as soon as we _____ (find) a place to live, we _____ (send) you our address.

David I can always email you.

Jack Yes, email's brilliant for keeping in touch, but you _____ (have to) wait until we _____ (set up) our computers.

Annie And David, I promise, you _____ (be) our first guest when we _____ (move) into our new home.

David Excellent. I'll look forward to that!

GRAMMAR SPOT

1 Which sentence expresses a future certainty, and which a future possibility?

If I see Anna, **I'll tell** her.
When I see Anna, **I'll tell** her.

2 Underline the time expressions in the following sentences:

When we get there, we'll give you a call.
As soon as we find a place to live, we'll send you our address.
You'll have to wait until we've set up our computers.

3 Which tenses are used in the time clauses?

▶▶ **Grammar Reference 8.1 and 8.2 pp145–146**

PRACTICE

Another busy day

1 Put *if, as soon as,* or *before* into each box. Put the verbs in the correct form.

David Bye, darling! Good luck with the interview!

Sue Thanks. I'll need it. I hope the trains are running on time. [If] I 'm_____ (be) late for the interview, I _____ (be) furious with myself!

David Just stay calm! Call me when you can.

Sue I will. I _____ (call) you on my mobile [   ] I _____ (get) out of the interview.

David When _____ you _____ (know) [   ] you've got the job?

Sue They _____ (tell) me in the next few days. [   ] they _____ (offer) me the job, I _____ (accept) it. You know that, don't you?

David Of course. But we'll worry about that later.

Sue OK. Are you going to work now?

David Well, I _____ (take) the children to school [   ] I _____ (go) to work.

Sue Don't forget to pick them up [   ] you _____ (finish).

David Don't worry, I won't forget. You'd better get going. [   ] you _____ (not hurry), you _____ (miss) the train.

Sue OK. I _____ (see) you this evening. Bye!

T 8.3 Listen and check. Practise the conversation with a partner.

2 With your partner, ask and answer questions using the prompts.

- How/Sue feel if/late for the interview?
- When/call David?
- When/know if she's got the job?
- What/she/do if they offer her the job?
- What/David do before/go to work?
- When/David pick up the children?

How will Sue feel if she's late for the interview?

She'll be furious with herself.

WINNING THE LOTTERY
Second conditional

1 **T 8.4** Listen to five people saying what they would do if they won £5 million in the lottery and take notes.

2 Use your notes from exercise 1 to complete sentences 1–5.

1 I _____ my own island in the Caribbean.
   I _____ loads of money to charity.
2 I _____ my job and travel. But it _____ me.
3 I _____ lots of land, so I _____ peace and quiet.
4 I _____ a space tourist and fly to Mars on the space shuttle.
5 I _____ away a penny. I _____ it all on myself.

Practise the sentences.

GRAMMAR SPOT

1 Look at the conditional sentences.

> If I **have** time, I'**ll do** some shopping.
> If I **had** £5 million, I'**d buy** an island.

Which sentence expresses a possible situation?
Which sentence expresses an unlikely or unreal situation?

2 Complete each of these sentences to show the real situation.

> If I **had** a lot of money, I'**d travel** around the world.
>   (But unfortunately, *I don't have a lot of money.*)
> If I **had** a car, I'**d** never **catch** a bus again.
>   (But unfortunately, . . .)
> If I **didn't have to work** today, I'**d go** to the beach.
>   (But unfortunately, . . .)

▶▶ **Grammar Reference 8.3–8.5 p146**

PRACTICE

What would you do?

1 What would *you* do with £5 million? Work in groups. Ask and answer the questions.

- What . . . buy?
  What would you buy?

- How much . . . give away?
  Who . . . give it to?
- . . . travel? Where . . . to?

- What about your job?
  . . . keep on working or
  . . . give up your job?

- . . . go on a spending spree, or . . . invest the money?
- . . . be happier than you are now?

Conversations with *will* and *would*

2 Look at the situations. Decide if they are possible or unlikely.

1 There's a good documentary on TV tonight. **possible**
2 You find a burglar in your home. **unlikely**
3 You see a ghost.
4 Your friend isn't doing anything this weekend.
5 You are president of your country.
6 You don't have any homework tonight.
7 You can speak perfect English.

3 Ask and answer questions about what you will do or would do.

What will you do if there's a good documentary on TV tonight?

I'll watch it.

What would you do if you found a burglar in your home?

I'd call the police.

Conditional forms

4 Match a line in **A** with a line in **B** and a sentence in **C**.

A	B	C
1 If Tony calls,	don't wait for me.	It would be really useful for work.
2 If you've finished your work,	I might take up an evening class.	He can reach me there.
3 If I'm not back by 8 o'clock,	you have to have a visa.	Keep warm and drink plenty of fluids.
4 If you have the flu,	please let me know.	I'd love to show you around.
5 If you're ever in London,	tell him I'm at Alex's.	Just be back in 15 minutes.
6 If you go to Russia,	you can take a break.	I'd love to learn more about photography.
7 I'd buy a computer	if I could afford it.	You can get one at the embassy.
8 If I had more time,	you should go to bed.	Go without me and I'll meet you at the party.

T 8.5 Listen and check. Practise the sentences.

5 Look at the verb forms in these questions.
- What do you do if you can't sleep at night?
- What will you do if the weather's nice this weekend?
- What would you do if you found a wallet with a lot of money in it?

In groups, answer the questions.

READING AND SPEAKING
Who wants to be a millionaire?

1 **T 8.6** Listen to the song 'Who Wants to Be a Millionaire?' What do/don't the singers want to do?

Look at the tapescript on p128. Listen again and check.

2 Look at the chart below. Do you think these are good (✓) or bad (✗) suggestions for people who win a lot of money? Write your opinions on the chart.

If you win a lot of money, . . .	Your opinion	The article's opinion
1 you should give up your job.	☐	☐
2 you should buy a new house.	☐	☐
3 you shouldn't tell anyone.	☐	☐
4 you should give money to everyone who asks for it.	☐	☐
5 you should go on a spending spree.	☐	☐
6 you should give lots of it away.	☐	☐

3 Read the article. What does it say about the six suggestions in exercise 2? Put (✓) or (✗) in the chart.

4 Complete the article with the phrases below.

a his unluckiest bet
b to move to a bigger house
c we feel at home
d among all the members of her family
e what the money would do to *us*
f as soon as possible
g most of their money will be spent
h nothing but misery

5 Answer the questions.

1 According to the article, is it a good thing or a bad thing to win a lot of money?
2 How does winning a large amount of money affect our work? Our home? Our friends? Our relatives?
3 In what way is our life like a jigsaw? How does a windfall smash the jigsaw?
4 How can money be wasted?
5 What are the two bad luck stories?
6 What made Jim Taylor happy?
7 How has Anita Cotton survived?

What do you think?

• How would you answer the questions in the last paragraph of the article?
• What advice would you give to someone who has won a lot of money?

Who wants to be a millionaire?

All over the world, lotteries create new millionaires every week. But what is it actually like to wake up one day with more money than you can imagine?

Nearly all of us have fantasized about winning the big prize in a lottery. We dream about what we would do with the money, but we rarely stop to think about (1)___!

For most of us, our way of life is closely linked to our economic circumstances. The different parts of our lives fit together like a jigsaw – work, home, friends, hobbies, and sports make up our world. This is where we belong and where (2)___. A sudden huge windfall would dramatically change it all and smash the jigsaw.

For example, most people like the idea of not having to work, but winners have found that without work there is no purpose to their day and no reason to get up in the morning. It is tempting (3)___ in a wealthy area, but in so doing, you leave old friends and routines behind.

Winners are usually advised not to publicize their address and phone number, but charity requests and begging letters still arrive. If they are not careful, (4)___ on solicitors' fees to protect them from demanding relatives, guards to protect their homes and swimming pools, and psychiatrists to protect their sanity!

Winners who lost it all

There are many stories about people who couldn't learn how to be rich. In 1999 **Abby Wilson** from Brixton, London, won £7 million on Thunderball, and it brought her (5)___. She immediately went on a spending spree that lasted for four years and five marriages. She is now penniless and alone. 'I'm a miserable person,' she says. 'Winning that money was the most awful thing that ever happened to me.'

We do

Then there is the story of **William Church**, 37, a cafeteria cook from Blackpool. He won the National Lottery, but it turned out to be (6)_____. Three weeks after winning, he dropped dead of a heart attack, brought on by ceaseless hounding from the press, the public, and relatives, after his £3.6 million win was made public.

Winners who survived

For some people, the easiest thing is to get rid of the money (7)_____. **Jim Taylor**, a sailor from Scotland, won £2 million, and blew the money in 77 days. He withdrew thousands of pounds a day from the bank and handed it to former shipmates and strangers in the street. On one occasion, he handed out £150,000 to homeless people in a Glasgow park. Later he said he had no regrets about his wasted fortune.

Anita Cotton was the biggest lottery winner at the time when she won £12 million. It has taken her years to get used to the changes in her life. 'I couldn't have done it without my family,' she says. 'There were so many lies about me in the press. They said I had dumped my husband and children, bought an island in the Indian Ocean, and become a drug addict. All wrong.' Her fortune has been divided (8)_____.

A final thought

When you next buy a lottery ticket, just stop for a minute and ask yourself why you're doing it. Do you actually want to win? Or are you doing it for the excitement of thinking about winning?

Language work

Match the words from the text in **A** with their definitions in **B**.

A	B
fantasized	took out (money from the bank)
linked	attractive, inviting
windfall	connected
smash	dreamed
tempting	having no money
begging	break violently
penniless	asking for something very strongly
withdrew	an unexpected sum of money you receive

VOCABULARY AND SPEAKING
Base and strong adjectives

1 Some adjectives have the idea of *very*. Look at these examples from the article on p66–67.

> a huge windfall = a very big windfall
> a miserable person = a very unhappy person

2 Match the base adjectives in **A** with the strong adjectives in **B**.

A Base adjectives	B Strong adjectives
tired	great, wonderful, fantastic, superb
frightened	exhausted
good	delicious
tasty	filthy
bad	terrified
pretty, attractive	starving
hungry	horrible, awful, terrible, disgusting
angry	thrilled, delighted
dirty	astonished, amazed
surprised	hilarious
happy	beautiful, gorgeous
funny	furious

> **!**
> **1** We can make adjectives more extreme with adverbs such as *very* and *absolutely*.
> Their house is **very** big.
> Their garden is **absolutely** enormous.
> **2** We can use *very* only with base adjectives.
> very tired   NOT ~~very exhausted~~
> **3** We can use *absolutely* only with strong adjectives.
> absolutely wonderful   NOT ~~absolutely good~~
> **4** We can use *really* with both base and strong adjectives.
> really tired   really exhausted

3 **T 8.7** Listen to the conversations. What are they about? Write the adjectives and adverbs you hear.

1 _film_   _good, absolutely superb_
2 _____   _____
3 _____   _____
4 _____   _____
5 _____   _____
6 _____   _____

> **WRITING:** A narrative (2)
> ▶▶ Go to p114

LISTENING
Charity appeals

1 Work with a partner. Choose three of these charities. Discuss why you think people should donate to them.

- a charity that helps elderly people with food and housing
- a hospice for people who are dying of an incurable disease
- an organization that provides emergency supplies and medicine for disaster victims
- a charity that helps homeless people
- cancer research
- a charity that helps people with AIDS
- animal rescue shelters

Compare your answers with other pairs.

2 **T 8.8** Listen to information about three more charities and complete the chart.

	Who or what the charity tries to help	How the charity helps
1 Amnesty International		
2 WWF		
3 Crisis Now!		

What do you think?

Imagine that you have £10,000 that you want to give to charity. Who would you give the money to? How would you divide it?

Think about what you would do, and then discuss your ideas with a partner.

If I had £10,000 to give away, I'd give it to three charities ...

EVERYDAY ENGLISH
Making suggestions

1 Maria is bored and Paul is broke. Look at the suggestions made by their friends. Are they talking to Maria or Paul? Write **M** or **P**.

M	Let's go shopping!
☐	If I were you, I'd get a better job.
☐	Why don't you ask your parents?
☐	You ought to ask your boss for a pay-rise!
☐	I don't think you should go out so much.
☐	Why don't we go for a walk?
☐	You'd better get a loan from the bank.
☐	Shall we see what's on television?

I'm broke!

I'm bored!

<u>Underline</u> the words used to make suggestions. Which suggestions include the speaker?

2 **T 8.9** Listen to the conversations. Notice how Maria and Paul accept and reject the suggestions.

T 8.9 Check with the tapescript on p128. Practise the conversations with a partner.

Roleplay

With your partner, make conversations for the situations. Use different ways of making suggestions.

- You have a terrible cold.

  A My head is killing me! And my nose is running!
  B I think you should go to bed with a hot drink.
  A That's a good idea. I'll go right now.
  B How about a hot lemon drink? I'll make it for you.
  A Oh, that would be great!

- You both have the evening free, and there's nothing good on TV.
- Your best friend is having a birthday party next week. You don't know what to give your friend as a present.
- Your neighbour leaves his dog home alone every night while he's at work. The dog barks all the time when nobody's home, and the noise is keeping you awake.
- Your flat is a mess, the carpets and curtains are ragged, and the furniture is ancient. Suddenly, you inherit some money!
- You've just got a job in Moscow, so you need to learn the Russian language, and find out about Russian people and culture as quickly as possible.

9 Relationships

Modal verbs 2 – probability · Character adjectives · So do I! Neither do I!

TEST YOUR GRAMMAR

1 Read each pair of sentences. If the sentence is a fact, put (✓). If the sentence is only a possibility, put (?).

1 [?] I must be in love!
   [✓] I'm in love!

2 [?] She could be having a shower.
   [✓] She's having a shower.

3 [✓] That isn't your bag.
   [?] That can't be your bag.

4 [?] You must have met my brother.
   [ ] You've met my brother.

5 [✓] They haven't met the president.
   [?] They can't have met the president.

6 [ ] Shakespeare might have lived there.
   [✓] Shakespeare lived there.

Shakespeare might have lived there.

2 Which sentences talk about the present? Which talk about the past?

I NEED HELP!
must, could, might, can't

1 Do you ever read advice columns in magazines or newspapers? What kind of problems do people write about?

2 Lucy and Pam have problems. They wrote to 'Susie's Problem Page' in *Metro Magazine*. Read Susie's advice. What do you think the problems are?

Susie's problem

Got a problem? *Metro Magazine*'s agony aunt

Lucy's problem:
'I think about him night and day!'

Susie replies:

Hi Lucy,

Everyone has daydreams and there's nothing wrong with that. It's only a problem when you forget where dreams end and the real world begins. Don't write to him any more. You know in reality that a relationship with him is impossible, and that running away to Hollywood is a crazy idea. You need to find other interests and friends your own age to talk to. Sitting at home watching him on video won't help you. Your parents are clearly too busy to notice or listen. Your future is in your hands, so get a life, study hard, and good luck!

Yours,

Susie

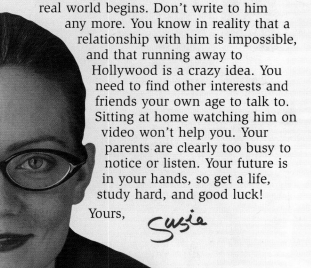

3 Look at Susie's replies. Say who *he*, *she*, or *they* refer to in these sentences.

1   She must be exhausted. **Pam**
2   She must be in love with a film star.
3   She could be a doctor or a nurse.
4   She can't have many friends.
5   He might have a gambling problem.
6   She can't be very old.
7   He must be unemployed.
8   They can't have much money.

4 Give reasons for each statement in exercise 3. Discuss with the class.
Pam must be exhausted because she works hard and she does all the housework.

5 Read Lucy and Pam's letters to Susie on p154 to find out if your ideas are correct.

page

Dr Susie Eden, gives expert advice.

Pam's problem:
'We don't communicate any more!'

Susie replies:

Hi Pam,

You're not helping your marriage by saying nothing to him. He doesn't seem to notice how you feel. I know he's worried about his mother, but it's unfair that he's always at her house and leaves you to do all the housework. You have a tiring and stressful job, caring for sick people all day. Make him understand this and ask him about the hundreds of lottery tickets you found. Encourage him to look for work – he'd feel better about himself if he had a job and it would help the family finances. In the meantime, don't hide your feelings; otherwise your anger and resentment will grow.

Yours, *Susie*

 Dr Susie Eden c/o Metro Magazine, PO Box 201, Lower-East Dockside, Newcastle-upon-Tyne NT12 5NP

Metro Magazine 114

Grammar Reference 9.1 p147

GRAMMAR SPOT

1 The following sentences all express *It's possible that she's in love*. Which sentence is the most sure? Which sentences are less sure?

She **must be** in love.
She **might be** in love.
She **could be** in love.

2 How do we express *I **don't** think it's possible that she's in love*?

PRACTICE

Grammar and speaking

1 Respond to the statements or question. Use the words in brackets.

1   I haven't eaten anything since breakfast. (must/hungry)
    You must be hungry.
2   Steve has three jobs. (can't/much free time)
3   The phone's ringing. (might/Jane)
4   The cat's soaking wet! (must/raining)
5   Listen to all those fire engines! (must/somewhere)
6   I don't know where Sam is. (could/his bedroom)
7   Marta isn't in the kitchen. (can't/cooking dinner)
8   Whose coat is this? (might/John's)

T 9.1 Listen and check. Practise the sentences with a partner. Pay attention to stress and intonation.

What are they talking about?

2 **T 9.2** Listen to five short conversations and guess the answers to the questions. Work with a partner.

1   **A** It's Father's Day next Sunday.
    B I know. Should we buy Dad a present or just send him a card?

    Who do you think they are? Friends? Brother and sister? Husband and wife?
    They can't be just friends. They could be brother and sister. They might be husband and wife.

2   Where do you think the people are? At home? In a pub? In a restaurant?
3   What do you think his job is? A lorry driver? A taxi driver? An actor?
4   What do you think she's talking about? Taking a test? Meeting her boyfriend's parents? A job interview?
5   Who or what do you think they are talking about? A cat? A dog? A baby?

Who's who in the family?

3 Work in small groups. Look at p154–155.

A HOLIDAY WITH FRIENDS
must have been/can't have been

1 **T 9.3** Andy is calling Carl. With a partner, read and listen to Andy's side of the conversation. What are they talking about?

Andy Hi! Carl? It's Andy. How are you? Feeling better?

Carl ...

Andy Really? Still on crutches, eh? So you're not back to work yet?

Carl ...

Andy Another week! Is that when the plaster comes off?

Carl ...

Andy No, I'm fine. We're both fine. Julie sends her love, by the way.

Carl ...

Andy Yes, yes, we have. Julie picked them up today. They're good. I didn't realize we'd taken so many of us all.

Carl ...

Andy Yes, the sunset. It's a good one. All of us together on Bob and Marcia's balcony, with the mountains and the snow in the background. Brings back memories, doesn't it?

Carl ...

Andy Yes, I know. I'm sorry. But at least it happened at the end; it could have been the first day. You only missed the last two days.

Carl ...

Andy Yeah, and it was noisy too! We didn't have any views of the mountains. Yeah, we've written. We emailed the manager yesterday, but I don't know if we'll get any money back.

Carl ...

Andy Yeah. The airline found it and put it on the next flight. Marcia was very relieved.

Carl ...

Andy Absolutely. It was a great holiday. Some ups and downs, but we all had fun, didn't we? Shall we go again next year?

Carl ...

Andy Great! It's a date. And next time go around the trees! I'll call you again soon, Carl. Take care!

Carl ...

Andy Bye.

Andy

Carl

2 Read the questions. Tick (✔) the sentence you think is possible. Cross (✗) the one you think is not possible.

1 What is the relationship between Andy and Carl?
  - ☑ They must be friends.
  - ☐ They could be business colleagues.

2 Where have they been?
  - ☑ They could have been on a skiing holiday.
  - ☐ They can't have been on a skiing holiday.

3 What happened to Carl?
  - ☑ He must have broken his leg.
  - ☐ He might have broken his arm.

4 How many people went on holiday?
  - ☐ There must have been four.
  - ☑ There might have been five or more.

5 Where did they stay?
  - ☐ They could have stayed with friends.
  - ☑ They must have stayed at a hotel.

6 What did they do on holiday?
  - ☑ They must have taken a lot of photos. (sunsets)
  - ☐ They can't have taken any photos.

7 Why did Andy and Julie send an email to the manager?
  - ☐ They could have written to thank him.
  - ☑ They might have written to complain about their room. (no view)

8 What did Marcia lose?
  - ☐ It might have been her skis.
  - ☑ It could have been her suitcase. (it)

3 Use some of the ideas in sentences 1–8 to say what you think happened to Andy and Carl.

Andy and Carl must be friends and they could have been on ...

4 **T 9.4** Listen to the full conversation between Andy and Carl. Which of your ideas were correct?

GRAMMAR SPOT

1 What is the past tense of these sentences?

| She | must
can't
could
might | be on holiday. |

2 What is the past tense of these sentences?

I must buy some sunglasses.
I have to go home early.
I can see the mountains from my room.

▶▶ **Grammar Reference 9.2 p147**

PRACTICE
Grammar and speaking

1 Respond to the statements and questions. Use the words in brackets.

1 I can't find my homework. (must/forget)
   You must have forgotten it.
2 Mark didn't come to school last week. (must/ill)
3 Why is Isabel late for class? (might/oversleep)
4 I can't find my notebook. (must/drop)
5 The teacher's checking Maria's work. (can't/finish already)
6 How did Bob get such good marks in that test? (must/cheat)

T 9.5 Listen and check. Practise the sentences with a partner.

Discussing grammar

2 How many different modal auxiliary verbs can you fit naturally into each sentence? Discuss as a class the differences in meaning.

| can | can't | could | must | might | should | shall |

1 He _____ have been born during World War II.
2 _____ you help me with the dishes, please?
3 You _____ see the doctor immediately.
4 It _____ be raining.
5 _____ we go out for dinner tonight?
6 I _____ stop smoking.
7 It _____ have been Bill that you met at the party.
8 I _____ learn to speak English.

READING AND SPEAKING
A father and daughter

1 Discuss these questions with a partner and then with the class.

- Who do you look more like, your mother or your father?
- Who are you more like in character, your mother or your father?
- Do you want to bring up your children in the same way you were brought up?

2 In the magazine article on the right, two different members of the same family describe their relationship with each other.

Work in two groups.

Group A Read what Oliver Darrow says about his daughter, Carmen.

Group B Read what Carmen Darrow says about her father, Oliver.

3 In your groups, discuss the answers to the questions about your person.

1 Which two sentences best describe their relationship?
  a It was closer when Carmen was a child.
  b They get on well and have similar interests.
  c They don't have much in common.

2 Which two sentences best describe Oliver?
  a He's done a lot for his daughter.
  b He isn't very sensitive to how she feels.
  c He's more interested in himself than his family.

3 Which two sentences best describe Carmen?
  a She is selfish and spoilt.
  b She tried to please her father.
  c She was never really happy until she married George.

4 How did Oliver behave in front of Carmen's friends?

5 Why did she leave school?

6 Is she happily married? How do you know?

7 What does Carmen think of her father's career?

8 Why don't they see each other very much?

FAMILY MATTERS

Oliver Darrow, actor, talks about his daughter, Carmen.

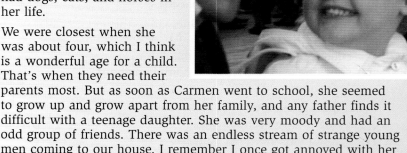

' My first wife and I only had one child. It might have been nice to have more. I would have liked a son, but we just had Carmen.

I see her as my best friend. I think she always comes to me first if she has a problem. We have the same sense of humour and share many interests, except that she's crazy about animals, obsessed with them – she has always had dogs, cats, and horses in her life.

We were closest when she was about four, which I think is a wonderful age for a child. That's when they need their parents most. But as soon as Carmen went to school, she seemed to grow up and grow apart from her family, and any father finds it difficult with a teenage daughter. She was very moody and had an odd group of friends. There was an endless stream of strange young men coming to our house. I remember I once got annoyed with her in front of her friends and she didn't talk to me for days.

I've always wanted the best for her. We sent her to a good school, but she wasn't happy there. She left because she wanted to become an actress, so with my connections I got her into drama school, but she didn't like that either. She worked for a while doing small roles in films, but she must have found it boring because she gave it up, though she never really said why. She got married a few years ago; her husband's a vet. They must be happy because they work together, and she loves animals.

'I see her as my best friend.'

We have the same tastes in books and music. When she was younger, I used to take her to the opera – that's my passion – but she can't have liked it very much because she hasn't come with me for years. I don't think she goes to the cinema or watches TV much. She might watch my films, but I don't know. It's not the kind of thing she talks to me about.

I'm very pleased to have Carmen. She's a good daughter, but I don't think she likes my new wife very much because she doesn't visit us very often. I'm looking forward to being a grandfather one day. I hope she'll have a son. '

Carmen Darrow, veterinary assistant, talks about her father, Oliver.

'I don't really know my father. He isn't easy to get on with. I've always found him difficult to talk to. He's a bit reserved, but he loves to be recognized and asked for his autograph.

I think people see his films and think he's very easygoing, but he really isn't. He's won some awards for his films, and he's really proud of them. He used to show them to my friends when they came to the house and that really embarrassed me.

'He's like a stranger.'

He can't have been home much when I was a small child because I don't remember much about him. His work always came first, and he was often away from home making films. I wasn't surprised when he and my mother split up.

He must have wanted the best for me, but the best was always what *he* wanted. He chose my school and I hated it. I had no friends there, I was miserable and didn't do well, so I was asked to leave. He must have been very disappointed, but he said nothing to me. He wanted me to be an actor like him but I'm not at all like him. I tried it for a while, but I was miserable until I met my husband. He's a vet and I'm his assistant. Now I'm doing what I always wanted to do, working with animals.

My father and I have always been so different. I love animals and he loves books and music, and above all opera, which I hate. If he comes to see us (we live on a farm), he always wears totally the wrong clothes, but we still don't see much of each other. It's because he didn't really want me to marry George. He wanted me to marry a famous film star or something, but of course I didn't. George and I don't want children, we have our animals, but my father would love to have a grandson. Maybe his new wife will give him the son he wants, but probably not. She cares too much about being slim and beautiful.

I occasionally see one of his films on TV. I find it hard to believe he's my father. He's like a stranger.'

4 Find a partner from the other group and compare your answers. Then read the other text.

What do you think?

Who has the more realistic view of the relationship? Oliver or Carmen? Why?

Language work

Use the modal verb in brackets in either the present or past to rewrite the first part of each sentence. Complete the sentences with your own ideas.

1 I'm sure Carmen likes animals a lot because … (must)
   She must like animals because she enjoys working with them.
2 I don't think Oliver is a very famous actor because … (can't)
3 I think maybe he has won an Oscar® because … (might)
4 I'm sure she had a lot of friends when she was a teenager because … (must)
5 I don't think she worked hard at school because … (can't)

VOCABULARY AND SPEAKING
Character adjectives

1 Do the personality quiz to discover what type of person you are. Write **Y** for *Yes*, **N** for *No*, and **S** for *Sometimes*.

What type of person are **you**?

1 ☐ Are you usually smiling and happy?

2 ☐ Do you enjoy the company of other people?

3 ☐ Do you find it difficult to meet new people?

4 ☐ Do you have definite plans for your future career?

5 ☐ Does your mood change often and suddenly for no reason?

6 ☐ Do you notice other people's feelings?

7 ☐ Do you think the future will be good?

8 ☐ Can your friends depend on you?

9 ☐ Is your room often a mess?

10 ☐ Do you get annoyed if you have to wait for anyone or anything?

11 ☐ Do you put off until tomorrow what you could do today?

12 ☐ Do you work hard?

13 ☐ Do you keep your feelings and ideas to yourself?

14 ☐ Do you often give presents?

15 ☐ Do you talk a lot?

16 ☐ Are you usually calm and not worried by things?

2 Work with a partner. Ask your partner to do the quiz about *you*. Compare your ideas and your partner's ideas about you. Are they the same or different?

3 Match these adjectives with the questions in the quiz.

☑ 8 reliable
☐ optimistic
☐ sociable
☐ talkative
☐ reserved
☐ shy
☐ impatient
☐ ambitious
☐ lazy
☐ generous
☐ moody
☐ hardworking
☐ easygoing
☐ untidy
☐ cheerful
☐ sensitive

Which adjectives describe you?

4 Which adjectives describe positive qualities and which describe negative? Which describe both?

Positive	Negative	Both
reliable		

5 Write the opposite of the adjectives in exercise 3. Remember that the prefixes *in-* and *un-* can sometimes be used to make negatives. Which of the adjectives can use these?

6 Describe someone in the class to your partner, but don't say who it is. Can your partner guess who it is?

WRITING: A description (2)
▶▶ Go to p116

LISTENING AND SPEAKING
Brothers and sisters

1 Do a class survey.
   1 Find out who has got any brothers and/or sisters.
   2 Who has got the most? How many? Do they like having lots of brothers and sisters?
   3 Has anyone got a twin brother or sister? Do they like being a twin?
   4 Is anyone in the class an only child? Do they like being an only child?

2 **T 9.6** Listen to two people talking about their families. Complete the chart.

Louisa

Rose

	Louisa	Rose
How many brothers and sisters has she got?		
Was she happy as a child? Why/Why not?		
Is she happy now? Why/Why not?		
What do you learn about other members of her family?		

What do you think?

Discuss these questions.
- How many children have you got/would you like to have?
- What size is the perfect family?
- Would you like to have twins?

EVERYDAY ENGLISH
So do I! Neither do I!

1 **T 9.7** Listen to Sue's friends talking to her about themselves. Put a (✓) if it's the same for Sue and a (✗) if it's different.

Sue's friends	Sue	Sue's words
1 I want to travel the world.	✓	*So do I.*
2 I don't want to have lots of children.		
3 I can speak four languages.		
4 I can't drive.		
5 I'm not going to get married until I'm 35.		
6 I went to London last year.		
7 I've never been to Australia.		
8 I don't like politicians.		
9 I'm bored with Hollywood actors.		
10 I love going to parties.		

2 Write in Sue's words. Choose from the lists below.

So am I.	Neither am I.	I am.	I'm not.
So do I.	Neither do I.	I do.	I don't.
So can I.	Neither can I.	I can.	I can't.
So did I.	Neither did I.	I did.	I didn't.
So have I.	Neither have I.	I have.	I haven't.

T 9.7 Listen again and check your answers.

What does Sue say when it is the same for her?
What does she say when it is different?

▶▶ **Grammar Reference 9.4 and 9.5 p147**

3 Work with a partner. Read the statements in exercise 1 and give true answers.

4 Go around the class. Everyone must make a statement about themselves or give an opinion about something. The others in the class must respond.

I love chocolate!

So do I. / Me too.

I don't!

I didn't do my homework.

Neither did I. / Me neither.

I did!

10 Obsessions

Present Perfect Continuous · Time expressions · Compound nouns · Quantity

TEST YOUR GRAMMAR

1 For each pair, match a line in **A** with a line or picture in **B**.

	A	**B**
1	What do you do What are you doing	on the floor? for a living?
2	He speaks He's speaking	three languages. to the teacher.
3	She has She's having	a baby next month. a house by the sea.
4	What have you done What have you been doing	with my pen? I can't find it. since I last saw you?
5	Who drank my beer? Who's been drinking my beer?	 
6	I read that book. I was reading that book	It was really good. when you called.

2 Look at the second sentence in each pair. What do the verbs have in common?

TONY'S PHONE BILL
Present Perfect Continuous

1 **T 10.1** Read and listen to the newspaper article. Answer the questions.

1 How much was the phone bill?
2 Why did his father buy him a mobile?
3 What has he done with the phone now?
4 Where has Tony been working?

Dad bans phone after 3,500 texts!

A Manchester teenager has received a phone bill for over £450 after sending 3,500 text messages in just one month.

Tony Russell has had his new 'state of the art' mobile phone for only three months, but now his father, Lionel, has taken it away.

'He's been asking me for a mobile for years because all his friends have got one,' explained Lionel. 'I finally bought one for his birthday because he's been doing so well at school, but he and his mates are "texting-crazy". They do it all the time – on buses, in the street. They even text each other from different sides of the school playground. They've got "textitis".'

Tony said 'I thought texting was much cheaper than phoning, so I've been texting my friends all day long and even into the early hours of the morning. I've been going to bed at 2.00 most nights. Sometimes my hand hurt from pressing the buttons so much, but I was having such good fun that I couldn't bear to stop!'

His father said, 'I have forgiven him, but I am angry with the phone company as they are encouraging this craze.' He has made his son promise to pay back the money, so Tony has been working on Saturdays. He has found a job in a shoe shop. So far he has paid back £46. 'I reckon it will take me about a year to clear this debt,' he said.

2 Here are the answers to some questions about Tony. Write the questions using *he*.

1 Three months. (*How long … ?*)
2 For years. (*How long … ?*)
3 Because all his friends have got one. (*Why … want … ?*)
4 His friends. (*Who … texting?*)
5 2.00 (*What time … ?*)
6 Yes, he has. (*… forgiven … ?*)
7 £46. (*How much … ?*)
8 About a year. (*How long … ?*)

T 10.2 Listen and check.

GRAMMAR SPOT

1 <u>Underline</u> examples of the Present Perfect Simple and the Present Perfect Continuous in the text.

2 Look at the questions below. Which one asks about an activity? Which one asks about a quantity?

How long have you been learning English?
How many teachers have you had?

▶▶ **Grammar Reference 10.1 and 10.2 p148**

PRACTICE

Conversations

1 Write questions with *How long … ?* Use either the Present Perfect Simple or Continuous. (If both are possible, use the continuous form.)
1 I live in the country. **How long have you been living in the country?**
2 I play tennis.
3 I know Jack well.
4 I work in Hong Kong.
5 I have a Japanese car.

2 Make sentences using the same verbs about yourself. With a partner, ask and answer questions with *How long … ?*

3 For each sentence in exercise 1, write a question in the Past Simple.
1 When _____ move there?
2 How old _____ when _____ started _____ ?
3 Where _____ meet _____ ?
4 Why _____ decide _____ ?
5 How much _____ pay _____ ?

4 **T 10.3** Read and listen to the conversation.

> **A** You look happy. What have you been doing?
> **B** I'm really excited! I've been getting ready to go on holiday.
> **A** Have you done everything?
> **B** Well, I've picked up the tickets and I've been to the bank, but I haven't packed yet.

Make similar conversations with a partner.
1 **A** covered in paint/what/do?
   B redecorate the bathroom.
   A finish yet?
   B paint the door and the ceiling/not put up the wallpaper yet.
2 **A** hands dirty/what/do?
   B filthy/work in the garden.
   A finish yet?
   B cut the grass/not water the flowers yet.
3 **A** your eyes red/what/do?
   B exhausted/revise for my exams.
   A finish them yet?
   B do chemistry and history/not do English yet.

T 10.4 Listen and compare. Practise the conversations again.

Discussing grammar

5 Why are these sentences strange? What would be better?
1 Ouch! I've been cutting my finger.
2 'Why is your hair wet?' 'I've swum.'
3 You've got tears in your eyes. Why have you cried?
4 I'm really sorry, but I've been crashing into the back of your car.
5 I've written my autobiography this afternoon.

A LIFELONG PASSION

Time expressions

1 Astrid Johnsson is a cellist. She has had an interesting life so far. Look quickly through the chart of events in her life. What are some of the things she has done?

Age	Life Event
0	Born on **4 March, 1960**, in Sweden
3	Started playing the cello
8	Won award for *Young Musician of the Year*, toured with the Swedish Youth Orchestra
11	**August 1971**, performed in classical music festival in Stockholm
18–22	Won scholarship and studied at the Royal Academy of Music, London
19	Met her first husband
21	Got married in **spring 1981**
22	Received Master of Music Degree. Played in world concerts and festivals. Appeared on British TV with the London Symphony Orchestra
23	Daughter born **9 July, 1983**
29	Got divorced. Toured Japan, the US, and Canada with the Chamber Orchestra of Great Britain
31	Bought a flat in New York
33–37	Composed concertos and European film soundtracks. Met Georges Leveaux, a conductor
38	**3 August, 1998**, married Georges; moved to Paris
40	Won *Best European Film Soundtrack* 1999
42	Began teaching at the Music Centre, in Paris, and working as a visiting lecturer to music schools worldwide
NOW	Still teaching cello and lecturing

Astrid Johnsson

2 Answer the questions.

1 How long has she been playing the cello?
2 Which orchestras has she played with?
3 What sort of music has she composed?
4 What has she won?
5 How long has she been married to Georges?
6 How many times has she been married?
7 How long was she married to her first husband?
8 How long has she been teaching the cello and lecturing?

PRACTICE

Questions and answers

1 Ask and answer the questions about Astrid.

1 When … born?
2 When … given the award of *Young Musician of the Year*?
3 When … go to the Royal Academy of Music?
4 What … her daughter born?
5 Which countries … lived in?
6 When … appear on British TV?
7 How many children … ?
8 How long … in Paris?

> *When was she born?*
>
> *In 1960.*

T 10.5 Listen and check.

2 Make a similar chart of the events in your life or the life of someone you know well. Ask and answer questions with a partner.

A lecture tour

3 Astrid is on a two-week lecturing tour of England and Scotland. Look at her schedule.

	WEEK 1	WEEK 2
SUNDAY	London	Birmingham
MONDAY	London	Manchester
TUESDAY	London	Manchester
WEDNESDAY	London	Edinburgh
THURSDAY	Oxford	Edinburgh
FRIDAY	Oxford	Edinburgh
SATURDAY	Birmingham	Fly home to Paris

4 It is Monday of the second week, and Astrid is being interviewed by a journalist. How does she answer these questions?

1 How long are you here in Britain for? **Just two weeks.**
2 How long have you been in Britain?
3 Where were you the day before yesterday?
4 Where were you this time last week?
5 Where will you be the day after tomorrow?
6 Where will you be a week today?

T 10.6 Listen and check.

Discussing grammar

5 Correct the mistakes in the questions.

1 What time did you go to bed at last night?
2 What have you done last weekend?
3 What are you doing this night?
4 Are you going to study English the next month?
5 Have you been studying English since three years?
6 How long you live in this town?
7 When is your mother born?
8 How long have you been knowing your teacher?

6 Ask and answer the questions with a partner.

3 Complete these sentences with the phrases from the box.

> while she was at music school
> after winning the award
> at the age of three
> until she married Georges
> since she married Georges
> while she was composing
> two years after she got married
> between 1978 and 1982

1 She started having cello lessons
_____ .
2 _____ for *Young Musician of the Year*, she toured schools with the Swedish Youth Orchestra.
3 She was at the Royal Academy of Music _____ .
4 She met her first husband _____ .
5 Her daughter was born _____ .
6 She met Georges _____ concertos and European film soundtracks.
7 She lived in New York _____ .
8 She's been living in Paris _____ .

▶▶ **Grammar Reference 10.3 p148**

WRITING: Writing a biography
▶▶ Go to p117

READING AND SPEAKING
A big name in Hollywood

1 Discuss the questions about your favourite film star.

- What films has he/she been in?
- What kind of films does he/she act in? Action? Romance? Comedy?
- What is the best role he/she has ever played?
- What do you think he/she is like as a person? What does he/she look like?
- Where does he/she live?
- What do you know about his/her family?
- What is he/she most famous for? Looks? Acting ability? Behaviour off-screen?

2 Match a line in **A** with a line in **B**.

A	B
I was once	as the bad guy.
In films he is always cast	She has real talent.
She auditioned	the big time.
He's going to make	a production company.
She was turned down	for the part of Mary. (x2)
Give her a break!	an extra in a film.
He set up	

3 Read the magazine article. Answer as many questions as you can in exercise 1 about Dennis Woodruff.

4 Answer the questions.
1 Who will you probably *not* see if you go to Hollywood?
2 Is Dennis famous?
3 How does he try to sell himself?
4 Will he make the big time?
5 Where does he audition? How do people react?
6 Why is he tired?
7 How did he get the idea of promoting himself?
8 Is Dennis optimistic?

Language work

5 Here are the answers to some questions about Dennis. Write the questions.
1 _____? For 25 years.
2 _____? Over 300 times.
3 _____? 20 years ago.
4 _____? For 30 years.
5 _____? 15,000.

6 The words in **A** are in the text. Match them with similar meanings in **B**.

A	B
trendy	improbable
unlikely	stories
fake	caught so you can't move
trapped	enormous
ignore	different from what is considered usual
unconventional	not real
tales	pay no attention to
huge	fashionable

Fam
for not

If **you go** to Hollywood and look around the trendy coffee shops and restaurants, it is unlikely that you will meet your favourite film star. However, it is almost certain that you will meet Dennis Woodruff.

Dennis is a 'movie' star – well, sort of. You learn this quickly because he tells everyone he meets. He wears a T-shirt that says 'Dennis Woodruff, world-famous actor'. On his modified Chevrolet convertible he has five Oscars® (fake, unfortunately) and other awards that he has won. He also hands out videotapes of his films in exchange for a modest $10.

If fame is a matter of being known by influential people, then Dennis Woodruff is certainly famous. He describes himself as Hollywood's best known out-of-work actor. He has been looking for work for 25 years. It is true that he has been on television over 300 times and has worked in about 45 motion pictures, invariably as an extra.

OUS being famous

Dennis Woodruff
Hollywood 'movie' star – sort of

KNOWN ACTOR DENNIS WOODRUFF SEEKS HIS BIG BREAK 818 761-0580

WOODRUFF

DENNIS WOODRUFF

ACTOR DENNIS WOODRUFF

CAST ME!

HOLLYWOOD

But mostly he is known as the hippie guy with the long blond ponytail, who is trapped in the only role he has been able to play with any success – playing Dennis. Everything about Dennis has to do with selling himself. He talks constantly about his life, his talent, his artistic abilities, his ambitions. His never-ending search for work in the film industry no longer has any realistic chance of success, so now he acts out the role of an actor looking for work. 'Cast me!' shouts the writing on his car. 'Buy my movie!'

'Actually,' says Dennis, 'I am a movie star. It's just that no one has realized it yet.' His 'movies', titled *Dennis Woodruff the Movie, Parts I and II* and *Double Feature, starring Dennis Woodruff* are heavily autobiographical – more documentaries of his life than anything else. You can watch him auditioning for parts in front of the security cameras at local restaurants. People recognize him and then, sadly, ignore him.

He has rugged, unconventional good looks, though he seems tired. 'I've been making another movie about me. It's called *Life Is Art*. I want to show everyone how my life is like a work of art.'

One of the most miserable tales he tells is about how he nearly made the big time. The famous actor John Wayne was going to give him a break, but unfortunately he died. Legendary producer Otto Preminger wanted to make him a star. He also died.

Now nearly 50, Dennis first had the idea of promoting himself over 20 years ago when he asked a casting director why he had been turned down for a part. 'Because you're not a big name in Hollywood,' came the answer. Dennis immediately wrote his name in huge letters on the top of his car. It didn't get him any work, but it did get him noticed.

He's been living in a mobile home in East Hollywood for 30 years, and to his credit, he manages to earn a living. He has set up a production company with his brother, and he has sold 15,000 copies of his video. True success, he feels, is just around the corner. Now there's optimism for you.

VOCABULARY
Compound nouns

1 Nouns can be combined to make a new word or phrase. These are called compound nouns. They are written in different ways. Look at these words from the article about Dennis Woodruff.

One word	Two words
ponytail	mobile home
videotape	movie star

2 Put one word in each box to form three compound nouns.

1 ache
   tooth brush
   paste

2 **dining**
   changing ☐
   waiting

3 lights
   ☐ warden
   jam

4 news
   travel ☐
   estate

5 place
   ☐ engine
   works

6 **credit**
   birthday ☐
   business

7 brush
   ☐ dresser
   cut

8 mail
   ☐ **port**
   conditioning

9 **cup**
   ☐ spoon
   pot

10 set
    ☐ glasses
    tan

11 **wrapping**
    writing ☐
    toilet

12 centre
    ☐ **spree**
    list

3 Here are definitions of some compound nouns from exercise 2. What are the words?

- A pain in your tooth or teeth.
- A place where aeroplanes take off and land.
- A person whose job is to cut and style people's hair.
- The time when the sun goes down and night begins.
- A place where there are lots of different kinds of shops.

4 Write definitions of more words from exercise 2 and test the other students.

LISTENING AND SPEAKING
Collectors

1 Discuss these questions as a class.

- What kinds of things do people often collect?
- Why do people collect things?
- Do you collect anything? Did you use to collect things when you were younger? What? Why?

2 You are going to listen to two people who are both passionate collectors. Look at the pictures. What can you see? What do they collect? What questions would you like to ask them?

3 Work in two groups.

Group A `T 10.7` Listen to Andrea Levitt who collects dolls.

Group B `T 10.8` Listen to Jeff Parker who collects *Star Wars* memorabilia.

Andrea Levitt and her doll collection

4 Answer the questions.

1 Where does she/he live? Who with?
2 What does she/he do for a living?
3 How long has she/he been collecting?
4 How many items has she/he collected?
5 How many rooms of the house are taken up with the collection?
6 What's her/his favourite item?
7 Where do the items come from?
8 Is she/he in touch with other people who share the same hobby?

5 Find a partner from the other group. Compare and exchange information.

Jeff Parker and his *Star Wars* collection

EVERYDAY ENGLISH
Expressing quantity

1 Complete the sentences with the words below. Some are used more than once.

a few   How many
a little   **enough**   too much
as much as   too many
all   **How much**   any
as many as

1 A ~~How much~~ coffee do you drink?
  B At least six cups a day.
  A That's ~~too much~~. You shouldn't drink ~~as much~~ that.
2 A ~~How many~~ aspirins do you usually take when you have a headache?
  B About four or five.
  A That's ~~too many~~. You shouldn't take ~~as many~~ that!
3 A ~~How much~~ do you earn?
  B Not ~~enough~~ to pay all my bills!
4 A ~~How many~~ people are there in your class?
  B Forty.
  A I think that's ~~too many~~.
5 A Have you got ~~any~~ homework tonight?
  B Far ~~too much~~. I'll never be able to do it ~~all~~.
6 A How old are you?
  B Seventeen. I'm old ~~enough~~ to get married, but not old ~~enough~~ to vote!
7 A When did you last go to the dentist?
  B Very recently. Just ~~a few~~ days ago.
8 A Do you take milk in your tea?
  B Just ~~a little~~.

T 10.9 Listen and check. Practise the conversations with a partner.

2 With your partner, ask and answer the questions in exercise 1 about you.

11 Tell me about it!

Indirect questions · Question tags · The body · Informal English

TEST YOUR GRAMMAR

1 All of these sentences are correct.
Why is there no *does* in sentences 2 and 3?

1 Where does she live?
2 I know where she lives.
3 Can you tell me where she lives?

2 Choose the correct question tag.

1 It's a beautiful day,	did he?
2 You like learning English,	isn't it?
3 You've been to Australia,	didn't they?
4 Henry didn't say that,	don't you?
5 They had a good time,	haven't you?

It's a beautiful day, isn't it?

A STRANGER IN TOWN
Indirect questions

1 **T 11.1** Flavia has just checked into her hotel in Toronto. Look at the information she wants, then listen to the conversation. Complete her sentences.

What Flavia wants to know	What Flavia says
1 Could you help me?	I wonder if _____ help me.
2 Are we near the CN Tower?	I'm not sure _____ near the CN Tower.
3 Are there any good restaurants nearby?	Can you tell me _____ any good restaurants nearby?
4 What time do the banks close?	I don't know what time _____.
5 Which restaurant did you suggest?	I'm sorry, but I can't remember which restaurant _____.

GRAMMAR SPOT

1 Look at what Flavia says. These are indirect questions. How does the word order change?

2 What happens to *do/does/did* in indirect questions?

3 When do we use *if* in indirect questions?

▶▶ **Grammar Reference 11.1 p149**

2 Read tapescript 11.1 on p131 and practise the conversation. Then close your books and do it again.

3 Here is some more information that Flavia wants. Use the prompts to ask indirect questions.

1 What's the population of the city?
(*Do you know … ?*)

2 Is there an underground?
(*Could you tell me … ?*)

3 Where are the best shops?
(*Can you tell me … ?*)

4 Where can I go for a run in the mornings?
(*Do you happen to know … ?*)

5 Is there an art gallery near here?
(*Do you have any idea … ?*)

6 What do people do in the evening?
(*I wonder … .*)

4 Work with a partner. Ask and answer similar indirect questions about a city or town that you know well.

PRACTICE

Asking polite questions

1 Match a word in **A** with a line in **B** and a line in **C**.

A	B	C
What How Which	newspaper football team long far kind of many much	times have you been on a plane? do you support? music do you like? do you read? is it to the station from here? time do you spend watching TV? does it take you to get ready in the morning?

2 Work with a partner. Ask and answer indirect questions using the ideas in exercise 1.

Could you tell me . . . ?
Would you mind telling me . . . ?

Finding out about Madonna

3 What do you know about Madonna?

She's American.

She's a singer and an actress.

4 Ask about Madonna using these phrases and the prompts 1–8.

I wonder . . .	I'd like to know . . .
I have no idea . . .	Does anybody know . . .

1 where/born
2 how old/when/start/singing
3 go to university
4 ever win any awards
5 where/live
6 how many times/married
7 how many children/have
8 how many number one hits/have

I wonder where she was born.

5 Work with a partner.

Student A Look at p155. **Student B** Look at p156.

WE LIKE ANIMALS, DON'T WE?
Question tags

1 **T 11.2** Listen to Gabriella, aged 4, talking to Karen, her mother. <u>Underline</u> the question tags.

G Mummy?
K Yes, Gaby?
G I've got ten fingers, haven't I?
K Yes, that's right, sweetie. Ten pretty little fingers.
G And Daddy didn't go to work this morning, did he?
K No, it's Saturday. He's working in the garden today.
G And we like animals, don't we, Mummy?
K Yes, we do. Especially our cats, Sammy and Teddy.
G Can I have a biscuit now, Mummy?

T 11.2 Listen again. Does Gabriella's intonation go up or down on the question tags?

2 Complete the conversation between Karen and her assistant with a question tag from the box.

| didn't I? | isn't it? | am I? | haven't I? |

K Now, what's happening today? I've got a meeting this afternoon, _____?
A Yes, that's right. With Henry and Tom.
K And the meeting's here, _____?
A No, it isn't. It's in Tom's office at 3 o'clock.
K Oh! I'm not having lunch with anyone, _____?
A No, you're free for lunch.
K Phew! And I signed all my letters, _____?
A No, you didn't, actually. They're on your desk, waiting for you.
K OK. I'll do them now. Thanks a lot.

T 11.3 Listen and check. Does Karen's intonation go up or down on the question tags?

GRAMMAR SPOT

1 Which speaker, Gabriella or Karen, uses question tags to mean . . . ?
- I'm not sure, so I'm checking.
- Talk to me, I want to have a conversation with you.

2 How do we form question tags?

▶▶ **Grammar Reference 11.2 p149**

3 Practise the conversations with a partner.

PRACTICE

Question tags and intonation

1 Look at the sentences and write the question tags.

1	It isn't very warm today, _____?	↗
2	You can cook, _____?	
3	You've got a CD player, _____?	
4	Mary's very clever, _____?	
5	There are a lot of people here, _____?	
6	The film wasn't very good, _____?	
7	I'm a silly person, _____?	
8	You aren't going out dressed like that, _____?	

T 11.4 Listen and check. Write ↗ if the questions tag goes up and ↘ if it goes down.

2 Match a response with a sentence in exercise 1.

- ☑4 Yes. She's extremely bright.
- ☐ Believe it or not, I haven't. I've got a cassette player, though.
- ☐ Why? What's wrong with my clothes? I thought I looked really cool.
- ☐ No, it's freezing.
- ☐ No, you're not. Everybody makes mistakes.
- ☐ Me? No! I can't even boil an egg.
- ☐ I know! It's absolutely packed. I can't move!
- ☐ It was terrible! The worst I've seen in ages.

T 11.5 Listen and check. Practise the conversations with a partner.

Conversations

3 Add three question tags to the conversation below. Do they go up or down?

> **A** It's so romantic.
> **B** What is?
> **A** Well, they're really in love.
> **B** Who?
> **A** Paul and Mary.
> **B** Paul and Mary aren't in love.
> **A** Oh yes, they are. They're mad about each other.

T 11.6 Listen and compare.

4 Look at p156. Choose one of the conversations and add question tags. Learn it by heart, and act it out for the rest of the class.

T 11.7 Listen and compare.

READING AND SPEAKING
How well do you know your world?

1 Do you know the answers to these questions?

1 **Do animals have feelings?**
2 **What are the Earth's oldest living things?**
3 **What man-made things on Earth can be seen from space?**
4 **What is the most terrible natural disaster to have hit the Earth?**
5 **Why isn't there a row 13 on aeroplanes?**
6 **Why do women live longer than men?**
7 **Was Uncle Sam a real person?**

2 Put one of these lines before each question in exercise 1. What is true for you?

> I think I know . . .   I'm not sure . . .
> I think . . .   I have no idea . . .
> I don't know . . .   I wonder . . .

> *I think animals have feelings.*

> *I have no idea what the Earth's oldest living things are.*

Discuss your ideas as a class.
Which question interests you the most?

3 Read the answers to the questions. How much did you already know?

4 Here are the last lines of the seven answers. Which answer do they go with?

   a The country with the highest life expectancy is Japan – 84 years for women and 77 for men.

   b Less than 24 hours after the meal, Christ was crucified.

   c It is very likely that this explosion wiped out all the dinosaurs.

   d Fear is instinctive and requires no conscious thought.

   e You can also see fires burning in the tropical rainforest.

   f It has also endured climatic catastrophes, and nuclear bomb testing – and still it lives on!

   g Over the years, various cartoonists gave him his characteristic appearance.

5 Here are seven questions, one for each text. What do the underlined words refer to?

   1 Where is the oldest <u>one</u> in the world?
   2 Why is <u>this</u> difficult to see from space?
   3 Do <u>they</u> have the full range of emotions?
   4 How did <u>they</u> become extinct?
   5 What did <u>he</u> say 'US' stood for?
   6 Do <u>they</u> have a thirteenth floor?
   7 Why are <u>they</u> more likely to have accidents?

Answer questions 1–7.

6 These numbers are from the texts. What do they refer to?

4,600	15	200	1906	1815
65 million	14	six	84	1766

Producing a class poster

7 What else would you like to know about the world? Work in groups and write some questions. Think of:

- places (countries, cities, buildings)
- people (customs, languages, superstitions, famous people)
- things (machines, gadgets, transportation, etc.)
- plants and animals

8 Choose two questions you wrote in exercise 7 and research the answers. You could use the Internet or an encyclopedia.

Make them into a poster for your classroom wall.

How well do

1 Q Do animals have feelings?

A All pet owners would say 'Yes'. Molly the dog and Whiskers the cat can feel angry, depressed, neglected, happy, even jealous and guilty.

Many scientists, however, are sceptical about giving animals the full range of emotions that humans can feel. Part of the problem is that it is impossible to prove that even a human being is feeling happy or sad. In fact, it is only because we can observe body language and facial expression that we can deduce it. And of course humans can express the emotion with language.

However, most researchers do agree that many creatures experience fear. Some scientists define this as a primary emotion. ☐

2 Q What are the Earth's oldest living things?

A The White Mountains of California are home to our oldest living things – trees! The oldest tree in the world, Methuselah, has roots that go back over 4,600 years. This makes it older even than the Great Pyramids. The 26-foot bristlecone pine tree is the oldest of many that have outlived civilization after civilization. ☐

3 Q What man-made things on Earth can be seen from space?

A *'When humans first flew in space, they were amazed to discover that the only man-made object visible from orbit was the Great Wall of China.'* Although this is a nice idea, it's not true. The Great Wall is mostly grey stone in a grey landscape and, in fact, is very difficult to see even from a plane flying at a mere 15 kilometres above. What can be seen when orbiting the Earth (from about 200 kilometres up) are the lights of the world's large metropolitan areas. ☐

4 Q What is the most terrible natural disaster to have hit the Earth?

A Earthquakes, volcanic eruptions, and hurricanes are responsible for the deaths of thousands of people every year.

One of the most violent earthquakes ever recorded was in Ecuador in 1906. It was the equivalent of 100 H-bombs, but it was nothing compared to a volcanic eruption in Tambora, Indonesia in 1815. This was the equivalent of 10,000 H-bombs. But, even these are nothing compared to many tropical hurricanes: they regularly have the energy of an amazing 100,000 H-bombs.

However, there is one natural disaster that beats all of these by a very long way – a meteor that hit the Earth 65 million years ago and caused an explosion the equivalent of 10 million H-bombs. ☐

6 Q Why do women live longer than men?

A Women generally live about six years longer than men. Evidence suggests that boys are the weaker sex at birth, which means that more die in infancy. Men also have a greater risk of heart disease than women, and they have heart attacks earlier in life. Men smoke and drink more than women, and their behaviour is generally more aggressive, particularly when driving, so they are more likely to die in accidents. Also, men are more often in dangerous occupations, such as construction work.

Historically, women died in childbirth and men in wars. So nuns and philosophers often lived to great ages. Now childbearing is less risky and there are fewer wars. ☐

5 Q Why isn't there a row 13 on aeroplanes?

A In many countries, the number 13 is considered to be very unlucky. In France, there is never a house with the number 13. In the United States, modern high-rise buildings label the floor that follows 12 as 14.

Where did this fear of a number come from? The idea goes back at least to Norse mythology in ancient times. There was a banquet with 12 gods. Loki, the spirit of evil, decided to join without being invited. In the fight that followed, Balder, the favourite of the gods, was killed.

In Christianity, this theme was repeated at the Last Supper. Jesus Christ and his apostles numbered 13 people at the table. ☐

7 Q Was Uncle Sam a real person?

A Yes, he was! This symbol of the United States with a long white beard, wearing striped trousers and top hat, was a meat packer from New York state.

Uncle Sam was Samuel Wilson, born in Arlington, Massachusetts in 1766. At the age of eight, he was a drummer boy in the American Revolution. Later in life he moved to New York and opened a meat-packing company. He was a good and caring employer and became affectionately known as Uncle Sam.

Sam Wilson sold meat to the army, and he wrote the letters US on the crates. This meant 'United States', but this abbreviation was not yet common. One day a company worker was asked what the letters US stood for. He wasn't sure, and wrongly said that perhaps the letters stood for his employer, Uncle Sam. Nevertheless, the mistake continued. Soon soldiers started referring to all military goods as coming from Uncle Sam. They even saw themselves as Uncle Sam's men. ☐

LISTENING AND SPEAKING
The forgetful generation

1 **T 11.8** Listen to the introduction to a radio programme called *What's Your Problem?* and answer the questions.

- What problem are they talking about?
- What do they think is causing it?

2 Discuss these questions.

- Does your lifestyle mean that you have a lot to remember to do each day?
- Do you think modern society is busier and more stressful than 100 years ago?
- How do you remember all the things that you have to do each day?

3 **T 11.9** Listen to Ellen, Josh, and Fiona, and take notes.

	What did they forget?	**What did they do?**
Ellen		
Josh		
Fiona		

4 **T 11.10** Listen to the rest of the radio programme and answer the questions.

1 What is Professor Alan Buchan's job?
2 What is it about some modern day working practices that causes forgetfulness?
3 Why did the woman think that she was going insane?
4 What was the woman's problem?
5 What helped the woman feel more relaxed?
6 Does Professor Buchan advise using a computer to help remember things?
7 What does he advise? Why?
8 How does the presenter try to be funny at the end of the interview?

What do you think?

- Do you think Professor Buchan's explanation for forgetfulness is true?
- Do you know any stories of forgetfulness, either your own or somebody else's?

VOCABULARY AND IDIOMS
What can your body do?

1 As a class, write all the parts of the body that you know on the board.

2 Work with a partner. Which parts of the body do you use to:

kick   chew
lick   **think**   stare
bite   hold   point
hug   climb   drop
hit   kiss
whistle

3 Match a verb from exercise 2 with a noun or phrase from the box.

a ladder	into an apple
litter on the ground	me on the cheek
into space	a tune
about the meaning of life	a football
your grandmother	a gun
a nail with a hammer	gum
an ice-cream	me in your arms

4 Look at these idioms. Can you guess their meaning?

hold your breath
kiss something goodbye
hit the roof
think twice (about something)
kick the habit
drop someone a line

Complete the sentences. Use the idioms above. If necessary, change the form of the verb. The first letter of each missing word is given.

1 The best way to stop hiccups is to
   h_____ your b_____ and
   count to ten.

2 My parents h_____ the r_____
   when I said I'd been to an all-night
   party.

3 I've tried so many times to stop biting
   my nails, but I just can't k_____
   the h_____.

4 I almost bought a new sports car, but
   then I t_____ t_____ about it
   and realized it wasn't such a great idea.

5 **A** I lost my purse with £200 in it.
   B Well, you can k_____ that
       money g_____ !

6 D_____ me a l_____ when
   you know what time you're coming,
   and I'll meet you at the station.

WRITING: Words that join ideas
▶▶ Go to p118

EVERYDAY ENGLISH
Informal English

1 When we speak, we use a lot of informal language, depending on who we're speaking to.

These trainers cost ninety quid!

You're kidding!

In the conversations, choose the correct expression.

1 **A** What do you say we break for lunch?
  B ☐ Great idea.   We can grab a sandwich at the deli.
      ☐ I get it.

2 **A** ☐ How are you doing?
      ☐ What are you up to?
  B Nothing much. Just sitting around watching TV.
  A You're such a couch potato.
  B ☐ Hey, take a break!   I work hard all week. I like
      ☐ Hey, give me a break!   to relax at weekends.

3 **A** Quick! Give me your homework so I can copy it.
  B ☐ Look out!   Do your own homework!
      ☐ No way!

4 **A** Did you mend the TV?
  B ☐ Kind of.   Channel 4's OK, but we still can't get Sky.
      ☐ All right.
  A Anything good on tonight?
  B ☐ Dunno.   Look in the paper.
      ☐ What's up?

5 **A** What do you call that stuff you use to clean between
       your teeth?
  B What do you mean?
  A ☐ You see!   It's like string. White.
      ☐ You know!
  B ☐ Wow!   You mean dental floss.
      ☐ Oh!
  A Yeah. That's it!

T 11.11 Listen and check. Practise the conversations with a partner.

2 Underline the examples of informal language. How do we say them more formally? Be careful if you try to use them!

12 Life's great events!

Reported speech · Reporting verbs · Birth, marriage, and death · Saying sorry

TEST YOUR GRAMMAR

1 Read the story of John and Moira in **A** and complete their actual conversation in **B**.

THE MARRIAGE PROPOSAL

A **John** greeted **Moira** and asked how she was. She told him she was fine. He said it was great to see her. He added that they hadn't seen each other since Paris. She said that she had loved Paris and asked if they could go back next spring. John said there was something he had to ask her. He told her that he loved her and asked if she would marry him and come to Paris on honeymoon. She said that she would and that she loved him too.

B **J** Hi, Moira. How __are you__ ?
M I _____, thanks.
J It _____ to see you again. We _____ seen each other since Paris.
M I _____ Paris. _____ we _____ back next spring?
J There _____ something I _____ to ask you.
I _____ you. _____ you _____ me and come to Paris on honeymoon?
M Yes, I_____. I _____ you, too.

2 Which is direct speech and which is reported speech?

3 **T 12.1** Listen and check. What are the differences?

THE WEDDING
Reported statements and questions

1 Adam and Beatrice meet at John and Moira's wedding. Match a line in **A** with a line in **B**.

A Adam	B Beatrice
1 How do you know John and Moira?	Yes, we have. We flew in from Dublin yesterday.
2 Are you married?	Sure. I'll introduce you to my husband.
3 Where did you meet your husband?	We're staying at the Four Seasons Hotel.
4 Have you travelled far to get here?	Yes, I am. That's my husband over there.
5 Do you live in Dublin?	I went to the same school as Moira.
6 So, where are you staying?	Actually, I met him at a wedding.
7 So am I. Can we meet there later for a drink?	Yes, we do.

T 12.2 Listen and check.

2 Beatrice is telling her husband, Ron, about the conversation with Adam. Read what she says.

*'I just met this really nice guy called Adam. He was very friendly. Do you know what he said? First, he asked me how I **knew** John and Moira. I told him that I **had gone** to the same school as Moira. Then he asked if I **was** married. Of course I said that I **was**! And next …'*

GRAMMAR SPOT

1 Complete the reported speech.

Direct speech	Reported speech
'Are you married?' he asked.	He asked if I ___was___ married.
'We're married,' she said.	She said that they _____ married.
'How do you know John and Moira?' he asked.	He asked me how I _____ John and Moira.
'I went to the same school as Moira,' she told him.	She told him that she _____ to the same school as Moira.

2 What happens to tenses in reported speech?

3 What is the difference in the way *say* and *tell* are used?

4 When is *if* used?

▶▶ Grammar Reference 12.1–12.3 p150

PRACTICE

What did Adam say?

1 Work with a partner. Continue reporting the conversation.
'… *next he asked where we'd met and I told him that we …*'

T 12.3 Listen and compare.

He's a liar!

2 After having a drink with Adam, Ron and Beatrice go back to their hotel room. Complete their conversation.

1 **R** Adam lives in Birmingham.
  B He told me he _____! (Cambridge)
2 **R** He doesn't like his new job.
  B He told me he _____ it! (love)
3 **R** He's moving to Manchester.
  B Hang on! He told me _____! (Australia)
4 **R** He went to Brighton on his last holiday.
  B Strange. He told me _____! (Florida)
5 **R** He'll be 40 next week.
  B Really! He told me _____! (30)
6 **R** He's been married three times.
  B But he told me _____! (never/married)
  R You see! I told you he was a liar!

T 12.4 Listen and check. Notice the stress and intonation. Practise the conversation with a partner.

Discussing grammar

3 Work with a partner. What is the difference in meaning in the pairs of sentences below? When does *'d = had*? When does *'d = would*?

1 He asked them how they'd travelled to the wedding.
  He asked them how they'd travel to the wedding.
2 She told her mother that she loved John.
  She told her mother that she'd love John.
3 She said they lived in Dublin.
  She said they'd lived in Dublin.

What did the people actually say in direct speech?

4 Report these sentences.
1 'I'm tired!' he said.
2 'Are you leaving on Friday?' she asked me.
3 'We haven't seen Jack for a long time,' they said.
4 'We flew to Tokyo,' they said.
5 'Which airport did you fly from?' I asked them.
6 'The flight has been cancelled,' the announcement said.
7 'I'll call you later,' he said.
8 'We can't do the exercise,' they told the teacher.

GO TO PRISON!
Reported commands and requests

1 Read the newspaper article. Name the people in the photos.

2 Who is speaking? Find the lines in the text that report these sentences.

   1 'You have to go to prison for 14 days.'
     Judge Pickles ordered them to spend 14 days in prison.

   2 'It's terrible. We can hear them shouting from across the street.'

   3 'Please will you stop making a noise? My baby can't get to sleep.'

   4 'Stop making that noise!'

   5 'Please, can you come right away?'

   6 'OK. OK. It's true. We were arguing.'

   7 'You've been wasting our money on drinking and gambling again!'

   8 'We didn't throw the chair.'

   9 'Remember that you have already had two warnings from the police.'

  10 'I think you should see a marriage guidance counsellor.'

'We can hear them shouting through the walls.'

'A MARRIAGE MADE IN HELL!'

This is how Judge Margaret Pickles described the marriage of Kenny and Kathleen Brady as she ordered them to spend 14 days in prison.

'My husband's been wasting money on drinking and gambling.'

THE COUPLE married only six months ago, and already they are famous for their fights. Neighbours complained that they could hear them shouting from across the street. Ann West, who lives next door, said, 'First I asked them nicely to stop because my baby couldn't get to sleep, but they didn't. Then my husband knocked on their door and told them to stop, but they refused to listen. They threw a chair out of the window at him. It just missed him! So that was it! We called the police and asked them to come right away.'

The Bradys admitted they had been arguing. Mrs Brady said that she had accused her husband of wasting their money on drinking and gambling. However, they denied throwing the chair.

The judge clearly did not believe them. She reminded them that they had already had two previous warnings from the police. She advised them to talk to a marriage guidance counsellor.

Mr and Mrs West and their baby are looking forward to getting some sleep!

GRAMMAR SPOT

1 Which sentence is a reported statement?
Which is a reported command?

> He **told them to stop** making a noise.
> She **told them that she lived** next door.

2 Which sentence is a reported question?
Which is a reported request?

> I **asked them to stop** making a noise.
> She **asked me if I had met** them before.

3 *Say, tell,* and *ask* are all used in reported speech. <u>Underline</u> other verbs in the article that can be used to report conversations.
She <u>ordered</u> them …

▶▶ **Grammar Reference 12.4 p150**

PRACTICE

Other reporting verbs

1 Match these reporting verbs with the direct speech below.

a ask	d invite	g beg
b tell	e remind	h refuse
c order	f advise	

1 **b** 'Sign on the dotted line,' the postman said to me.

2 ☐ 'Please can you translate this sentence for me?' Maria said to Mark.

3 ☐ 'Don't forget to send Aunt Judy a birthday card,' Mary said to her son.

4 ☐ 'Please, please, please marry me. I can't live without you,' John said to Moira.

5 ☐ 'We would like you to come to our wedding,' John said to his boss.

6 ☐ 'I won't go to bed!' Tommy said.

7 ☐ 'You should talk to your solicitor,' Ben said to Tim.

8 ☐ 'Take that chewing gum out of your mouth right now!' the teacher said to Joanna.

2 Report the sentences in exercise 1 using the verbs a–h.

The postman told me to sign on the dotted line.

▶▶ **Verb patterns p158**

T 12.5 Listen and check.

Listening and note-taking

3 You are police officers taking statements. Work in two groups.

T 12.6 **Group A** Listen to Kathleen Brady and take notes.

T 12.7 **Group B** Listen to Ann West and take notes.

4 Find a partner from the other group and report what you heard. Find the differences. Begin like this:

A Kathleen admitted that they sometimes argued. She said that …
B Ann complained that they argued every night. She said that …

5 Write the reports for the police records. Use the verbs in the box.

admit	apologize	complain	offer	order	promise	refuse	say	tell

VOCABULARY AND SPEAKING
Birth, marriage, and death

1 Write these words and phrases in the correct column.

wedding	funeral	get engaged
have a baby	bouquet	wreath
pregnant	reception	bury
groom	midwife	widow
cot	mourners	honeymoon
nappy	get divorced	coffin

Birth	**Marriage**	**Death**

2 Here are the opening and closing lines of a short story of a long life.

Victor Parrot was born one cold, stormy night in …

… He died, aged ninety-five, with a smile on his face. Over five hundred mourners came to his funeral.

Work with a partner. Write the story of the main events of Victor's life. Use as many of the words from exercise 1 as possible. Read your story to the class.

3 What happens at births, weddings, and funerals in your country?

LISTENING AND SPEAKING
A birth

1 Work in small groups. What have you been told about the day you were born? Who told you? What did they say? Tell any interesting stories to the class.

2 **T 12.8** Jane Banner lives on the Isle of Mull off the west coast of Scotland. She has recently had a baby. Listen to her sister, Catherine, telling the story of the baby's birth. Who can you identify in the photo?

3 Underline the correct answer.
1 Jane was taken off the isle by … helicopter / ferry / lifeboat.
2 She ended up giving birth … in the aisle of a plane / on the lifeboat / on the mainland.
3 At the birth there was/were … a doctor / a midwife / two midwives.
4 One of the problems was … Jane's husband wasn't present / lack of space / it was a difficult birth.
5 The crew drank to the health of the baby with … champagne / whisky / a cup of tea.
6 The baby was named … Edith Mora / Caledonian McBrayne / Hazel Beth Mora.
7 To commemorate the baby's birth they … put her name on the bell / put a notice in the newspaper / named a ferry after her.

Roleplay

Work with a partner.

Student A You are one of the lifeboat crew. Tell the story of the birth to a friend.

Student B React to the story and ask questions to get more information.

> *Did you see the story in the local paper?*

> *Which story was that?*

READING AND SPEAKING
A death

1 You are going to read and listen to a poem by WH Auden (1907–1973). The poem is called 'Funeral Blues'. What does the title tell you about the poem?

2 **T 12.9** Close your books and close your eyes and listen to the poem. Don't try to understand every word.
- What has happened?
- How does the writer feel about the world now?
- What words or lines can you remember?

Share what you can remember with the rest of the class.

3 **T 12.9** Listen again, and read the poem. Answer the questions. Use your dictionary to check new words.
1 A loved one has died. What, in general, does the poet want the rest of the world to do? Why does the poet feel like this?
2 Which lines describe things that could possibly happen? Which lines describe impossible things?
3 Which verse describes the closeness of the relationship?
4 When you fall in love it is said that you see the world through 'rose-coloured glasses'. What does this mean? In what ways is the poem the opposite of this?

Learning by heart

4 Divide into four groups.
1 Each group choose one verse and learn it by heart.
2 Recite the poem around the class.

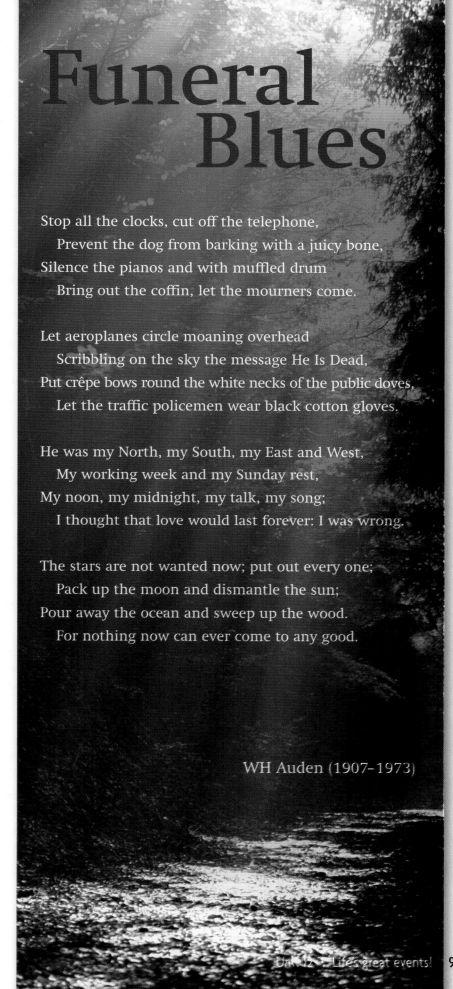

Funeral Blues

Stop all the clocks, cut off the telephone,
    Prevent the dog from barking with a juicy bone,
Silence the pianos and with muffled drum
    Bring out the coffin, let the mourners come.

Let aeroplanes circle moaning overhead
    Scribbling on the sky the message He Is Dead,
Put crêpe bows round the white necks of the public doves,
    Let the traffic policemen wear black cotton gloves.

He was my North, my South, my East and West,
    My working week and my Sunday rest,
My noon, my midnight, my talk, my song;
    I thought that love would last forever: I was wrong.

The stars are not wanted now; put out every one;
    Pack up the moon and dismantle the sun;
Pour away the ocean and sweep up the wood.
    For nothing now can ever come to any good.

WH Auden (1907–1973)

LISTENING AND SPEAKING
My Way

1 **T 12.10** Listen to the song 'My Way', made famous by Frank Sinatra.

- What is the message about life in this song?
- At what stage in his life is the singer?

2 Work with a partner. Discuss which words on the right best complete the lines.

T 12.10 Listen again and check. Sing along if you can!

Frank Sinatra

WRITING: Correcting mistakes (2)

▶▶ Go to p119

My Way

And now, the end is near
And so I (1)_____ the final curtain
My friend, I'll say it clear
I'll (2)_____ my case, of which I'm certain
I've lived a life that's full
I've (3)_____ each and every highway
And more, much more than this,
I did it my way

Regrets, I've had (4)_____
But then again, too few to mention
I did what I (5)_____ to do
and saw it through without exemption,
I planned each charted course,
each careful (6)_____ along the byway
And more, much more than this,
I did it my way

Yes, there were (7)_____ ,
I'm sure you knew,
When I bit off
more than I could (8)_____
But through it all,
when there was doubt
I ate it up and spit it out
I faced it all and I stood (9)_____
and did it my way

I've loved, I've (10)_____ and cried
I've had my fill, my share of losing
And now, as tears subside,
I find it all so (11)_____
To think I did all that
And may I say, not in a (12)_____ way,
'Oh, no, oh, no, not me, I did it my way.'
For what is a man, what has he got?
If not himself, then he has (13)_____.
To say the things he truly (14)_____
and not the words of one who kneels,
The record shows I took the (15)_____
and did it my way
Yes, it was my way.

1	**meet / face**
2	**state / say**
3	**travelled / ridden**
4	**a lot / a few**
5	**had / wanted**
6	**step / stop**
7	**days / times**
8	**chew / eat**
9	**tall / up**
10	**joked / laughed**
11	**exciting / amusing**
12	**sad / shy**
13	**nothing / naught**
14	**feels / knows**
15	**blows / time**

EVERYDAY ENGLISH
Saying sorry

1 Complete the conversations with the expressions from the box.

> (I'm) sorry   I'm so sorry   Pardon
> Excuse me   What

1 **A** Excuse me, can you tell me where the post office is?
  B _____, I'm a stranger here myself.

2 **A** Ouch! That's my foot!
  B _____. I wasn't looking where I was going.

3 **A** _____, what's that creature called?
  B It's a Diplodocus.
  A _____?
  B A Diplodocus. D-I-P-L-O-D-O-C-U-S.
  A Thank you very much.

4 **A** I failed my driving test for the sixth time!
  B _____.

5 **A** _____! We need to get past. My little boy isn't feeling well.

6 **A** Do you want your hearing aid, Grandma?
  B _____?
  A I said: Do you want your hearing aid?
  B _____?
  A DO YOU WANT YOUR HEARING AID?!
  B _____, I can't hear you. I need my hearing aid.

T 12.11 Listen and check. Practise the conversations with a partner.

2 What exactly would you say in the following situations? Use two to four sentences in your response.

- You were cut off in the middle of an important phone call to a business colleague. You call your colleague back.

- You want to get off a very crowded train at the next stop. You have a large suitcase.

- You want the attention of the waiter in a very crowded restaurant. You want another large bottle of mineral water for your table.

- A friend tells you that she can't meet you for lunch as planned next Thursday because she suddenly has to go to an aunt's funeral.

- You thought you had bought a medium-size jumper, but when you get home you see it is the wrong size. You take it back to the shop.

- Your dinner guest reminds you that he is a vegetarian. You have just put a huge steak on his plate.

> *Hello? I'm sorry about that.*
> *I think we must have been cut off.*

WRITING

REFERENCE

Writing

UNIT 1 *p13*

CORRECTING MISTAKES (1)

1 It is important to try to correct your own mistakes when you write. Look at the letter that a student has written to her friend. Her teacher has used symbols to show her the kind of mistakes she has made. Read the letter and correct the mistakes.

T Tense	WW Wrong word
Prep Preposition	P Punctuation
Gr Grammar	Sp Spelling
WO Word order	⅄ Word missing

                              23, St. Mary's Road,
                              Dublin 4, Ireland
                              Tuesday, 10 May

Dear Stephanie

    How are you? I'm very well. I came <u>in</u> [Prep] Dublin two weeks ago <u>for to</u> [Gr] study at a language school. I want⅄learn english [P] because⅄is a very important language. I'm <u>stay</u> [Gr] with <u>a</u> [Gr] Irish family. They've got two <u>son</u> [Gr] and a daughter. Mr Kendall is⅄teacher and Mrs Kendall wor<u>k</u> [Gr] in a hospital. The Irish <u>is</u> [Gr] very kind, but they speak very quickly!

    I study in the morning. My teacher<u>s</u> [P] name is Ann. She <u>said</u> [WW] me that my English is OK, but I <u>do</u> [WW] a lot of mistakes. Ann <u>don't</u> [Gr] give us too much homework, so in the afternoons I <u>go always</u> [WO] sightseeing. Dublin is much <u>more big</u> [Gr] than my town. I like <u>very much painting</u> [WO] and I'm very interestin<u>g</u> [Gr] <u>for</u> [Prep] modern art, so I visit galleries and museums. I've met a girl named Martina. She <u>came</u> [T] from Spain and <u>go</u> [Gr] to Trinity College. Last night we <u>go</u> [T] to the cinema, but the film wasn't very <u>exiting</u> [Sp].

    <u>Do</u> [WW] you like to visit me? Why don't you come for a weekend?

I'd love to see you.

Write to me soon.

Love, *Kati*

2 Answer the questions.
1 Where is Kati? Where is she staying?
2 Why is she there?
3 What does she do each day?
4 What does she do in her free time?
5 Who has she met?

3 Imagine that you are a student in another town. Answer the questions in exercise 2 about *you*.

4 Write a similar letter to a friend back in your country. Write 150–200 words.

LETTERS AND EMAILS
Beginnings and endings

1 How many different ways can you think of to start and end a letter or email?

wishes **madam** **All** **Hi!** sir
Dear Lots of **love** best
sincerely Yours faithfully

Annie Souch
27 Salford Road
Chipping Norton

Matilda Bayes <mpbayes@calverton.com>
Barnabas Henryroy <BHR1508@conwyinc.co.uk>

ESSEX CARS
OFFICIAL FORD DEALER
ON ROAD, Braintree
044 1778 33221144
044 1765 44335689
cars-braintree.co.uk

9 Llewellyn Street
Llandudno
Wales LL32 9PQ

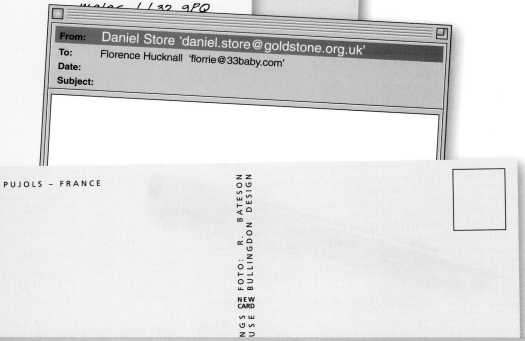

From: Daniel Store 'daniel.store@goldstone.org.uk'
To: Florence Hucknall 'florrie@33baby.com'
Date:
Subject:

PUJOLS – FRANCE

FOTO: R. BATESON
BULLINGDON DESIGN
NGS
USE
NEW
CARD

2 Read extracts 1–11 from some letters and emails. Which are beginnings and which are endings? Write **B** or **E**.

1 <u>Just a note</u> to say thank you so much for having me to stay last weekend. **B**

2 Thank you for your letter of 16 April. Please find enclosed a cheque for £50.00.

3 Write or better still, email me soon.

4 How are you doing? You'll never guess who I saw last week at Dan's.

5 I am writing in response to your advertisement in yesterday's *Daily Star*.

6 We trust this arrangement meets with your satisfaction.

7 I'm sorry I haven't been in touch for such a long time.

8 I look forward to hearing from you at your earliest convenience.

9 I thought I'd write rather than email for a change.

10 Give my regards to Robert.

11 Take care and thanks again.

3 Look again at the sentences in exercise 2. Which are formal, and which are informal? <u>Underline</u> the words and phrases which helped you decide.

4 Match the beginnings and endings of these different letters and emails.

Beginnings	Endings
1 Dear Mary and Dave, Any chance that you two are free next Sat. p.m.?	• Many thanks. I look forward to hearing from you in the near future. Yours faithfully, James Fox
2 Dear Jane, Thanks for your letter. It was great to hear from you after such a long time. You asked me what I've been doing. Well, . . .	• We apologize for the inconvenience and will have pleasure in processing your order as soon as we receive the additional amount. Yours sincerely, Thames Valley Computer Software
3 Dear Sir/Madam, I saw an advertisement in the *Daily Telegraph* for weekend breaks at your hotel.	• It would be lovely to see you some time. Do you ever come to London? We could meet for lunch. Love Pat
4 Hi Pete, Thanks for the invite.	• Let me know asap. All the best, Martin
5 Dear Mr Smith, We received your order for the Encyclopedia World CD ROM, and your cheque for £75.	• Can't wait to see you. Let's hope it stays fine. Love to Ellie. See you then. Deborah

5 Continue the beginnings with one of these lines.

☐ Could you please send me your brochure and a price list? I would be most grateful.

☐ I've changed my job a few times since I last spoke to you, and as you know, I've moved to a new flat.

☐ Unfortunately, this amount did not include packing and postage, which is £7.50.

☐ We've got four tickets for that open-air concert in Woodstock. Interested?

☐ We'd love to come.

6 Which one . . .

• asks for information?
• invites?
• asks for further payment?
• accepts an invitation?
• gives news?

Underline the words and phrases which helped you decide.

7 You have just found the email address of an old friend on the website *Friends Reunited*. Write an email to him/her. Give your news, describe some things that you have done recently, and say what your future plans are. Ask about his/her news and family.

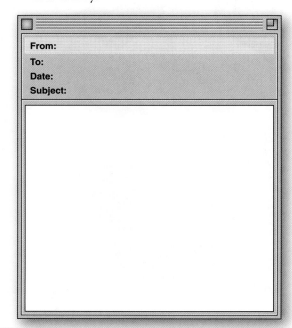

From:
To:
Date:
Subject:

A NARRATIVE (1)
Telling a story – linking ideas

1 Read the story. Where do clauses a–f go?

a as soon as their father had died

b who had worked hard in his vineyard all his life

c what their father had meant by the great treasure

d and while they were working they thought about what their father had said

e because they felt that all their hard work had been for nothing

f Soon they had dug up every inch of the vineyard

Complete the moral.

THE FARMER AND HIS SONS

There was once an old, dying farmer (1)___. Before he died he wanted to teach his three sons how to be good farmers. So he called them to his bedside and said, 'My boys, I have an important secret to tell you: there is a great treasure buried in the vineyard. Promise me that you will look for it when I am dead.'

The sons gave their promise and (2)___ they began looking for the treasure. They worked very hard in the hot sun (3)___. They pictured boxes of gold coins, diamond necklaces, and other such things. (4)___ but they found not a single penny. They were very upset (5)___. However, a few months later the grapes started to appear on the vines. Their grapes were the biggest and best in the neighbourhood and they sold them for a lot of money. Now the sons understood (6)___ and they lived happily ever after.

THE MORAL OF THIS STORY IS: HARD WORK BRINGS . . .

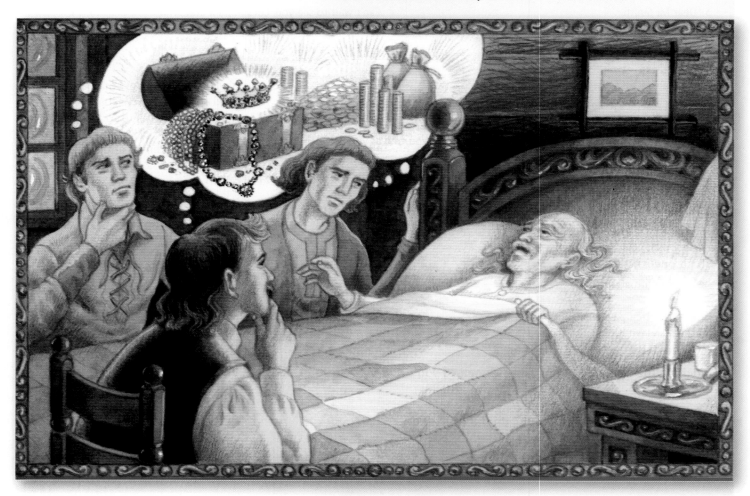

2 Complete the sentences using a linking word from the box. Use each linking word once only.

THE EMPEROR AND HIS DAUGHTERS

There was once an emperor _____ lived in a palace.
He had three daughters _____ no sons.
He wanted his daughters to marry _____ he died.
He found three princes. _____ his daughters didn't like them.
They refused to marry the princes, _____ the emperor became very angry.
He said they must get married _____ they were sixteen years old.
The three daughters ran away _____ the night and found work on a farm.
They fell in love with the farmer's sons _____ they were working there.
They married the sons _____ they were sixteen.

before **as soon as** **while** **during** **when** **but** **However,** **so** **who**

3 In what ways are these sentences different from the ones in exercise 2?

> There was once an old emperor who lived in an enormous, golden palace in the middle of the city Ping Chong. He had three beautiful daughters, but unfortunately no sons.

Continue rewriting the story, adding more detail to make it more interesting.

4 Write a folk tale or fairy story that you know. Write about 200 words.
Begin:

> There was/were once ...

or

> Once upon a time there was/were ...

End:

> ... and they lived happily ever after.

If your story has a moral, give it at the end.

FOR AND AGAINST

1 Read the text. Replace the underlined words and phrases with those in the box.

in my opinion,	One advantage is that	For instance
One disadvantage is that	pros and cons	All things considered
Finally	In conclusion	In fact,
Another point is that	Moreover	

CHILDHOOD
– the best time of your life

1 Some people say that childhood is the best time of your life. However, being a child has both <u>advantages and disadvantages</u>.

2 <u>On the plus side,</u> you have very few responsibilities. <u>For example</u>, you don't have to go to work, pay bills, or do the shopping, cooking, or cleaning. This means you have plenty of free time to do whatever you want – watch TV; play on the computer; go out with friends; play sports, or pursue other hobbies. <u>On top of that</u>, public transport, cinema, and sports centres cost much less for children. <u>All in all</u>, being a child is an exciting, action-packed time in life.

3 However, for every plus there is a minus. <u>For one thing,</u> you have to spend all day, Monday to Friday, at school. Studying usually means you have to do homework, and you have to take exams. <u>What is more</u>, you may have a lot of free time, but you are rarely allowed to do whatever you want. You usually have to ask your parents if you can do things, from going shopping in town to staying out late or going to a party. <u>Last of all</u>, although there are often cheaper prices for children, things are still expensive – and parents are not always generous with pocket money. There's never enough to do everything you want. <u>The reality is that</u> sometimes there's not enough to do anything at all!

4 <u>To sum up</u>, although some people see childhood as the best time in life, <u>I think that</u> children have no real choice, independence, or money. Nevertheless, it is true that choice, money, and independence all bring responsibilities and restrictions – which increase with age.

2 There are four paragraphs. What is the purpose of each one?

3 Match the pros with the cons.

	Pros	Cons
1	don't have to go to work	are never given enough pocket money
2	can go out to parties with friends	have to do homework and take exams
3	don't have to cook and clean	have to go to school Monday to Friday
4	costs less to do things	need to ask your parents' permission

4 You are going to write a 'for and against' essay. Write a list of pros and cons for one of these topics.

1 Getting older
2 Having a university degree
3 Having children while young

5 Use your ideas from exercise 4 to write four paragraphs. Write about 250 words.

MAKING A RESERVATION

1 Janet Cooper wants to go on holiday with her family. She faxes the Sea View B&B to see if they have the accommodation she wants. Look at the advert for the Sea View B&B and fill in the details at the top of the fax.

2 Put the words in order, and write them into the message part of Janet's fax.

Get away from the city.
Escape to the peace and quiet
of Cornwall!

For reservations and enquiries contact
Anne Westcombe:
  Phone/Fax: 01326 230579
  email: reservations@seaviewb&b.com

FAX TRANSMISSION

To: _____   Page 1 of 1

From: Janet Cooper   Date: _____

Subject: _____   To fax no.: _____

                           From fax no.: 01259 67821

a two / rooms / bed and breakfast / I / to / would like / reserve / at / your

b 27 August / We / on / are / arriving

c six / hope / stay / to / We / for / nights / departing / 2 September / on

d and / husband / would like / room / I / My / double / with / en-suite bathroom / an / preferably / a

e also / reserve / two / to / I / a / room / for / would / like / teenage / our / daughters

f should / non-smoking / rooms / be / Both

g sea / the / possible / Would / have / it / rooms / to / facing / be / ?

h available / for / you / Do / have / dates / these / rooms / ?

i also / me / you / Could / tell / room / each / price / the / of / ?

j from / I / forward / look / you / to / hearing

3 Write a reply letter or fax to Janet. Include the following information:

- thank her for her enquiry
- say you are pleased to confirm her reservation for the rooms she wants and for the dates she wants
- tell her that all the rooms come with en-suite bathroom and a sea view
- each room is £50 per night
- end the letter saying that you look forward to welcoming her and her family to the B&B
- finish with **Yours sincerely, Anne Westcombe**

A DESCRIPTION (1)

Describing a room – relative pronouns, participles

1 Think of your favourite room. Draw a plan of it on a piece of paper. Write down why you like it and some adjectives to describe it.

My favourite room is . . .   I like it because . . .

Show a partner your plan and talk about your room.

2 Read the description. Why is this kitchen more than just a room where you cook and eat?

3 Complete the description using these relative clauses:

> which tells the story
> that we're going to next Saturday
> where we cook and eat
> whose family have all emigrated
> which is the focal point of the room
> which means
> we haven't seen
> I like best
> who are cross and sleepy
> where family and friends come together

GRAMMAR SPOT

1 Underline the relative pronouns in exercise 3. What do they refer to? When do we use *which, who, that, where,* and *whose*?

2 Look at the these sentences. We can omit the relative pronoun from one in each pair. Which one? Why?

This is the room **which** I like best. / This is the room **which** has a good view of the sea.

He's a friend **who** we haven't seen for years. / He's a friend **who** lives in London.

3 Look at these examples of participles. Rewrite them with relative pronouns.

I have so many happy memories of times **spent** there.

There is a large window **looking** out onto two apple trees in the garden.

▶▶ **Grammar Reference 6.5 and 6.6 p143**

My favourite room

The room in our house (1)_____ is our kitchen. Perhaps the kitchen is the most important room in many houses, but it is particularly so in our house because it's not only (2)_____, but it's also the place (3)_____.

I have so many happy memories of times spent there: ordinary daily events such as making breakfast on dark, cold winter mornings for children (4)_____, before sending them off to school; or special occasions such as homecomings or cooking Christmas dinner. Whenever we have a party, people gravitate with their drinks to the kitchen. It always ends up the fullest and noisiest room in the house.

So what does this special room look like? It's quite big, but not huge. It's big enough to have a good-sized rectangular table in the centre, (5)_____. There is a large window above the sink, looking

out onto two apple trees in the garden. There's a big, old cooking stove at one end, and at the other end a wall with a huge notice board (6)_____ of our lives, past, present, and future: a school photo of the kids; a postcard from Auntie Nancy, (7)_____ to Australia; the menu from a take-away Chinese restaurant; an invitation to a wedding (8)_____; a letter from a friend (9)_____ for years. All our world is there for everyone to read!

The front door is seldom used in our house, only by strangers. All our friends use the back door (10)_____ they come straight into the kitchen and join in whatever is happening there. The kettle goes on immediately and then we all sit round the table, drinking tea and putting the world to rights! Without doubt some of the happiest times of my life have been spent in our kitchen.

4 Link these sentences with the correct relative pronoun: *who, which, that, where, whose.*

1 The blonde lady is Pat. She's wearing a black dress.
2 There's the hospital. My sister works there.
3 The postcard arrived this morning. It's from Auntie Nancy.
4 I passed all my exams. This made my father very proud.
5 Did you meet the girl? Her mother teaches French.

5 Complete the sentences with a word from the box in the present or past participle.

| play | give | stick | listen | arrange |

1 I spend hours in my room, _____ to music.
2 I have lots of posters _____ on the walls.
3 My brother is in his bedroom, _____ on his computer.
4 There are photos of my family _____ on my shelves.
5 I also have a colour TV _____ to me on my last birthday.

6 Write a similar description of your favourite room in about 250 words. Describe it and give reasons why you like it. Use relative pronouns and participles to link your sentences.

A LETTER OF APPLICATION

1 Read Nancy's letter of application and complete it using the phrases and words in the box.

I consider myself	experience	widely
As you will see	hard-working	fluently
I am writing in response	advertisement	CV
I look forward to hearing	on business	deadlines

Worldwatch Europe IPA
56 Merritts Avenue
Overland Park
Reading
RG2 6HD

Dear David Benton,

_____ to your _____ in today's *Guardian* for a journalist based in Geneva.

_____ from the enclosed _____, I studied journalism and modern languages at University College, London, and went on to do a master's in journalism at Queen Mary's College, London.

_____ the ideal candidate for the job because I have all the relevant _____. In my present job I am in charge of Eastern Europe publications for Intertec Publishing. Before this, I worked for the BBC World Service, at first covering Mexico and Argentina, then Europe. I have travelled _____ in South America and Europe. In my present job I frequently go to Japan _____. I speak French, German, and Spanish _____.

I am an enthusiastic and _____ person. I am good at organizing people and can meet _____.

_____ from you in the near future.

Yours sincerely,

Nancy Mann

2 Answer the questions.

1 What job is Nancy applying for?
2 Where did she hear about the vacancy?
3 What is she sending with her letter?
4 Look at her letter and the advert. Why does she think she is right for the job?

Worldwatch Europe

Business Journalist

This international business magazine, with 1,000,000 readers worldwide, is seeking a journalist, based in Geneva, to cover business news in Europe.

Requirements:

- a master's degree in journalism
- at least two years' experience in business journalism
- fluent in French and German. If possible, some knowledge of Spanish
- excellent communication skills
- international travel experience is a plus

Please send CV and letter of application to:

David Benton, Worldwatch Europe IPA
56 Merritts Avenue, Overland Park, Reading RG2 6HD

Visit us on the web: **http://www.wep@ipc.co.uk**

3 You are going to write a letter of application. Read the job advertisement below.

TRANS-GLOBE TOURS

TOUR GUIDES

We are looking for enthusiastic, hard-working, friendly people who

- have good interpersonal skills
- speak two or more languages fluently
- have a genuine interest in other countries and cultures
- want to see the world

Please apply with CV to:

Martin Ruane, Personnel Manager
Trans-Globe Tours, Victoria Square, London SW1 6VC

4 Answer the questions in exercise 2 about *you*. Use your answers to write your letter of application for Trans-Globe Tours. Write about 200 words.

A NARRATIVE (2)
A disastrous holiday – adverbs in a narrative

1 Think about the worst holiday you have ever had! Write some notes about it, then swap information with a partner.

2 Read the beginning of the story about Jack and Liza's holiday. Put the words on the right into the correct place in the lines, and make any necessary changes.

A HOLIDAY HORROR STORY

AFTER CHRISTMAS two years ago Jack and Liza decided to go away for New Year. They didn't want to stay in a hotel with crowds of people and they were delighted when they saw an advertisement in *The Sunday Times* for a holiday flat in a village near Oxford. It was no ordinary flat. It was on the top floor of an old Elizabethan mansion. They booked it, and on New Year's Eve they set off in the car. It was raining and freezing cold, they were happy and excited.

    They had been driving for three hours when they saw the house in the distance. It looked magnificent with tall chimneys and a long, wide drive. They drove up to the house, went up the steps to the huge front door and knocked. Nothing happened. They knocked again. The door opened and a small, wild-looking old lady stood there.

just/suddenly/somewhere
so/really
However
immediately/Although
heavily
nearly/finally
incredibly
loudly
more loudly/Eventually/slowly

3 Work with your partner. Look at the pictures and complete the next part of the story using the prompts below to help.

The old lady was wearing . . .
In one hand she was carrying a large glass of whisky and . . .
The house was absolutely . . .
The old lady led Jack and Liza slowly up . . .
There were two huge dogs growling menacingly . . .
When they saw the rooms they couldn't believe their eyes because . . .
They hurriedly . . .

4 Read your story aloud to the class and compare ideas.

5 Read the end of the story. Put the words on the right into the correct place.

WHEN they got outside again the rain had turned to snow. They ran to the car, laughing. They felt that they had been released from a prison and now they wanted to be with lots of people. They drove to the next village and as midnight was striking they found a hotel with a room for the night. 'Happy New Year!' cried Jack, as he kissed the surprised receptionist on both cheeks. 'You have no idea how beautiful your hotel is!'

hysterically
desperately/quickly/fortunately/just

warmly

6 Write the story of your worst holiday in about 250 words.

- When was it?
- Where was it?
- Why was it bad?
- Who were you with?
- What did you do?

A DESCRIPTION (2)
Describing a person

1 Think of someone in your family.
Write answers to questions 1–6 about
him/her.

  1 What is his/her name?
  2 How is this person related to you?
  3 Why are you choosing this person?
  4 What is he/she like?
  5 What does he/she look like?
  6 What does he/she like to do?

Read your sentences to the rest of the class.

2 Look at the photo and read the description
of Emily Morgan. Write the words and
phrases used to describe her on the chart.

physical appearance	
character	
habits	

3 *not very tolerant* in paragraph 2 is
a polite way of saying *intolerant*.
Make polite forms of these words.

  1 rude
  2 boring
  3 cheap
  4 ugly
  5 cruel
  6 stupid

4 Use your sentences from exercise 1 to
write a similar description of one of
your relatives. Include:

- your relation to him/her
- your opinion of him/her
- physical description
- his/her character, habits, likes and dislikes

Emily Morgan, My Aunt

Of all my relatives, I like my Aunt Emily the best. She's
my mother's youngest sister. She has never married and
she lives all alone in a small village near Bath. She's in
her late fifties, but she's still quite young in spirit. She
has a fair complexion, curly grey hair, and deep blue
eyes. She has a kind face, and when you meet her, the
first thing you notice about her is her warm, friendly
smile. Her face is a little lined now, but I think she is
still rather attractive. She is the kind of person you can
always go to if you have a problem.

Aunt Emily likes reading and gardening, and she likes
to take her dog, Buster, for long walks in the park.
She's a very active person. Either she's making something
or mending something or doing something to help
others. She does the shopping for some of the old people
in the village. She's extremely generous, but not very
tolerant of people who don't agree with her. I hope that
I am as contented as she is when I am her age.

WRITING A BIOGRAPHY
Combining sentences

1 Read the sentences in **A** about Astrid Johnsson. Compare them with the paragraphs in **B**. Note all the ways the sentences combine. <u>Underline</u> the words in **A** that are not used again in **B**.

A

Astrid Johnsson is a cellist.
She is Swedish.
She is famous for her music.
She is famous worldwide.
She started playing the cello at the age of three.
She was born in Stockholm in 1960.
She left Stockholm in 1978.
She won a scholarship to the Royal Academy of Music in London.
She studied the cello.
She studied the history of music and composition.

She has travelled all over the world.
She has played in concerts and composed film music.
She has lived and worked in many places.
She has lived and worked in London, New York, and Paris.
She now lives in Paris.
She lives with her daughter and her second husband.
He is a conductor.
He is Georges Leveaux.

B

Astrid Johnsson, the Swedish cellist, who is famous worldwide for her music, started playing the cello at the age of three. Born in Stockholm in 1960, Astrid left there in 1978 when she won a scholarship to the Royal Academy of Music in London. Whilst there, she not only studied the cello, she also studied the history of music and composition.

Since then she has travelled all over the world, playing in concerts and composing film music. She has lived and worked in many places, including London, New York, and Paris, where she now lives with her daughter and her second husband, the conductor Georges Leveaux.

2 Alfred Nobel is also Swedish. Why is he famous? Combine these sentences about him to form a natural sounding paragraph. Use the first paragraph on Astrid to help.

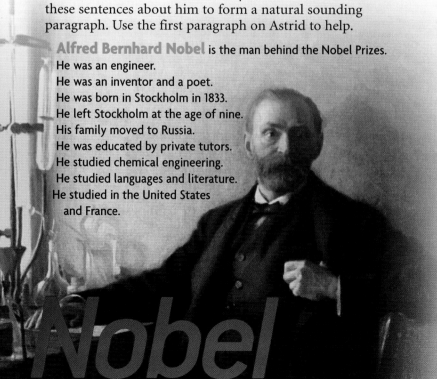

Alfred Bernhard Nobel is the man behind the Nobel Prizes.
He was an engineer.
He was an inventor and a poet.
He was born in Stockholm in 1833.
He left Stockholm at the age of nine.
His family moved to Russia.
He was educated by private tutors.
He studied chemical engineering.
He studied languages and literature.
He studied in the United States and France.

3 Starting as shown, continue the biography of Alfred Nobel.

Returning to Sweden with his brother Emil in 1852, he …

He returned to Sweden in 1852.
He returned with his brother Emil.
They worked in their father's factory.
The factory was an explosives factory.
An explosion in the factory killed Emil in 1864.
Alfred was deeply affected.
He wanted to invent a safer explosive.
He invented one in 1867.
He called it 'dynamite'.
He started to set up dynamite factories.
He founded factories in many parts of the world.
Alfred made a fortune.
He died in 1896.
He left $9 million.
He left the money to set up yearly prizes for science, literature, and world peace.
The prizes are called the Nobel Prizes.

4 Research some facts about a famous man and a famous woman, dead or alive, who you admire. Write a short profile for each of them.

WORDS THAT JOIN IDEAS

1 Join the sentences in different ways using the words in brackets.

1 George was rich. He wasn't a happy man. (but / although / however)
2 Jo rang me from a phone box. She's lost her mobile. (because / so)

2 Look at these words and expressions. They prepare people for what you are going to write or say next. Read and complete the sentences.

1 **In fact/Actually** (*I'm going to add more information to support this statement.*)
Peter doesn't like working in London. **In fact**, he's thinking of changing jobs.
Peter and I are in love. **Actually**, we _____ .

2 **Of course/Naturally** (*What I am going to say is obvious.*)
Of course, having a baby has totally changed our lives.
Naturally, when I was a child I didn't _____ .

3 **Fortunately/Unfortunately** (*What I am going to say is/is not good news.*)
She tried really hard, and **fortunately**, she passed the exam.
She stood and waited for over an hour, but **unfortunately**, _____ .

4 **Nevertheless** (*I am going to tell you about a result or effect which is unexpected.*)
The accident wasn't her fault. **Nevertheless**, she felt terrible.
My father didn't do very well at school. **Nevertheless**, _____ .

5 **Anyway** (*I am going to finish talking about the subject and move on to something new.*)
What traffic! I thought I'd never get here. **Anyway**, now let's get on with the meeting.
Anyway, you've heard enough about me. What _____ ?

3 Read the email and write the word or words that fit best.

To: Melodycat@hyp.org
Subject: Hi from Jackie and Joe

Hi Melody,

I hope you're all well. Things are busy here. Maya moved out last week. She found a small apartment not far from here, (1)_____ (so / anyway) we still see her all the time. She also got a new job at a radio station. (2)_____ (Unfortunately, / Because) it doesn't pay very well, (3)_____ (of course / but) at least she likes it. Now that Maya has moved out, it's only Joe and me at home. After 24 years of having kids around the house, it's a little strange to have the place all to ourselves. (4)_____, (However / In fact) it's nice to come home to a clean house at the end of the day. :-)

Samantha is going to graduate from Oberlin College this year. We're all very proud and (5)_____ (however / of course) we're going to have a party for her. (6)_____, (So / Actually) it's going to be a surprise party! So, shhh! Samantha says she wants to travel somewhere interesting this summer, (7)_____ (but / because) she hasn't decided where to go yet. Joe's fine, (8)_____ (although / so) he's been in a bad mood lately. He hasn't been able to do much in the garden (9)_____ (because / actually) it's rained every day for the last two weeks! (10)_____, (In fact / Nevertheless) it's been the rainiest summer for 20 years. (11)_____, (Anyway / Of course) that's enough of our news. How are you all? What are you up to?

Write back and tell me everything!
Love, Jackie

CORRECTING MISTAKES (2)

1 Kati was a student of English in Dublin, where she stayed with the Kendall family. She has now returned home. Read the letter she has written to Mr and Mrs Kendall. Her English has improved, but there are still over 25 mistakes. How many can you find?

Szerencs u. 43
3300 Eger
Hungary

Friday, 14 June

Dear Mr and Mrs Kendall

I am home now since two weeks, but I have to start work immediately, so this is the first time is possible for me to write. How are you all? Are you busy as usual? Does Tim still work hard for his exam next month? I am miss you a lot and also all my friends from Dublin. Yesterday I've received a letter from my Spain friend, Martina, and she told me about some of the other people I met. She say that Atsuko and Yuki will write me from Japan. I am lucky because I made so many good friend during I was in Ireland. It was really interesting for me to meet people from so many different countries. I think that we not only improved our English (I hope this!) but we also knew people from all over the world and this is important.

My family are fine. They had a good summer holiday by the lake. We are all very exciting because my brother will get married just before Christmas and we like very much his girlfriend. They have looked for a flat near the city centre but it is no easy to find one. If they won't find one soon, they will have to stay here with us.

Please can you check something for me? I can't find my red scarf. I think maybe I have forgotten it in the cuboard in my bedroom.

Please write soon. My family send best wishes to you all. I hope I can come back next year. Stay with you was a very wonderful experience for me. Thank you for all things and excuse my mistakes. I already forget much words.

Yours faithfully,

Kati

PS I hope you like the photo. It's nice, isn't it?

2 Compare the mistakes you have found with a partner. Correct the letter.

3 Write a thank-you letter to someone you have stayed with.

Tapescripts

Unit 1

T 1.1 **General knowledge quiz**

1 The modern Olympic Games started in 1896.
2 It takes eight minutes for the sun's rays to reach the Earth.
3 He was walking on the moon.
4 If you are flying over the International Date Line, the Pacific Ocean is below you.
5 A vegetarian doesn't eat meat.
6 www. stands for World Wide Web.
7 Glasses were invented in Italy around 1300 AD.
8 Brazil has won the World Cup five times.
9 John Lennon was returning to his apartment when he was assassinated.
10 Chinese is spoken by the most people in the world.
11 Nelson Mandela didn't become president of South Africa until he was 76 years old because he was in prison for 27 years.
12 People have been sending emails since the 1970s.

T 1.2

1 The sun doesn't rise in the west! It rises in the east!
2 Cows don't eat meat! They eat grass!
3 Mercedes-Benz cars aren't made in Canada! They're made in Germany!
4 Neil Armstrong didn't land on the moon in 1989! He landed in 1969!
5 John Lennon wasn't performing on stage when he was assassinated! He was returning to his apartment!
6 The Pyramids weren't built by the Chinese! They were built by the Egyptians!
7 We haven't been in class for five hours! We've been in class for one hour!
8 We aren't studying Italian! We're studying English!

T 1.3

1 A What did you do last night?
  B I stayed at home and watched television.
2 A What kind of books do you like reading?
  B Horror stories and science fiction.
3 A Have you ever been to the United States?
  B Yes, I have. I went there last year.
  A Did you like it?
  B Yes, I really enjoyed it.
4 A What's the teacher doing?
  B He's helping Maria with this exercise.
5 A What does your mother do?
  B She works in a bank.
6 A Why didn't you do your homework last night?
  B Because I didn't feel well.
7 A What are you doing next weekend?
  B I'm going to a party.
8 A Have you got a TV in your bedroom?
  B No, I haven't. Just a CD player.

T 1.4

1 My sister's a teacher.
2 She's on holiday at the moment.
3 She's in France.
4 She's never travelled to Europe before.
5 She's been there for two weeks.
6 She's going back to work next week.
7 Her husband's a builder.
8 He's got his own business.

T 1.5 **See p8**

T 1.6 **Making conversation**

D = Dad, E = Emma

D Good morning! Did you have a nice time last night?
E Yes, I did. I went round to Bill's house.
D Do you want breakfast?
E No, I don't, thanks. I'm not hungry.
D Have you had any coffee?
E Yes, I have. I don't want any more, thanks.
D Is Bill coming round tonight?
E No, he isn't. He's going out for dinner with his family.
D OK. Are you leaving for school soon?
E Yes, I am. I'm going right now. Bye!

T 1.7

1 Is it hot today?
2 Is it raining?
3 Are you wearing trainers?
4 Do you usually come to class by bus?
5 Are you going out tonight?
6 Did you have a good day yesterday?
7 Have you got a dictionary?
8 Have you got any pets?

T 1.8

1 A Do you like studying English?
  B Yes, I do. It's my favourite subject.
2 A Is it a nice day today?
  B No, it isn't. It's freezing.
3 A Have you seen my pen?
  B No, I haven't. You can borrow mine if you want.
4 A Are you staying at home this evening?
  B Yes, I am. Do you want to come round?
5 A Did you go on holiday last summer?
  B No, I didn't. I couldn't afford to.

T 1.9 **My wonders**

K = Kelly, S = Sam, P = Peter

K We were doing the wonders of the world in school today. You know, the seven ancient wonders, the pyramids and such like and we got to talking about what modern wonders would be and well we all thought that …
S Huh! I know what the best modern wonder is for me. I know what's changed *my* life more than anything else …
P What's that, Dad?
S The dishwasher.
K Uh? What d'you mean – the dishwasher?
S I mean the dishwasher. I think it's marvellous! Every time I use something – cups, plates, dishes, knives, forks, you know, I just put it in, and after a few days it fills up, I turn it on and 'bingo' – all clean, bright and sparkling and I start again. Helps keep my kitchen tidy. I'm not very good at tidyi …
K Yeah, and the rest of the house is a mess! Come on Grandpa, be a bit more serious, we …
S I *am* serious!
K Well, anyway, *we* all said at school the very best thing was the mobile phone …
P I knew it!
S Huh! I don't even know how to use one.
K Oh, I couldn't live without mine. It's brilliant. I can call or text my friends all the time …
P Don't I know …
K … from wherever I am and they can call or text me. Or if I need a lift from you or Mum …
P You mean like when you need picking up from a friend's house in the evening?
K Yeah, that kind of thing … or if I'm going to be home late, or like staying late at school or whatever – I can just let you and Mum know what's happening.
S OK, OK that's good, but the problem is that people use them too much for every little thing, you're never alone …
K You're never alone with a mobile phone, you're never alone …
P *(laughs)* All right, all right Kelly you can stop that. What *I* really hate is when people shout into them in public places and *every*one has to listen to their boring conversations – you know the kind of thing – er 'Hello sweetheart, it's me. I'm on the train, you can put the dinner in the oven.'
S Sometimes it's not just boring, it's really dangerous, you know, when people use them when they're driving – I've seen lots of …
K And teachers go absolutely mad if we forget to turn them off and they ring in class or you hear the 'beep' 'beep' 'beep' of a text message.
S I'll bet they do. Good manners certainly aren't a wonder of the modern world!
P Well, I have to say for me the most amazing wonder is an obvious one … it's the Internet and email. It's changed the whole world and it's totally transformed *my* business. Everyone at work is always on the computer, checking emails, sending emails. It's where most of our business is done nowadays.
S Yeah, but the bad part is that you're glued to your computer all day – er I reckon people'll forget how to communicate face to face soon, it'll all be through machines. Just because you've got all these different ways to communicate doesn't mean there's any more to say! I'm glad I didn't have emails and texting in my day.
K Ah, but Grandpa, the way things are going, you'll probably be able to send messages through your dishwasher soon!
S Huh, not in my lifetime I hope!

T 1.10 **See p12**

T 1.11

1 food 3 stood 5 read 7 phone
2 near 4 paid 6 work 8 walk

T 1.12

1 **A** Sorry I'm late. I got stuck in traffic.
  B Never mind. You're here now. Come in and sit down.
2 **A** Bye, Mum! I'm off to school now.
  B Take care, my love. Have a nice day!
3 **A** Have you heard that Jenny's going out with Pete?
  B Really? I don't know what she sees in him!
4 **A** How long did it take you to do the homework?
  B Ages! How about you?
5 **A** I don't know about you, but I'm sick and tired of this weather.
  B So am I. I can't stand all this rain.
6 **A** Who was that I saw you with last night?
  B Mind your own business!
7 **A** I'm tired. I'm taking next week off.
  B That sounds like a good idea. The break will do you good.
8 **A** Let's go for a run in the park!
  B Me? Run? You must be joking!
9 **A** Can we get together this afternoon at 3.00?
  B I'm sorry. I can't make it then. What about a bit later?
10 **A** What a gorgeous coat! Was it expensive?
  B Yes, it cost a fortune!

T 1.13

1 I'm taking this Friday and next Monday off. We're going away for a long weekend.
2 Can we meet at about 7 o'clock?
3 I'm really sorry I'm late. I overslept.
4 John's going to take Sue to the party next week.
5 Dad, how much do you earn?

Unit 2

T 2.1 See p15

T 2.2

1 Is he married?
 Yes, he is.
2 What does he do?
 He's a lawyer.
3 Where does he live?
 In a big house in Dallas, Texas.
4 Has he got any children?
 Yes, he's got two.
5 What does his wife do?
 She's an interior designer.
6 Which sports does he play?
 He sometimes plays golf.
7 Where is he working at the moment?
 In Mexico.
8 Is he paid very well?
 Yes, he is.

T 2.3

45-year-old college graduate makes $60,000 a year as a paperboy!

People think it's a joke that a man my age with a college degree is a paperboy! But, hey, it's great. I'm paid good money – $60,000 a year for four hours' work a day. On top of that I often get $50 a week in tips. Not bad!
My job isn't easy. I get up at 2.00 a.m. every day, seven days a week. The first newspaper is delivered at 2.30 a.m. I finish four hours, 65 miles, and 1,000 newspapers later. I drive a red Chevy Blazer and the newspapers are packed into the back.
I love the peace and quiet in the early morning. Most of the time I have the world to myself. Occasionally, I meet a jogger. I usually get back home by 7.00 a.m. Then I have the rest of the day to be with my family and do what I want. I have two teenage children and my wife works at the University of Iowa. Some days I coach my kids' baseball team, other days I play golf. I'm also studying for my master's degree at the moment. I want to be a marriage counsellor eventually, but I'm not in a hurry. I'm enjoying life too much. Some people think it's not much of a job but, hey, when they're sitting in an office, I'm playing golf! So I ask you – who has the better life?

T 2.4

1 I'm paid good money – $60,000 a year. And I often get $50 a week in tips.
2 I get up at 2.00 a.m. … The first newspaper is delivered at 2.30 a.m.
3 I drive a red Chevy Blazer and the newspapers are packed into the back.
4 I love the peace and quiet.
5 Occasionally, I meet a jogger.
6 I usually get back home by 7.00 a.m.
7 My wife works at the University of Iowa.
8 Some days I coach my kids' baseball team, other days I play golf.
9 I'm also studying for my master's degree at the moment. I want to be a marriage counsellor.
10 Some people think it's not much of a job, but, hey, when they're sitting in an office, I'm playing golf.

T 2.5 See p17

T 2.6 Interview with Lucy

I = Interviewer, L = Lucy

1 **I** Do you like your job?
  L Oh yes, I do. I enjoy my job very much.
2 **I** Why do you like it so much?
  L Because I love working with children and making them laugh.
3 **I** What do you wear to work?
  L I wear crazy clothes. A fancy coat and stripy tights.
4 **I** Who are you working with now? Anyone special?
  L Well, at the moment I'm working with a very sick little girl from Bosnia. She's had so many operations. She's very special to me.
5 **I** Does she speak any English?
  L No, she doesn't. We communicate through laughter.
6 **I** Isn't it tiring?
  L Yes, it is. It's very tiring indeed. I'm exhausted at the end of each day.
7 **I** What do you do in the evenings? Do you just go home and relax?
  L No, I don't. I often go out with friends. I have the best friends and the best job in the world.

T 2.7 Sport and leisure

Mary

I'm 85 years old, but I've always been interested in keeping fit. Recently, I started doing aerobics. I go once a week – on – erm – a Thursday morning to the local old people's day centre. It's really nice there. They run a special aerobics class for us. Erm – first thing we do is exercise … for about three quarters of an hour. We go through all the exercises to music. There are between four and eight of us depending on the weather, really. We just wear loose-fitting clothes and comfortable shoes or trainers and, – erm – apart from the music, and Julianne, our lovely instructor, we don't need anything else! I'm quite good at it now. I can do most of the exercises, although there are one or two that are a bit energetic for me at my age – erm – I'm one of the oldest – erm – some of the others are just babies of about sixty! Afterwards we all go for a cup of tea and a piece of cake in the coffee bar. It's a really nice morning.

Jenny

I didn't start skiing until my mid 40s. Now I go once or twice a year for two weeks, usually in early spring. I live in London, so I go to ski resorts in Europe – in France, Italy, or Austria. At first it was really difficult, starting in my 40s. I spent most of my time on my bottom! But I was determined to learn so I took some classes. My husband thought I was mad – but my children said 'You go for it Mum!' so I did and now my husband's taken up skiing, too. I have my own skis, ski poles, and boots and stuff – that I take with me, and of course all the latest clothes – it's important to be fashionable on the ski slopes, you know. I have a lovely ski suit – I like to look good. Now my instructor says I'm a very good skier and in fact I even give lessons to friends – and my husband! If you've never been skiing, you should try it. Hey, I could give you your first lesson!

Thomas

I absolutely love football. I'm crazy about it. It's the best! I love watching it but I 'specially enjoy playing it. I am nine years old and I play for the local team at my school's football pitch. I play matches twice a week – on Friday evenings after school and on Sunday mornings. And we also have football coaching on Tuesday evenings when we just practise all our football skills. It's brilliant! Er – we all have a special kit – a football shirt with a number on the back – er – I'm number 7, it's my lucky number! And we wear shorts, socks and stuff, all in matching colours and of course our football boots – oh – and we also have to wear shin pads for protection, you know. We have a team tracksuit, too – but we only wear this before and after matches and for training. Erm – my mum always comes to support us – even when it's raining. Mmm – my team isn't very good, in fact, we nearly always lose – but we don't care! Er – our football coach, Martin, says winning doesn't matter – it's taking part that counts – mmm – maybe he's right, but d'you know what I think? I think it's just fantastic when we win! Yeah.

T 2.8 See p21

T 2.9 See p21

T 2.10

1 'When are you going away on holiday?'
 'On the fifteenth.'
 'And when do you get back?'

'On the twenty-fourth. I'll give you a ring when we get home.'

2 And now the business news. The unemployment rate has risen slightly this month. The national unemployment rate is now 4.2%, and in our area, an estimated 15,000 people are out of work.

3 'Thank you for calling the Blackpool Concert Hall. This is Matt speaking. How can I help you?'
'Oh, hi. Erm – do you still have seats for tonight's concert?'
'Yes, we do.'
'Great. I'd like two tickets, please. Can I reserve them by phone?'
'Yes, that's fine. Erm – tickets are £35 each. Could I have your name please?'
'Yes, Sarah Dawson.'
'Thanks.'
'Can I pay by visa?'
'Yes that's fine. Erm – what's your card number please?'
'It's 4929 … 7983 … 0621 … 8849.'
'Let me read that back. 4929 … 7983 … 0621 … 8849.'
'That's right.'

4 'Hey, I really like your shoes! Where d'you buy them?'
'At that new shop in town.'
'Oh yeah? Next to the post office.'
'Yeah.'
'How much were they, if you don't mind me asking?'
'£39.99 in the sale. Everything's half price you know, so they were reduced from £79.99.'
'What a bargain!'

5 'Hello?'
'Hi Jim. How're things?'
'Fine. Listen – we're having a party this Saturday, and we were wondering if you'd like to come. It's our tenth wedding anniversary.'
'Congratulations. When is it?'
'It starts at seven o'clock.'
'Saturday at seven? Sounds good.'

Unit 3

T 3.1

The Tale of Gluskap and the Baby

Gluskap the warrior was very pleased with himself because he had fought and won so many battles. He boasted to a woman friend: 'Nobody can beat me!'
'Really?' said the woman. 'I know someone who can beat you. His name is Wasis.' Gluskap had never heard of Wasis. He immediately wanted to meet him and fight him. So he was taken to the woman's village. The woman pointed to a baby who was sitting and sucking a piece of sugar on the floor of a teepee.
'There,' she said. 'That is Wasis. He is little but he is very strong.' Gluskap laughed and went up to the baby. 'I am Gluskap. Fight me!' he shouted. Little Wasis looked at him for a moment, then he opened his mouth. 'Waaah! Waaah!' he screamed. Gluskap had never heard such a terrible noise. He danced a war dance and sang some war songs. Wasis screamed louder. 'Waaah! Waaah! Waaah!' Gluskap covered his ears and ran out of the teepee. After he had run a few miles, he stopped and listened. The baby was still

screaming. Gluskap the fearless was terrified. He ran on and was never seen again in the woman's village.

T 3.2

/t/
laughed
stopped
looked
danced
/d/
covered
listened
opened
screamed
/ɪd/
wanted
shouted
boasted
pointed

T 3.3

1 What was she doing at 7 o'clock yesterday morning?
She was packing her suitcase.
2 What was she doing at 8 o'clock?
She was driving to the airport.
3 What was she doing at 10 o'clock?
She was flying to Glasgow.
4 What was she doing at half past eleven?
She was having a meeting.
5 What was she doing at half past one in the afternoon?
She was having lunch.
6 What was she doing at 3 o'clock?
She was visiting Dot Com Enterprises.
7 What was she doing at 6 o'clock?
She was writing a report on the plane.
8 What was she doing at half past eight in the evening?
She was putting the baby to bed.
9 What was she doing at 10 o'clock?
She was relaxing and listening to music.

T 3.4

1 A I didn't laugh at his joke.
  B Why? Had you heard it before?
2 A Were you surprised by the ending of the film?
  B No, I'd read the book, so I already knew the story.
3 A I went to the airport, but I couldn't get on the plane.
  B Why? Had you left your passport at home?
4 A I was homesick the whole time I was living in France.
  B That's really sad! Had you never lived abroad before?
5 A The hotel where we stayed on holiday was awful!
  B That's a pity. Hadn't you stayed there before?
6 A I met my girlfriend's parents for the first time last Sunday.
  B Really? I thought you'd met them before.
7 A My grandfather had two sons from his first marriage.
  B Really? I didn't know he'd been married before.

T 3.5

An amazing thing happened!

N = Nicola, W = Wanda

N Hi, Wanda. Did you have a good holiday?
W Oh, yeah, we had a great time. But I have to tell you – the most amazing thing happened.
N Really? What was that?
W Well, Roy and I were at the beach near the hotel and we were swimming in the sea – it was our first day – and this huge wave came along and knocked my sunglasses into the water. I …
N Why were you swimming in your sunglasses?
W Oh, I don't know. I'd just left them on top of my head. I'd forgotten they were there. Anyway, they were gone. I couldn't find them anywhere. I was really upset. You know Roy had given me those sunglasses for my birthday and they were really expensive.
N I remember – nearly £100.
W Yeah. Anyway, I had to have sunglasses, so I bought a new pair – just a cheap pair this time. The next day I was lying on the beach, sunbathing. Then, suddenly another huge wave …
N You didn't lose another pair of sunglasses?
W No, no. You'll never believe this – there was another huge wave. It completely covered me. I was so wet and …
N Are you sure this was a good holiday?
W Yeah – but listen! When I looked down, there on the sand, right next to me, were my expensive sunglasses. The ones I had lost the day before! I couldn't believe my eyes!
N You're joking! That is *amazing*!

T 3.6 Books and films

V = Vinnie, W=Will, S = Sue, M = Maeve,

V Hey, I just read a great book.
W A book? Hey Vinnie, we're impressed! What was it?
V *The Philosopher's Stone*
M Isn't that a Harry Potter book?
V Well, yeah, yeah, but … . No, no, come on you guys, – really, it was terrific. I was so amazed. JK Rowling's a really good writer. Lots of adults read her books, they're not just for kids.
W Sure, Vinnie. You believe that, if you want.
S No, come on, he's right. I mean, I've seen people reading Harry Potter on the Underground and I've seen the video – my nephew has it – it's excellent!
M Actually, I've just bought *Captain Corelli's Mandolin* on DVD. Has anyone read that book?
S Oh no, no, please! Not *Captain Corelli's Mandolin*. I could *not* read that book. Everybody said it was great. I could *not* read it.
W You have to skip the first hundred pages and after that it's great.
V Hey guys! Call me old-fashioned but I like to begin a book at the beginning.
W But it is a great story, though – 'specially when it, y'know, moves to him and the girl on the Greek island.
M Yeah, it's a fantastic love story. But sooo sad! Actually, I read it on holiday, on a beach on a

Greek island – would you believe – and I just cried and cried. People kept asking me if I was OK!

V Hey, didn't Nick Cage star in the film?

W Yeah, with Penelope Cruz … she is just so lovely …

M Er well right so …what *is* your favourite book then Sue?

S Oh … well … my all time best is … right, you'll never believe this … it's – it's *Dracula*!

M *Dracula?* You're kidding!

S No – no, I'm not. I know everybody's *heard* of *Dracula* and *seen Dracula* films, but I bet not many people have read the book. It's by a man called Bram Stoker and it's brilliant.

W Yeah – there are loads of *Dracula* films. Er, I saw one not long ago actually, with – er – Tom Cruise.

V Yeah, yeah, I love horror movies – the scarier the better!

M Well, actually, I think *Frankenstein*'s a much better horror movie. You feel really sorry for that poor monster.

S Well, it's good but not that good. I mean that's only *my* opinion of course.

V *Dracula* is more scary … with huge teeth that he sinks into the necks of beautiful women. Aaargh!

M Aaargh! That's disgusting!

S OK Vinney. OK. So what else do *you* read – I mean other than Harry Potter that is?

V Hey – come on, come on! I had to read Ernest Hemingway at school and I quite enjoyed it … oh … what was it called? Oh yeah, yeah, yeah, *The Sun Also Sets*

W *Rises*. – *The Sun Also Rises*.

V Whatever.

W No I read it years ago – it's a great read, actually. It's all about Hemingway's travels through France and Spain, isn't it? Oh, … and his drinking.

M Yeah, Hemingway drank a lot, didn't he? Well, we're going on holiday to Florida next month. Maybe we can hang out in the bars where he used to drink and …

V What? What? Hemingway lived in Florida?!

W You're the American!

V Well …

W Yeah, in – in Key West, but we'll only visit *some* of the bars he went to!

T 3.7

1 **A** Did you like the film?
  B It was excellent. Have you seen it yet? It stars Julia Kershaw and Antonio Bellini.
2 **A** What did you think of the play?
  B It was really boring! I fell asleep during the first act.
3 **A** Did you like your pizzas?
  B They were delicious. John had tomato and mozzarella and I had tuna and sweetcorn.
4 **A** Do you like Malcolm Baker's novels?
  B I didn't like his first one, but I couldn't put his latest one down until the last page.
5 **A** What do you think of their children?
  B I think they spoil them. They always give them whatever they want.
6 **A** What was your holiday like?
  B It was a nice break, but the weather wasn't very good.
7 **A** What did you think of Sally Cotter?

  B She's usually good, but I don't think she was right for this part.
8 **A** What was the match like?
  B It was really exciting, especially when David Stuart scored in the closing minutes.

Unit 4

T 4.1 Teenagers and parents

I = Interviewer, S = Sarah, L = Lindsay

I Tell me, what are some good things about being a teenager and not an adult?

S Um … well, for one thing, you don't have to go to work.

L Yeah. And you don't have to pay bills.

I OK …

L And you can go out with your friends, and you can go shopping, and you can go to the cinema, and you can …

S Oh, come on, Lindsay. Adults can do all that too! But what's different is how much freedom teenagers have.

L Don't have, you mean.

S Right. How much freedom we don't have. I mean, I always have to tell my mum and dad where I'm going and what time I'm coming home.

L Mmm.

I And what time do you have to get back home?

S Mmm – by 10 o'clock on a week-day, maybe 11 or 12 at the weekend.

L It doesn't matter because you never have enough money anyway!

S Definitely. You get pocket money from your parents, but it's never enough. And you aren't allowed to buy whatever you want.

I OK, OK. Life's tough for kids. But what do you think it's like being an adult? Lindsay?

L Well, adults have to worry about paying the bills and taking care of their family. They can't always do what they want when they want.

I They have responsibilities, you mean?

L Yeah. I feel more sorry for my mum than my dad. She's always rushing around and she has to go to work as well. She doesn't have to work on Thursdays and Fridays, but she still has loads of different things to do in a day, like shopping and cooking, and taking me to dance classes.

I So, do you think your dad has an easier life?

L Well, I don't know. He has to drive over 500 miles a week.

I Sarah, tell me about school. What are some of the rules at your school?

S Oh! There are so many! Let's see. We can't wear make-up. We aren't allowed to chew gum. We aren't allowed to bring mobile phones to class . . .

L There are millions of rules – all of them stupid.

S And if you break one of the rules, you have to stay after school!

L Well, speaking of school, I've got to go. I've got to do my homework!

T 4.2

1 You don't have to go to work.
2 You don't have to pay bills.
3 You can go out with your friends.

---

4 I always have to tell my mum and dad where I'm going.
5 What time do you have to get back home?
6 You aren't allowed to buy whatever you want.
7 Adults have to worry about paying the bills.
8 They can't always do what they want.
9 We aren't allowed to bring mobile phones to class.
10 I've got to go. I've got to do my homework.

T 4.3

1 Where's my briefcase? I've got to go to work!
2 Look at those dirty plates! We've got to do the washing-up.
3 Pamela and Charles don't have any food in their house. They've got to go shopping.
4 John needs to get an alarm clock. He's got to get up early tomorrow.
5 I haven't got any clean socks. I've got to do the washing.
6 The chef's ill, so the waiter's got to do the cooking.

T 4.4 See p32

T 4.5 See p33

T 4.6 G=Grandma, A = Antony

G You must look after your money.
A Yes, Grandma! I will.
G You mustn't talk to strangers.
A No, Grandma! I won't.
G You mustn't go out when it's dark.
A No, Grandma! I won't.
G You mustn't drink too much beer.
A No, Grandma! I won't.
G You must make sure you eat well.
A Yes, Grandma! I will.
G You must have a bath regularly.
A Yes, Grandma! I will.
G You must phone us if you're in trouble.
A Yes, Grandma! I will.
G You mustn't go anywhere that's dangerous.
A No, Grandma! I won't.

T 4.7 A new job

D = Dave, M = Manager

D So, um … what time do I have to start?
M 11.00 in the morning or 4.00 in the afternoon.
D And do I have to wear a uniform?
M Definitely. You have to wear the same uniform as everyone else – a short-sleeved white shirt, black trousers, and a red hat. And a name tag.
D So … what do I do exactly?
M You serve the customers. Remember – you must always be polite. You say 'Good morning' or whatever the time of day, and then 'Can I help you?' When they tell you what they want, you have to enter it into the computer, and when they're finished, you should read back what they've ordered. Then you take their money, and you put together their food. That's it.
D Great. When can I start?
M You start at 4.00 tomorrow afternoon.
D Cool.
M Here's your hat. And your name tag. You're all set. Welcome to Burger Heaven, Dave.

T 4.8

The Italians eat a lot of pasta.
The Chinese cook lots of noodles and rice.

The British invented football.
The Canadians often watch ice hockey on TV.
The French produce champagne.
The Japanese eat raw fish.
The Scots wear kilts on special occasions.

T 4.9 **Come round to my place!**

Sumie

My name is Sumie. I come from Nagano, Japan. In my country, we usually invite guests home at the weekend for dinner, at about 7 o'clock in the evening. Before they come, we must tidy the front garden and clean the entrance hall. Then we must spray it all with water to show that we welcome our guests with cleanliness. The guests usually bring a gift, and when they give you the gift they say, 'I'm sorry this is such a small gift,' but in fact they have chosen it very carefully. When the meal is ready the hostess says, 'We have nothing special for you today, but you are welcome to come this way'. You can see that in Japan you should try to be modest and you should not show off too much. If you don't understand our culture, you may think this is very strange. When we have foreign guests, we try to serve traditional Japanese meals like sushi, tempura, or sukiyaki, but when we have Japanese guests, we serve all kinds of food such as spaghetti, Chinese food, or steaks.
When guests leave, the host and hostess see them out of the house and wait until their car turns the corner of the street; they wait until they can't see them any more.

Kate

My name is Kate and I'm from Bristol in England. We like to have people over for lunch and they usually get here around noon. We often have people over to eat, but sometimes when we invite a lot of people over, for a family gathering for example, we have what's called a 'potluck lunch'.
A potluck is an informal occasion, so people dress casually. If the weather is nice we'll have it outside in the garden. What makes it fun is that everyone who comes has to bring a dish of food. They're given a choice: starter, main course, salad or vegetable, or dessert. As the host, I'll know how many of each kind of dish the guests will bring, but not exactly what the foods will be. That's why it's called 'potluck' – it's a surprise, having a dinner party and not knowing what you're going to feed the guests! All I have to do is make one dish myself and get cups, glasses, and knives and forks together, and supply the drinks. As the guests arrive, they put their dish on the table, and people help themselves. Some guests might bring a bottle of wine or flowers as a gift but I don't expect anything. It's a fun, relaxed way of getting together with friends or family.

Lucas

My name is Lucas and I'm from Porto Alegre which is in the southern part of Brazil. We like to invite our friends over at weekends, on a Friday or a Saturday night for a 'Churrasco', or Brazilian barbecue. These are very popular in this part of Brazil.
People come about 8.00 in the evening and stay to midnight or even later – sometimes until 2.00 in the morning, whenever people start getting sleepy. People stay a long time; there is no set time for dinner to end. We'll sit around and play cards or just talk. It's very informal. If people

want to bring something, I'll tell them to bring something for the meal like a bottle of wine or something for dessert.
Ah, but what about the food? At a 'Churrasco', we cook different kinds of meat on long metal skewers over an open flame. We have all kinds of meat: beef, pork, and maybe Brazilian sausage. Sometimes chicken too. Then we cut off slices of meat from the skewers to serve the guests. It's really delicious. We usually have potato salad or rice as side dishes. After the meal we drink coffee or espresso.

T 4.10

1 A Could you bring us the bill, please?
   B Yes, sir. I'll bring it right away.
2 A Would you give me your work number, please?
   B Of course. Oh, shall I give you my mobile number, too?
3 A Can I help you?
   B Just looking, thanks.
4 A Two large coffees, please.
   B White or black?
5 A Can you tell me the code for Paris, please?
   B One moment. I'll look it up.
6 A I'll give you a lift if you like.
   B That would be great! Could you drop me off at the library?
7 A Would you mind opening the window?
   B No problem. It's stuffy in here.
8 A Could I have extension 238, please?
   B That line's engaged. Would you like to hold?

T 4.11

1 'So, anyway, there I was, sitting in my boss's office. All of a sudden, the phone rings and my boss says …'
   'Sorry to interrupt, darling, but I think the baby's crying. Could you go and check?'
2 'Can I help you?'
   'Yes, I bought these shoes here two days ago, and the heel on this one is already broken. Can I change them for a new pair?'
   'Of course. Let me see if we have another pair in your size.'
3 'Will you turn down that awful music?'
   'What?'
   'Will you turn down that awful music? Or better still – turn it off!'
   'Oh, all right.'
4 'Hi, Bob. Where are you going?'
   'I have a meeting with the web designer and the programmer about our new website this afternoon.'
   'Could you do me a favour? Would you mind asking the programmer to call me? I have a question for him about the budget.'
   'Sure. No problem.'

Unit 5

T 5.1 **Ben's list**

B = Ben, A = Alice

B I'm going shopping. Do we need anything?
A I don't think so. … Oh, hang on. We haven't got any sugar.
B It's OK. It's on my list. I'm going to buy some.
A What about bread?
B Good idea! I'll get a loaf.

A Er, what time will you be back?
B I don't know. I might stop at Nick's. It depends on how much time I've got.
A Don't forget we're playing tennis with Dave and Donna this afternoon.
B Don't worry. I won't forget. I'll be back before then.
A OK.

T 5.2 **What's going to happen?**

1 A Have you got the plane tickets?
   B Yes. They're with the passports and traveller's cheques.
   A What time is the taxi coming?
   B In about thirty minutes. What's the name of the hotel we're staying at?
   A The Grand Hotel.
   B Have you remembered your swimming costume this year?
   A Oh, yes. It's packed. What about tennis rackets?
   B I put them in my case, with the fifteen books.
   A Right. Let's get these cases closed.

2 A Well, darling, it's our big day soon.
   B I know. I can't wait. I hope the weather's good.
   A Yes, it makes such a difference, doesn't it?
   B The church is looking beautiful.
   A And the hotel's getting ready for the reception.
   B And then there's our honeymoon in Rome.
   A Ah!

3 A Have you packed the books and the pictures from the living room?
   B Yes. And all the kitchen things are packed, too.
   A That's it then. What time are the removal men coming?
   B Early, I hope. About 7.00 in the morning.
   A Good. It's a long drive, *and* it's right in the middle of the countryside.
   B I can't wait to be there.
   A And I can't wait to get the baby's room ready.
   B Tom if it's a boy and Natalie if it's a girl. How exciting!

T 5.3

1 I think Jerry will win the tennis match. He's been playing really well lately.
2 I think it'll be a nice day tomorrow. The forecast is for warm and dry weather.
3 I think I'll pass my exam on Friday. I've been studying for weeks.
4 I think you'll like the film. It's a wonderful story, and the acting is excellent.
5 I think we'll get to the airport in time. But we'd better get going.
6 I think you'll get the job. You have the right qualifications and plenty of experience.

T 5.4

1 I don't think Jerry will win the tennis match. He hasn't practised for weeks.
2 I don't think it'll be a nice day tomorrow. The forecast said rainy and windy.
3 I don't think I'll pass my exam on Friday. I haven't studied at all.
4 I don't think you'll like the film. It's a bit boring.
5 I don't think we'll get to the airport in time.

There's too much traffic.

6 I don't think you'll get the job. They're looking for someone with more experience.

T 5.5 **Arranging to meet**

L = Liz, MY = Min Young

L We need to meet some time this weekend to talk about our project.

MY OK. What are you doing today?

L Well, this afternoon I've got a dance class, but I'm not doing anything this evening. What about you?

MY Mmm – I'm going shopping this afternoon, and this evening I'm going ice-skating. What about tomorrow?

L Well, I'm having my hair cut tomorrow afternoon, so that'll take a while.

MY What time will you be finished at the hairdresser's?

L About 4 o'clock. What are you doing around that time?

MY I don't know. I might be free.

L OK. Why don't we meet at the Internet Café at about 5 o'clock? We can have a coffee and do our work.

MY Sounds good to me. Are you going out in the evening?

L Yes. I'm going out for dinner with a couple of friends. Do you want to join us?

MY That would be great! I'd love to.

L OK. So we'll meet tomorrow at 5 o'clock at the Internet Café.

MY Good.

T 5.6 **A weather forecast**

And here's the weather for some popular destinations in Western Europe for the next twenty-four hours.

A Let's begin in the north. I'm afraid spring isn't here yet! Another major frontal system will move in from the Atlantic affecting Northern Ireland and Scotland, before moving on to Scandinavia. It's going to bring plenty of rain, which could fall as snow on Scottish mountains. So it will feel very chilly everywhere. Temperatures around five or six degrees at best in the rain but much lower in snowy areas, where they will stay around freezing all day, you'll be lucky to see two degrees.

B Moving south now, into England and Wales, most of northern France, and across through Belgium and Holland. Things look more springlike here and it will be a lot brighter than in recent weeks. Along Channel coasts especially, there may be a little rain at first, with temperatures reaching only eight degrees. Inland, however, there will be more sunshine than showers, with all areas becoming warmer and drier as the day goes on. Towards the end of the day temperatures could be as high as 15 degrees in these regions. The winds will be light, coming from the south but it will feel very pleasant.

C If you're lucky enough to be going to southern France or Spain you'll find the best of today's weather. In the far south of Spain, mainly clear skies, lots of sun with high temperatures for the time of year up to 24 degrees, and everywhere else 18 or 19 degrees with some cloud. But it's not all good news. Strong winds along the southern French coast could spoil your evening walk.

D Further east, across the Alps, from Switzerland into northern Italy, there are the remains of another weather system. There will be stormy weather during the day with thunder and lightning, bringing over two inches of rain to some lowland areas and heavy snow to the mountains. Strong winds and rain will continue most of the day. The winds will make it feel much cooler for the time of year with temperatures struggling to reach ten degrees. And watch out for early morning fog.

So that's it, a quick tour of Western Europe – not bad in central countries, warm and sunny in Spain; cool, wet, and windy in parts of Italy, and Switzerland – oh, and stay away from those Scottish mountains unless you're wearing warm clothes.

T 5.7

1 A Do you think it'll be a rough crossing?
  B Well, the forecast is good, so it should be pretty smooth.
2 A Excuse me, I think those seats facing the front are ours.
  B Oh, I'm sorry. We didn't know they were reserved.
3 A We're going to Market Street. Could you tell us when it's our stop?
  B Just sit near the front and I'll call it out.
4 A Can you take us to the airport?
  B Of course. Hop in!
5 A Can I take these bags on with me?
  B I'm sorry. Only one item of hand luggage per passenger.
6 A That's all right. You can keep the change.
  B Thanks a lot. Do you want a hand with those bags?
7 A Excuse me, are we landing on time?
  B Yes. We're beginning our descent soon.
8 A No, no! He said turn *left* at the lights, not right!
  B Look! *You* drive and *I'll* give directions from now on! Right?
9 A How do I get to Oxford Circus?
  B Take the Piccadilly Line, eastbound, and change at Green Park.

Unit 6

T 6.1 **A student visitor**

S = Sandy, N = Nina

S Our student from Seoul arrived on Monday.

N What's her name?

S Soon-hee.

N That's a pretty name! What's she like?

S She's really nice. I'm sure we'll get on well. We seem to have a lot in common.

N How do you know that already? What does she like doing?

S Well, she likes dancing, and so do I. And we both like listening to the same kind of music.

N What does she look like?

S Oh, she's really pretty. She has big, brown eyes and long, dark hair.

N Why don't we do something with Soon-hee this weekend? What should we do? Get a pizza? Go clubbing? What would she like to do?

S I'll ask her tonight. She was a bit homesick at first, so I'm pretty sure she'll want to go out and make some friends.

N How is she now?

S Oh, she's OK. She called her parents and she felt much better after she'd spoken to them.

N Oh, that's good. I can't wait to meet her.

T 6.2

1 Thai food? It's delicious. It can be spicy, but it doesn't have to be.
2 Oh, she's very nice. You'd really like her. She's the kind of person you can always go to with a problem.
3 Not very well. He still has a temperature and a bad cough.
4 Well, she's crazy about horses. I don't think she has any other hobbies. Oh, she plays golf sometimes.
5 It's not very nice at all. It's raining, it's cold, and it's pretty miserable. What about where you are?
6 Mmm … a little like you, as a matter of fact. He's about the same height, tall with blond hair, but your hair's longer and straighter than his. Other than that, you two are quite similar.
7 It was great. Really relaxing. Lots of sunshine, good food. We did almost nothing but sit by the pool and read books for the whole two weeks.
8 I like all kinds, but I suppose I like biographies and detective stories best.

T 6.3 **A thank-you letter**

Dear Sandy and family,

I just wanted to say thank you for having me as your guest in your beautiful home. I had a great time. I really enjoyed meeting your friends. You all made me feel so welcome. You know how much I missed my family at first, but you were so kind that I soon stopped feeling homesick. I can't find the words to tell you how grateful I am. I'd like to call you. What's a good time to call?

You know that on my way home I stopped to visit my aunt in Perth. It was so hot! It was over 35 degrees all the time but I absolutely loved it. My aunt wanted me to stay longer, but I wanted to see my parents and my brother, Sang-chul. But she's invited me to go back and I'd love to do that. I'm thinking of going next year.

Anyway, I'm looking forward to hearing from you very soon. Let me know if you ever want to visit Seoul. My brother and I could take you to a 'norebang' (a singing room). It's a bit like karaoke!

Love to you all,

Soon-hee

P.S. Do you like the picture of Sang-chul and me?

T 6.4

1 They promised to bring the wine.
2 The teacher told them to do their homework.
3 I've just finished answering my emails.
4 Don't forget to take your passport.
5 He finally succeeded in passing his driving test.
6 We asked him to move his car.
7 I just need to go to the loo. I'll be back in a minute.
8 I don't mind looking after your cat.
9 Just let me finish what I'm saying.
10 Please can you help me carry this upstairs?
11 I hate shopping for clothes.
12 She's really looking forward to working with us.

T 6.5 See p50

T 6.6

1 A Nick's really quiet and shy. He never says a word.
  B Yeah, his brother is much more outgoing.
2 A What's Carrie's boyfriend like?
  B Well, he's tall, dark and handsome, but he's not very polite. In fact, he's even ruder than Carrie!
3 A How was your lunch?
  B Ugh! It was awful. The pizza was disgusting. We were really starving, but we still couldn't eat it!
4 A Mmm! These tomatoes are really delicious. Did you grow them yourselves?
  B Yes, we did. All our vegetables are home-grown.
5 A Did you have a good time in London?
  B We had a great time. There's so much to do. It's a really exciting city. And there are so many people from all over the world. I think it's nearly as cosmopolitan as New York.

T 6.7 New York

I = Interviewer, J = Justin, C = Cinda

I How long have you been here in New York?
J Nearly three years.
I And are you enjoying it?
J We love it.
C It's great.
I So what do you like best?
C Oh, the atmosphere, the mixture of all kinds of people. The speed of everything – it's exciting.
J I love the architecture, it's so different from London. Walking the streets and looking up at all those skyscrapers.
I And what about the people?
C Well, New Yorkers have a reputation for being rude and unfriendly, but I don't think that's true. People are always in a hurry, but they're not unfriendly.
J What I love is the – the great mixture of nationalities and cultures. It's got to be the most cosmopolitan city in the world.
I More than London?
J Hmm … well, I think so, but they're both very mixed.
C Life here seems much faster than in London. Everyone's in such a rush. Everything's done for speed. For example, I – I don't think people cook at home much – everyone seems to eat out or get food delivered because it's quicker and easier.
I Have you made many friends here?
J I've made friends at work mostly. But it's – it's difficult to make friends outside of work – people are so busy. But mostly I find people pretty friendly.
C Except the taxi drivers! Some of the rudest people I've ever met are New York taxi drivers!
J And some of the worst drivers. Every time I sit in a taxi I say a prayer. They drive so fast and suddenly they change lanes. And worst of all they don't seem to know where anything is.
C Yeah – you spend the entire journey giving directions. Anyway, I like using the subway. It's cheap.
J Yeah, and easy to use and it seems safe to me. We walk a lot as well. It's a lot safer now than it was ten years ago. It's still not very clean but it's getting better.
I Do you have a car?
J No. No, we don't. Not many of our friends do, actually. You don't really need one.
C I'd hate to drive in the city, I'd be terrified. Anyway, you can get everything delivered to your door – not just food.
I Don't you go shopping?
J Oh yeah, of course we do. Not all of us can afford to shop on 5th Avenue, you know, but it's – it's fun to look.
C Actually, the shops – sorry, the stores – are great. Always open – well nearly always – til 9.00 or 10.00 at night.
J People work much later here. I wasn't expecting to work such long hours! And the holidays – sorry, vacation time – and the – the public holidays they're, they're much shorter. I only get ten days a year. It's difficult for people like us with families in other countries. It's difficult to find time to visit them.
I But generally you're happy?
J Fantastic!
C It's an amazing place, but in a few years I think I'll be exhausted and ready for a quieter life!

T 6.8 London

I = Interviewer, A = Alan

I Alan, how long have you lived in London?
A Fifteen years.
I And do you like it here?
A Sure I like it – but London is one of those cities that you love and hate at the same time.
I So first – what do you hate?
A Oh the usual big city things – the crowds, the dirt, the traffic, and of course the Underground – it's so expensive compared with the subway in New York.
I And what do you like?
A Oh, a lot: fantastic theatres – I'm an actor so that's important for me – great art galleries, museums, I love the Natural History Museum. Concerts, wonderful orchestras. The best of everything comes to London.
I And what's best for you?
A For me? Oh, I just love standing on Waterloo Bridge and looking down the river at the Houses of Parliament and now, of course there's the London Eye – I think it's just wonderful. And – I like travelling in the black cabs. Taxi drivers here are great, so friendly! They tell you their life stories AND they know every street in London – not like in New York.
I And what about the people? What do you think of Londoners?
A Ah well – generally speaking, I think that they do live up to their reputation – they are reserved. It takes a while to get to know people. They won't tell you about themselves. You say to an American 'How are you?' and you get 'Oh man, I'm just great. I got the promotion and I love working here in Dallas, Denver, Detroit or Delaware etc. y' know. Ask an Englishman 'How are you?' and you get 'Er – fine, thank you'.
I So the stereotype's true?
A Yeah, they're – they're pretty reserved. They don't like giving personal details, but they complain a lot about life generally. They seem much less positive about life – much more cynical than Americans. They grumble about transport and politicians and money, how much things cost, their work …
I So, we're a miserable lot then!
A Not really. Leisure time – sorry – free time – is really important to the British. I think for many Americans, work is the most important thing in their lives. Americans work much longer hours. In Britain they get more vacation time and time off …
I … and still they grumble!
A Yeah.
I You've been in London 15 years. Has it changed in that time?
A Oh yeah a lot – especially the shops, they stay open much longer now. They used to close every Wednesday afternoon. People in the States could never believe that. Oh and the food!
I Everyone says English food is terrible. Is it?
A Well, when I first came it was terrible. It was so hard to get good food. Nowadays it's not hard at all. London has some great restaurants – my favourite here is the Indian food, it's fantastic. I think we have one of the best right here on our street. Just the best!
I You live in south London. Do you like it there?
A Very much. I love the mix of cultures and nationalities in every street.
I How long do you think you'll stay here?
A Oh, I don't know. Maybe five more years. Maybe forever!

Unit 7

T 7.1 The job interview

N = Nancy, D = David

D Who do you work for now, Nancy?
N I work for Intertec Publishing. We publish international business magazines.
D I see. And how long have you worked for them?
N I've worked there for nearly five years. No, exactly five years.
D And how long have you been in charge of Eastern Europe publications?
N For two years.
D And what did you do before you were at Intertec?
N I worked for the BBC World Service.

T 7.2

D As you know, this job is based in Geneva. Have you ever lived abroad before?
N Oh yes. Yes, I have.
D And when did you live abroad?
N Well, in fact I was born in Argentina and I lived there until I was eleven. Also, I lived in Berlin for one year when I was working for the BBC.
D That's interesting. Have you travelled a lot?
N Oh, yes, yes, absolutely. I've travelled to most countries in South America and many countries in Europe. I've also been to Japan a few times.
D Oh yes? And why did you go to Japan?
N It was for Intertec. I went there to interview some Japanese business leaders.

T 7.3

1 She was born in Argentina in 1969.
2 She went to school in Buenos Aires until she was eleven.
3 She studied modern languages and journalism for three years at University College, London.
4 She's worked for Intertec for the last five years.
5 She left the BBC five years ago.
6 She lived in Berlin while she was working for the BBC.
7 She's been married twice.
8 She's visited Japan a few times.
9 She hasn't heard if she got the job at Worldwatch Europe yet.

T 7.4 It's in the news

'Here are today's news headlines … Convicted murderer Charles Watkins has escaped from Belmarsh Prison in South London. … Two Spanish novelists have been awarded the Nobel Prize for literature. … Hurricane Jeffrey has hit the Caribbean, causing widespread damage in Puerto Rico. … Two thousand workers from a UK car factory have been laid off due to a slowdown in the economy. … Desmond Lewis has been knocked out in the fifth round of his heavyweight championship fight in Las Vegas.'

T 7.5

1 The murderer Charles Watkins has been recaptured by police.
2 A Sunny Vacations cruise ship has sunk off the coast of Florida near Miami.
3 Maria Martin, the famous ex-model, has left £3 million to her pet cat, Fluffy.
4 A priceless Van Gogh painting has been stolen from an art gallery in Madrid.
5 Floods have killed at least 20 people and 200 more have been left homeless in the West Country.
6 An 18-year-old student has been elected mayor of a town in California.
7 Company Director Paul Swan has been forced to resign because of a financial scandal.
8 The world champion runner Ken Quicksilver has failed a drugs test at the Olympic Games and is expected to be disqualified.

T 7.6 The busy life of a retired man

P = Philippa, T = Thomas

P How long have you been retired now, Grandpa?
T Oh, let me see. Uh, it's four years. Yes, I've been retired nearly four years now. I suppose I'm used to it after all this time. But, you know, I worked for *Courtauld's* for over forty years. Can you believe that? Forty years.
P One job for forty years. Incredible! I remember when you retired and they gave you that gold watch. Do you like being retired? I'd get bored, I'm sure I would. Don't you get bored?
T Well, I'm lucky. I've got my health so I can do a lot. I can get out a lot. I've just taken up golf, you know. It's a wonderful sport for an old man like me 'cos it's not really a sport at all, at least not the way your Grandpa plays it! It's just a good excuse for a walk, and I need an excuse since Rover died. I – I miss good old Rover; he and I were great friends … but I don't think I want another dog at my age. I go to the golf club twice a week. I've made some good friends there, you know. Have you met Ted and Marjorie? They're my age. They're a – oh, they're a lovely couple.
P Er, no … I don't think I've met them, but didn't you go on holiday with them?
T Yes, that's right. We went to Wales together last Easter. Oh, and we had a lovely time, lovely time. I do appreciate company since your grandma died … you know I really miss your grandma. 35 years we were married, 35 years and still as much in love as the day we met. She was a wonderful lady, your grandma.
P Oh, I know that, Grandpa. We all miss her so much. We all loved her so much.
T So I like to keep busy. I've been on all sorts of special holidays, y'know. Package holidays for senior citizens, and I've done a bit of …
P Well, I know you went to visit Uncle Keith in Australia. *And* you've just come back from a cruise round the Caribbean. You're so brown.
T I know. My word, that was an experience. I loved every minute of it! When you're older I'll tell you about the American widow I met! … Miriam, she was called. Oh, just a baby of fifty-five, but she seemed to like me.
P Grandpa!
T And yes, of course, Keith. I saw him two years ago. You've not met your Australian cousins yet, have you? Oh, you'd love the baby, Kylie, she's beautiful. Looks just like your grandma. But you know, I've also been to Spain, and Morocco, and Turkey. These package holidays are so good for people like me.
P Grandpa, next time, please think of me. Don't you want a companion? Can I come with you? I'd love a suntan like yours! We never go anywhere interesting.
T Oh, Philippa, you know your mum and dad wouldn't let me. Not until you've finished your exams. Helen says I'm a bad influence on you.
P Well, I think *you* have more fun than *I* do! All I have to look forward to is exams and more exams, and then years and years of work!
T Oh Philippa. Don't wish your life away. Just enjoy it all. You only get one go at it!

T 7.7

1 A Hello. Could I speak to Sam Jackson, please?
   B I'm afraid Mr Jackson's in a meeting. It won't be over until 3.00. Can I take a message?
   A Yes, please. Could you ask him to phone me? I think he's got my number, but I'll give it to you again just in case. It's 743 21 9186.
2 A Can I have extension 2173, please?
   B The line's busy at the moment. Would you like to hold?
   A Yes, please.
   Five seconds later.
   B I'm putting you through now.
   A Thank you.
3 A Could I speak to Alison Short?
   B I'm afraid she isn't at her desk at the moment. Do you want to hold?
   A No, don't worry. I'll phone back later.
4 A Can I speak to Terence Cameron, please?
   B Speaking.
   A Ah, Mr Cameron! This is Holly Lucas. I'm phoning about a letter I got this morning.
5 A Hello. This is Incom International. There's no one here to take your call at the moment. Please leave a message and we'll get back to you as soon as we can.

Unit 8

T 8.1 A place in the sun

D = David, J = Jack, A = Annie

D You're both mad. I think you'll regret it. You were earning good money here. You won't earn much growing lemons.
J We know that, but we won't need a lot of money to live there.
D But what will you do if you can't find anywhere to live?
A There are lots of cheap old farms. We'll have no trouble finding somewhere.
D But you don't even like gardening. What will you do if you don't like farming either?
J We'll only know if we don't like farming when we try it.
D Well, OK. But what if you …?

T 8.2 D = David, J = Jack, A = Annie

D Will you keep in touch with friends?
A Of course we will. When we get there, we'll give you a call.
D And how will I contact you?
J Well, as soon as we find a place to live, we'll send you our address.
D Hmmm, I can always email you.
J Yes, email's brilliant for keeping in touch, but you'll have to wait until we've set up our computers.
A And David, I promise, you'll be our first guest when we move into our new home.
D Excellent. I'll look forward to that!

T 8.3 D = David, S = Sue

D Bye, darling! Good luck with the interview!
S Thanks. I'll need it. I hope the trains are running on time. If I'm late for the interview, I'll be furious with myself!
D Just stay calm! Call me when you can.
S I will. I'll call you on my mobile as soon as I get out of the interview.
D When will you know if you've got the job?
S They'll tell me in the next few days. If they offer me the job, I'm going to accept it. You know that, don't you?
D Of course. But we'll worry about that later.
S OK. Are you going to work now?
D Well, I'm going to take the children to school before I go to work.
S Don't forget to pick them up as soon as you finish.
D Don't worry, I won't forget. You'd better get going. If you don't hurry, you'll miss the train.
S OK. I'll see you this evening. Bye!

T 8.4 Winning the lottery

1 What would *I* do if *I* won £5 million? Well, I'd make sure my family had enough money, and my friends, and then I'd buy my own island in the Caribbean. And I'd give loads of money to charity.
2 Oh, that's easy! I'd give up my job and travel. Anywhere. Everywhere. Oh but it wouldn't change me. I'd still live in the same area because I like it so much.
3 What would I do? I'd buy a nice house in the country. I'd make it the best place I could. And I'd have lots of land so I could have peace and quiet!

4 I'd be a space tourist and fly to Mars on the space shuttle.
5 I wouldn't give away a penny. I'd spend it all on myself!

T 8.5

1 If Tony calls, tell him I'm at Alex's. He can reach me there.
2 If you've finished your work, you can take a break. Just be back in fifteen minutes.
3 If I'm not back by 8 o'clock, don't wait for me. Go without me and I'll meet you at the party.
4 If you have the flu, you should go to bed. Keep warm and drink plenty of fluids.
5 If you're ever in London, please let me know. I'd love to show you around.
6 If you go to Russia, you have to have a visa. You can get one at the embassy.
7 I'd buy a computer if I could afford it. It would be really useful for work.
8 If I had more time, I might take up an evening class. I'd love to learn more about photography.

T 8.6

'Who wants to be a millionaire?'

Who wants to be a millionaire?
I don't.
Have flashy flunkies everywhere.
I don't.
Who wants the bother of a country estate?
A country estate is something I'd hate.

Who wants to wallow in champagne?
I don't.
Who wants a supersonic plane?
I don't.
Who wants a private landing field too?
I don't.
And I don't 'cos all I want is you.

Who wants to be a millionaire?
I don't.
Who wants uranium to spare?
I don't.
Who wants to journey on a gigantic yacht?
Do I want a yacht? Oh, how I do not!

Who wants a fancy foreign car?
I don't.
Who wants to tire of caviar?
I don't.
Who wants a marble swimming pool, too?
I don't.
And I don't 'cos all I want is you.

T 8.7

1 'What did you do last night?'
'We went to the cinema.'
'What did you see?'
'*Murder in the Park.*'
'Was it good?'
'It was absolutely superb!'
2 'Is it true that Liz won the lottery?'
'Yes! She won £2,000!'
'I bet she was really happy.'
'Happy? She was absolutely thrilled!'
3 'When I got home, I had to tell my parents that I'd failed the exam.'
'Oh, no! What did they say?'
'My mum was cross, but my dad was really furious.'

4 'We went out for dinner at that new restaurant last night.'
'Oh! What was the food like?'
'Well, the main course was really tasty, and as for the dessert, it was absolutely delicious!'
5 'We had a wonderful time at the beach last weekend.'
'Oh, yeah? Was the weather hot?'
'It was absolutely gorgeous!'
6 'How long was your flight?'
'14 hours.'
'14 hours! You must be really tired.'
'You bet! I'm absolutely exhausted!'

T 8.8 Charity appeals

1 Amnesty International

Amnesty International is a Nobel Prize-winning organization that works to support human rights around the world. It is independent of any government or political party and has over a million members in 162 countries. Amnesty International works to free all prisoners of conscience anywhere in the world. These are people who are in prison because of their beliefs, colour, ethnic origin, language, or religion. Amnesty International tries to help these prisoners in two ways: first, by publicizing their cases and, second, by putting pressure on governments to practise human rights.

2 WWF

WWF is the world's largest and most effective conservation organization. It is dedicated to protecting wild animals around the world and the places where these animals live. WWF directs its conservation efforts towards three global goals. Firstly, it works to save endangered species like the black rhino or the giant panda. Secondly, it works to establish and manage national parks and wildlife reserves around the world. Thirdly, it works to address global threats to our environment, such as pollution and climate change.

3 Crisis Now!

Drought and famine have come to Africa again this year, just as they have every year for the past fifteen years. In some parts of Africa it hasn't rained for three years. There have been no crops, and the animals on which many people depend died long ago. Refugees are pouring from the countryside into the towns in their desperate search for food, and it has been estimated that over 1,000 people are dying every day.
We are supplying towns and camps with food and medical supplies, but our efforts are drops in the ocean. We need a hundred times more food and medical supplies, as well as doctors, nurses, blankets, tents, and clothes. Your help is needed now before it is too late. Please give all you can. No pound or penny will ever be better spent or more appreciated.

T 8.9 Maria and Anna

M = Maria, A = Anna

M I'm bored!
A Well, it's a beautiful day. Why don't we go for a walk?
M No, I don't feel like it. I'm too tired.
A You need to get out. Let's go shopping!
M Oh, no! I'd rather do anything but that.
A OK, shall we see what's on television?
M That's a good idea.

A Do you want to watch the news?
M Mmm, I'd rather watch *The Simpsons*.

Paul and Mike

P = Paul, M=Mike

P I'm broke, and I don't get paid for two weeks. What am I going to do?
M If I were you, I'd get a better job.
P Oh, why didn't I think of that? Thanks, Mike. That's a big help.
M Well, you'd better get a loan from the bank, then.
P No, I can't. I owe them too much already.
M Why don't you ask your parents? They'd help you out.
P No, I'd rather not. I'd rather work out my problems for myself.
M You ought to ask your boss for a pay-rise!
P Good idea, but I've tried that and it didn't work.
M Oh, well, I suppose I could lend you some money.
P Really? Oh, that would be great! Thanks, Mike. You're a real mate.
M Yeah, well, OK then, but really, I don't think you should go out so much. That way, you won't be broke all the time.
P Yeah, yeah. I know. You're right.

Unit 9

T 9.1

1 'I haven't eaten anything since breakfast.'
'You must be hungry.'
2 'Steve has three jobs.'
'He can't have much free time.'
3 'The phone's ringing.'
'It might be Jane.'
4 'The cat's soaking wet!'
'Oh, it must be raining.'
5 'Listen to all those fire engines!'
'Ooh, there must be a fire somewhere.'
6 'I don't know where Sam is.'
'He could be in his bedroom.'
7 'Marta isn't in the kitchen.'
'She can't be cooking dinner.'
8 'Whose coat is this?'
'It might be John's.'

T 9.2

1 'It's Father's Day next Sunday.'
'I know. Should we buy Dad a present or just send him a card?'
2 'A half of lager and a fizzy mineral water, please.'
'Ice and lemon with the water?'
'Yes, please. And do you do bar meals?'
'Yes, we do.'
3 'I don't work normal hours and I like that. I'd hate one of those nine to five office jobs. Also I meet a lot of really interesting people. Of course, every now and then there's a difficult customer, but usually people are really nice. I took that really famous film star to the airport last week, now what was her name? Anyway she was lovely. Gave me a big tip!'
4 'So how did it go?'
'I'm not sure. I think it was OK.'
'Were you nervous?'
'Yeah, very, but I tried not to show it.'
'Could you answer all their questions?'

'Most of them.'
'And what happens now?'
'They said they'd phone me in a couple of days and let me know if I got it.'
5 'We've never had one before.'
'Really? We've always had them in our family. We're all crazy about them.'
'Well, we are now. The kids love her. And she's so good with them, very good-natured. But it wasn't fair to have one when we lived in a flat.'
'It's OK if they're small and you live near a park, but I know what you mean. What's her name?'
'Poppy.'

T 9.3 See p72

T 9.4 A holiday with friends

A = Andy, C = Carl

A Hi! Carl? It's Andy. How are you? Feeling better?
C Er – not really. I have to sit down most of the time. It's too tiring – walking with these crutches.
A Really? Still on crutches, eh? So you're not back to work yet?
C No. And I'm bored to death. I don't go back to the hospital for another week.
A Another week! Is that when the plaster comes off?
C I hope so. I can't wait to have two legs again! Anyway, how are you? Still missing the snow and the mountains?
A No, I'm fine. We're both fine. Julie sends her love, by the way.
C Thanks. Send her my love, too. I miss you all. By the way, have you got any of your photos back yet?
A Yes, yes, we have. Julie picked them up today. They're good. I didn't realize we'd taken so many of us all.
C What about that one with the amazing sunset behind the hotel?
A Yes, the sunset. It's a good one. All of us together on Bob and Marcia's balcony, with the mountains and the snow in the background. Brings back memories, doesn't it?
C Yeah. The memory of me skiing into a tree!
A Yes, I know. I'm sorry. But at least it happened at the end; it could have been the first day. You only missed the last two days.
C OK, OK. Oh, Andy, have you written to the hotel yet to complain about your room? That view you had over the car park was awful!
A Yeah, and it was noisy too! We didn't have any views of the mountains. Yeah, we've written. We emailed the manager yesterday, but I don't know if we'll get any money back.
C And Marcia's suitcase, did she find it?
A Yeah. The airline found it and put it on the next flight. Marcia was very relieved.
C I bet she was! All in all I suppose it was a pretty good two weeks, wasn't it?
A Absolutely. It was a great holiday. Some ups and downs, but we all had fun, didn't we? Shall we go again next year?
C I'd like to. All six of us again. Lisa wants to go again, too. It was her first time skiing and she loved it, but she says she'll only come if I don't break a leg!
A Great! It's a date. And next time go around

the trees! I'll call again soon, Carl. Take care!
C You too, Andy. Bye now.
A Bye.

T 9.5

1 A I can't find my homework.
   B You must have forgotten it.
2 A Mark didn't come to school last week.
   B He must have been ill.
3 A Why is Isabel late for class?
   B She might have overslept.
4 A I can't find my notebook.
   B You must have dropped it.
5 A The teacher's checking Maria's work.
   B She can't have finished already!
6 A How did Bob get such good marks in that test?
   B He must have cheated!

T 9.6 Brothers and sisters

Louisa

I = Interviewer, L = Louisa

L I'm the youngest of seven children. My oldest sister is still alive, aged ninety-three, and there are sixteen years between us. There were four girls, two boys, and then me.
I Seven children! Wow! How did you all get on together when you were children?
L Amazingly well. Being the youngest, my two brothers and I called our sisters 'the others', because they were either married or working by the time we were born. But the seven of us all got along very well. But it's different now, of course.
I Really? How?
L Well, when we were small, my older sisters often took care of us. Now my brothers and I are busy taking care of them.
I Tell me about your big sister Julia. How has your relationship with her changed over the years?
L Julia was the sister who used to … on her holidays … used to take me for walks and so on. But then she became a nun and went to Africa for twenty-three years. We wrote to one another and I was still her little sister. When she came back, it was shortly after my husband died. We became very close and our whole relationship changed and we became great friends.
I What do you see as the main advantage and disadvantage of coming from such a large family?
L Hmm. I think the main advantage was that we learned how to enjoy life without having a lot of money. I think our other relatives, my rich cousins in the city, envied us. We had old bikes, old clothes, but we had lots of freedom. In the city, they had to wear nice suits and behave correctly.
I Disadvantages?
L I think it was very difficult sometimes to have hand-me-down clothes, especially for a little girl like me. And I was sad that we didn't go away on holiday like some other children. But the advantages outweighed the disadvantages enormously, there's no doubt about that.
I Six out of the seven of you are still alive. How closely have you kept in touch over the years?
L Very closely. Of course we still phone each other all the time and see each other

whenever we can. And we have a big family reunion every year. My granddaughter's just had twins. That means we'll have four generations there this year. How marvellous!

Rose

I = Interviewer, R = Rose

I So, Rose, do you have any brothers or sisters?
R No, I don't. I'm an only child.
I So what was it like growing up as an only child? Were you happy?
R When I was little, I liked it. I had lots of cousins and most of them lived in the same town, so we all played together all the time. And I had a best friend who lived next door to me. She was the same age as me and so she was a bit like a sister I suppose. But she moved away and that was sad. It was hard when I was a teenager.
I Why was that?
R Well, you know what it's like being a teenager. You're kind of unsure of how to deal with things and how to deal with people, especially parents. It would have been nice to have a brother or sister to talk to.
I Some people who come from large families might envy you because you had all of your parents' attention.
R Yes. But I think it has its negative side as well as its positive side. I think you don't want all your parents' attention, especially as a teenager. It was hard to find myself and my place in the world, I suppose.
I What about now that you're an adult?
R Again, I think it's difficult really. My father died about ten years ago, so of course I'm the one who's left totally responsible for my mother. I'm the one who has to look after her if she has a problem and help her if she needs help in any way. There's nobody else to help at all.
I You're married now with two children of your own. Was that a conscious decision to have more than one child?
R Yes, definitely. And they seem very happy and they get along very well with one another. Usually.

T 9.7 S = Sue, A–J = Sue's friends

1 A I want to travel the world.
   S So do I.
2 B I don't want to have lots of children.
   S Neither do I.
3 C I can speak four languages.
   S I can't.
4 D I can't drive.
   S Neither can I.
5 E I'm not going to get married until I'm 35.
   S Neither am I.
6 F I went to London last year.
   S So did I.
7 G I've never been to Australia.
   S I have.
8 H I don't like politicians.
   S Neither do I.
9 I I'm bored with Hollywood actors.
   S So am I.
10 J I love going to parties.
   S So do I.

Unit 10

T 10.1 See p78

T 10.2

1 How long has he had his mobile phone?
2 How long has he been asking his father for a phone?
3 Why did he want one?
4 Who has he been texting?
5 What time has he been going to bed?
6 Has his father forgiven him?
7 How much has he paid back?
8 How long will it take him to clear the debt?

T 10.3 See p79

T 10.4

1 A You're covered in paint! What have you been doing?
  B I've been redecorating the bathroom.
  A Have you finished yet?
  B Well, I've painted the door and the ceiling, but I haven't put up the wallpaper yet.
2 A Your hands are dirty. What have you been doing?
  B They're filthy. I've been working in the garden.
  A Have you finished yet?
  B Well, I've cut the grass, but I haven't watered the flowers yet.
3 A Your eyes are red! What have you been doing?
  B I'm exhausted. I've been revising for my exams.
  A Have you finished them yet?
  B Well, I've done my chemistry and history, but I haven't done English yet.

T 10.5

1 'When was she born?'
  'In 1960.'
2 'When was she given the award of Young Musician of the Year?'
  'In 1968, when she was 8 years old.'
3 'When did she go to the Royal Academy of Music?'
  'In 1978. She won a scholarship.'
4 'What year was her daughter born?'
  'In 1983.'
5 'Which countries has she lived in?'
  'Sweden, England, the US, and France.'
6 'When did she appear on British TV?'
  'When she was 22.'
7 'How many children has she got?'
  'One daughter.'
8 'How long has she been living in Paris?'
  'Since 1998.'

T 10.6 A lecture tour

I = Interviewer, A = Astrid

1 I How long are you here in Britain for?
  A Just two weeks.
2 I How long have you been in Britain?
  A Eight days.
3 I Where were you the day before yesterday?
  A In Birmingham.
4 I Where were you this time last week?
  A In London.
5 I Where will you be the day after tomorrow?
  A I'll be in Edinburgh.
6 I Where will you be a week today?
  A Back in Paris.

T 10.7 Collectors

Andrea Levitt

I = Interviewer, A = Andrea

I First of all, a little bit about you. Are you originally from New York City?
A I'm from Wilmington, Delaware, but I've been living in New York a long time, 36 years. I came to New York to work in the fashion industry. I still work in the world of fashion. I love it.
I So, how long have you been collecting dolls?
A Hmm … it must be about 25 years. Yeah, 25 years.
I So what led you to having such a love of dolls? Have you always loved them?
A Well, no. I didn't play with dolls much when I was a girl, but uh these aren't children's dolls that I collect.
I No?
A No, they're really works of art. When you say the word 'doll' people think of a toy for little girls, but these are not. When I opened my business, *Dolls-at-Home*, two years ago, that was the message I wanted to get across to all art lovers – that dolls are another art form.
I I can see that these are not dolls for little girls. Some of them are really quite amazing. How many dolls do you have in your collection?
A Oh, I would say – um I think maybe three hundred.
I Wow! And where are they all?
A Well, I had to buy a new apartment …
I You bought an apartment for the dolls?!
A Yeah, I really did. My son, he's thirty-three now, he went off to college and I filled his room with dolls in two minutes so I realized that I needed a different apartment. I wanted to show off my dolls.
I So, you have what, maybe four or five rooms, all with dolls …
A Actually there are dolls in *every* room, even the bathroom and the kitchen.
I I was going to ask, is there one room where you don't allow dolls?
A No! Oh no, they're part of my life. I mean sometimes when people visit there's nowhere to sit. It's a problem.
I So, what about keeping them clean? Dusting them?
A Erm, yeah, that's a problem too. New York is dirty. Erm, I suppose they should be under glass but I don't want them under glass, I want to enjoy them. I dust them occasionally.
I Well, they look immaculate.
A Thanks.
I That's a very unusual doll. Is it valuable?
A No, not really. But that doll over there … It has an elephant mask. That's my favourite.
I Really?
A You see the mask goes up and it's a little boy's face and it goes down and it's an elephant's face. It's made by one of the best doll makers in the US, Akira Blount.
I And how do you find your dolls?
A I travel all over. I go to doll shows, and now that I have a website and I've started my own business, doll artists find me. As I said, it's been going on for two years now, and I have a mailing list of nine hundred people.
I Wow! What does your son think of all this?
A You know, he thinks I'm sort of … crazy. He loves this apartment but he can't understand …

I Why you fill it with dolls!
A Yeah, but two weeks ago he came to one of my doll shows, it was his first time, and I think he was impressed. Yeah, I think so.
I So, do you think you'll ever stop collecting them?
A No, there's always room for another doll. If you're a real collector you always find room.
I I'm sure you're right. Well, that's great Andrea. Thank you very much.

T 10.8 Collectors

Jeff Parker

I = Interviewer, J = Jeff

I First of all, erm, just a little bit about you, Jeff. Are you originally from New York City?
A No, I'm originally from the Philadelphia area. But I moved to New York about five years ago when I got a job working for a bank on Wall Street.
I Oh? And do you mind talking about your *Star Wars* collection?
J No, not at all.
I So, how did you get interested in *Star Wars*?
J Well, *Star Wars* was one of the first movies I ever saw. I think I was four years old. My dad took me to see it and I just loved it. Loved the story, loved the idea of being in space. I think I saw it ten times.
I Wow! You sure did love *Star Wars*!
J Yeah, I guess so. Then all the toys came out, so I started collecting the action figures.
I Action figures?
J They're these little metallic figures. Models of the characters in the movie.
I I see. And which character did you like best?
J Oh, I was a Han Solo fan. I think he was my favourite. You know, I still have that Han Solo action figure. It's worth a lot of money now, but I like it because it was the first Star Wars thing I ever owned.
I So, did you just collect the figures?
J Oh, no. I collected the figures first – Darth Vader, Luke, Obi-Wan Kenobi, R2-D2, and of course Princess Leia. Then I started collecting everything *Star Wars* – space ships, space stations, posters, videos …
I Well, you seem to have a lot of pieces in your collection. About how many pieces do you have all together?
J I'm not sure because most of my collection is at my parents' house in Philadelphia. I don't have the room for all of it here in New York … but I'd say I probably have about seven hundred pieces in all.
I Seven hundred pieces!? How did you get so many?
J Well, you know, I'd ask my mom for the newest toys, – every holiday, every birthday, and the collection just grew and grew. I think they really liked *Star Wars*, too. When I was a kid my mom gave me *Star Wars* birthday parties, and bought me *Star Wars* cereal for breakfast … I even had *Star Wars* pyjamas and *Star Wars* underwear.
I A real *Star Wars* family then?
J You could say that. They even called our family dog Princess Leia.
I And did you play with other kids who collected *Star Wars* stuff?
J No, not really. I liked to play with all the things by myself. I loved making up all these

Star Wars stories about the characters … and uh …

I And – and now? Are you in touch with other *Star Wars* collectors?
J No. I – I don't have the time really.
I So what are you going to do with your collection?
J I don't know. I'm not sure. Sometimes I think I might sell it. Other times I think I might just keep it and give it to my kids some day.
I Oh, that would be something, wouldn't it? Thanks, Jeff.

T 10.9

1 **A** How much coffee do you drink?
　 B At least six cups a day.
　 A That's too much. You shouldn't drink as much as that.
2 **A** How many aspirins do you usually take when you have a headache?
　 B About four or five.
　 A That's too many. You shouldn't take as many as that!
3 **A** How much do you earn?
　 B Not enough to pay all my bills!
4 **A** How many people are there in your class?
　 B Forty.
　 A I think that's too many.
5 **A** Have you got any homework tonight?
　 B Far too much. I'll never be able to do it all.
6 **A** How old are you?
　 B Seventeen. I'm old enough to get married, but not old enough to vote!
7 **A** When did you last go to the dentist?
　 B Very recently. Just a few days ago.
8 **A** Do you take milk in your tea?
　 B Just a little.

Unit 11

T 11.1　**A stranger in town**

F = Flavia, R = Hotel Receptionist

F Hi. I've just checked in and I wonder if you could help me.
R I'll be happy to try.
F Well, first, I'm not sure if we're near the CN Tower.
R The CN Tower? It's very close. It's only about a ten-minute walk.
F Oh, good. Can you tell me if there are any good restaurants nearby?
R Lots. Erm, one good one is the Café Giovanni. It's casual but they have very good food and live music in the evenings.
F Sounds wonderful. Oh, and I need to cash some traveller's cheques, but I don't know what time the banks close.
R Most banks don't close until 5.30 on weekdays, but some have extended hours.
F Thank you very much. Oh … I'm sorry but I can't remember which restaurant you suggested.
R The Café Giovanni.
F Café Giovanni. Got it. Thanks for your help.
R My pleasure.

T 11.2　**We like animals, don't we?**

K=Karen, G = Gabriella

G Mummy?
K Yes, Gaby?

G I've got ten fingers, haven't I?
K Yes, that's right, sweetie. Ten pretty little fingers.
G And Daddy didn't go to work this morning, did he?
K No, it's Saturday. He's working in the garden today.
G And we like animals, don't we, Mummy?
K Yes, we do. Especially our cats, Sammy and Teddy.
G Can I have a biscuit now, Mummy?

T 11.3　**K=Karen, A = Karen's assistant**

K Now, what's happening today? I've got a meeting this afternoon, haven't I?
A Yes, that's right. With Henry and Tom.
K And the meeting's here, isn't it?
A No, it isn't. It's in Tom's office, at 3 o'clock.
K Oh! I'm not having lunch with anyone, am I?
A No, you're free for lunch.
K Phew! And I signed all my letters, didn't I?
A Erm, no, you didn't, actually. They're on your desk, waiting for you.
K OK. I'll do them now. Thanks a lot.

T 11.4

1 It isn't very warm today, is it?
2 You can cook, can't you?
3 You've got a CD player, haven't you?
4 Mary's very clever, isn't she?
5 There are a lot of people here, aren't there?
6 The film wasn't very good, was it?
7 I'm a silly person, aren't I?
8 You aren't going out dressed like that, are you?

T 11.5

1 **A** It isn't very warm today, is it?
　 B No, it's freezing.
2 **A** You can cook, can't you?
　 B Me? No! I can't even boil an egg.
3 **A** You've got a CD player, haven't you?
　 B Believe it or not, I haven't. I've got a cassette player, though.
4 **A** Mary's very clever, isn't she?
　 B Yes. She's extremely bright.
5 **A** There are a lot of people here, aren't there?
　 B I know! It's absolutely packed. I can't move!
6 **A** The film wasn't very good, was it?
　 B It was terrible! The worst I've seen in ages.
7 **A** I'm a silly person, aren't I?
　 B No, you're not. Everybody makes mistakes.
8 **A** You aren't going out dressed like that, are you?
　 B Why? What's wrong with my clothes? I thought I looked really cool.

T 11.6

A It's so romantic, isn't it?
B What is?
A Well, they're really in love, aren't they?
B Who?
A Paul and Mary.
B Paul and Mary aren't in love, are they?
A Oh yes, they are. They're mad about each other.

T 11.7

1 **A** You broke that vase, didn't you?
　 B Yes, I did. I dropped it. I'm sorry.
　 A You'll replace it, won't you?
　 B Yes, of course I will. How much did it cost?
　 A £300.
　 B £300?! It wasn't *that* much, was it?

A Yes, it was.
2 **A** Have you paid the electricity bill yet?
　 B No, *you* paid it, didn't you?
　 A No, I haven't paid it. I thought you paid it.
　 B Me? But you *always* pay it, don't you?
　 A No, I don't. I always pay the phone bill.
　 B Oh, yes. Sorry.
3 **A** We love each other, don't we?
　 B Erm, I think so.
　 A We don't ever want to be apart, do we?
　 B Well …
　 A And we'll get married and have lots of children, won't we?
　 B What? You haven't bought me a ring, have you?
　 A Yes, I have. Diamonds are forever.
　 B Oh, dear!
4 **A** Helen didn't win the lottery, did she?
　 B Yes, she did. She won £2 million!
　 A She isn't going to give it all away, is she?
　 B As a matter of fact she is.
　 A Wow. Not many people would do that, would they?
　 B Well, *I* certainly wouldn't.
5 **A** I think we're lost. Let's look at the map.
　 B Uh-oh.
　 A What do you mean, 'Uh-oh'? You didn't forget to bring the map, did you?
　 B Sorry.
　 A How are we going to get back to the campsite without a map?
　 B Well, we could ask a police officer, couldn't we?
　 A There aren't many police officers on this mountain!

T 11.8　**The forgetful generation**

P = Presenter

P Hi, and welcome to *What's your problem?* How's your day been so far? Have you done all the things you planned? Kept all your appointments? Oh – and did you remember to send your mother a birthday card? If so, good for you! If not – well, you're not alone. Many of us in the busy twenty-first century are finding it more and more difficult to remember everything. Once upon a time we just blamed getting older for our absent-mindedness, but now experts are blaming our modern lifestyle. They say that we have become 'the forgetful generation' and that day after day we overload our memories.

T 11.9

Ellen

Last year I finished university and I got a job in the same town, Canterbury. And one day, for some reason, rather than go to work for 9 o'clock, I got the bus and went to the university for an 11 o'clock lecture. I was sitting there, in the lecture room, and I thought to myself, 'Why don't I know anybody?' Then suddenly I remembered that I'd finished university and that I was two hours late for work!

Josh

I'm studying law in London now, and, erm, at the end of last term I packed my suitcase as usual and went to King's Cross station to catch the train home. I was sitting reading on the train, revising for my exams, and the inspector came to check my ticket. He looked at it and said, 'Thank you, sir. We'll be in Newcastle in about an hour.' Suddenly I thought, 'Newcastle!?! I don't want to go to Newcastle. My parents live in Plymouth!' You see, when I was a child I lived with my parents in Newcastle, but we moved to Plymouth when I was ten. I couldn't believe it. How could I have been so stupid?

Fiona

Some time ago I got dressed, ready to go to work. I put on my smart black suit. I'd been working at home the night before – preparing for a very important meeting the next day, and I remembered to put all the right papers into my briefcase. I left home and walked down to the bus stop. Just before I got on the bus, I looked down, and I was still wearing my fluffy, pink bedroom slippers!

T 11.10   **P = Presenter, A = Alan**

P Stories of forgetfulness like these are familiar to many of us, and experts say that such cases as Ellen's, Josh's, and Fiona's show the loss of memory is not just related to age, but can be caused by our way of life. Alan Buchan is a Professor of Psychology and he explains why.

A One of the problems, these days, is that many companies have far fewer employees. This means that one person often does several jobs. Jobs that before were done by many people are now done by a few. If you have five things to do at once, you become stressed and forgetful. I think many people in work situations, at a meeting or something, have the experience where they start a sentence and halfway through it, they can't remember what they're talking about, and they can't finish the sentence.

P That's happened to me.

A It's a terrible feeling – you think you're going insane. I remember one patient who came to me so distressed because at three important meetings in one week, she found herself saying, mid-sentence, 'I'm sorry, I can't remember what I'm talking about.' This was a patient in a new job, which involved a lot of travelling. She also had a home and family to take care of and she'd recently moved. She had so many things to think about that her brain couldn't cope. It shut down.

P I can see the problem, but what's the solution? How did you help that patient?

A Well, part of the solution is recognizing the problem. Once we'd talked to this patient about her stressful lifestyle, she realized that she wasn't going crazy and she felt more relaxed and was able to help herself. But do you know one of the best ways to remember things, even in these days of personal and handheld computers?

P What's that?

A It's a notebook, or just a piece of paper! At the beginning of every day write yourself a list of things you have to do – and it gives you a really good feeling when you cross things off the list as you do them!

P Well, there you have it! Thank you very much Professor … uh … um … ? Oh – Professor Alan Buchan!

T 11.11

1 A What do you say we break for lunch?
   B Great idea. We can grab a sandwich at the deli.
2 A What are you up to?
   B Nothing much. Just sitting around watching TV.
   A You're such a couch potato!
   B Hey, give me a break! I work hard all week. I like to relax at weekends.
3 A Quick! Give me your homework so I can copy it.
   B No way! Do your own homework!
4 A Did you mend the TV?
   B Kind of. Channel 4's OK, but we still can't get Sky.
   A Anything good on tonight?
   B Dunno. Look in the paper.
5 A What do you call that stuff you use to clean between your teeth?
   B What do you mean?
   A You know! It's like string. White.
   B Oh! You mean dental floss.
   A Yeah. That's it!

Unit 12

T 12.1   **The marriage proposal**

J = John, M = Moira

J Moira! Hello there! How are you?
M John! I'm just fine, thanks.
J It's really great to see you again. We haven't seen each other since our trip to Paris.
M Oh, John! I loved every minute in Paris. I'll never forget it as long as I live. Can we go back there next spring?
J Moira, -er first, there's something I want to ask you, something I have to ask you. Moira, I love you so much. Will you marry me and come to Paris with me on honeymoon?
M Oh, John! Yes, I will. I love you, too.

T 12.2   **The wedding**

A = Adam, B = Beatrice

1 A How do you know John and Moira?
   B I went to the same school as Moira.
2 A Are you married?
   B Yes, I am. That's my husband over there.
3 A Where did you meet your husband?
   B Actually, I met him at a wedding.
4 A Have you travelled far to get here?
   B Yes, we have. We flew in from Dublin yesterday.
5 A Do you live in Dublin?
   B Yes, we do.
6 A So, where are you staying?
   B We're staying at the Four Seasons Hotel.
7 A So am I. Can we meet there later for a drink?
   B Sure. I'll introduce you to my husband.

T 12.3   **B = Beatrice, R = Ron**

B I just met this really nice guy called Adam.
R Oh, yeah?
B He was very friendly. Do you know what he said? First, he asked me how I knew John and Moira. I told him that I had gone to the same school as Moira. Then he asked if I was married. Of course I said that I was!
R He asked you that?
B … and next he asked where we'd met and I told him that we'd actually met at a wedding.
R You told him that?
B Sure. Then he wanted to know how long we had been here, and I said we had just got here yesterday and that we had flown in from

Dublin. He asked if we lived in Dublin, so I told him that we did.
R What else did this guy want to know?
B Well, he asked where we were staying and it turns out that he's staying at the Four Seasons, too. Then he asked if I could meet him later for a drink, and I said we could and that I would introduce him to you.
R I'm not sure I want to meet this guy.

T 12.4   **R = Ron, B = Beatrice**

1 R Adam lives in Birmingham.
   B He told me he lived in Cambridge.
2 R He doesn't like his new job.
   B He told me he loved it!
3 R He's moving to Manchester.
   B Hang on! He told me he was moving to Australia!
4 R He went to Brighton on his last holiday.
   B Strange. He told me he'd been to Florida!
5 R He'll be forty next week.
   B Really? He told me he'd be thirty!
6 R He's been married three times.
   B But he told me he'd never been married!
   R You see! I told you he was a liar!

T 12.5

1 The postman told me to sign on the dotted line.
2 Maria asked Mark to translate a sentence for her.
3 Mary reminded her son to send Aunt Judy a birthday card.
4 John begged Moira to marry him.
5 John invited his boss to his wedding.
6 Tommy refused to go to bed.
7 Ben advised Tim to talk to his solicitor.
8 The teacher ordered Joanna to take the chewing gum out of her mouth.

T 12.6

Kathleen Brady

OK. We argue sometimes but not that often. Usually we just sit quietly and watch TV in the evenings. But sometimes … sometimes we argue about money. We don't have much, so I get very upset when Kenny spends the little we have on drinking or gambling. He promised to stop drinking, but he hasn't stopped. It's worse since he lost his job. OK, we were shouting, but we didn't throw a chair at Mr West. It … um … it just fell out of the window. And I'm really sorry that we woke the baby. We won't do it again. We love children. We'll babysit for Mr and Mrs West anytime if they want to go out.

T 12.7

Ann West

Every night it's the same thing. They argue all the time. And we can hear every word they say. During the day it's not so bad because they're both out. But in the evenings it's terrible. Usually they start arguing about which TV show to watch. Then he slams the door and goes down the street to the pub. Last night he came back really drunk. He was shouting outside his front door, 'Open the door you … um … so and so.' I won't tell you the language he used! But she wouldn't open it; she opened a window instead and threw a plant at him. Tonight they threw a chair at my poor husband. They're so selfish. They don't care about our baby one bit.

T 12.8 A birth

Well, my sister was expecting her first child and – er – she was living on a Scottish isle, the island of Mull … just off the west coast, and – er – the plan was that she would – er – travel to a friend's house on the mainland – er – there's a ferry of course – er – a week before the baby was due. That was the plan but – er – of course babies don't always … and – er – anyway, two weeks before the baby was due, she was at home and the baby started coming early so my sister had to be taken off the island by lifeboat, not by ferry. You see, it was really early in the morning and the ferry hadn't started running. Erm – but even the lifeboat didn't make it in time to actually get her to the mainland. Er – you can imagine it's quite a small space to give birth in. She said it was kind of like lying in the aisle of an aeroplane or something, that's about all the space that you've got! Fortunately the lifeboat crew were marvellous, – er – they're nearly all volunteers who – who man the lifeboats. You have like the captain of the boat and four crew members, and – er – in this case, a midwife from the hospital – and another midwife who was just passing, just … on her way home, in fact.

So, in this small space there were all these people standing around as she was giving birth – oh, and of course her husband Nick was there too – so it was quite crowded! My sister was just pleased that there were no complications and that she managed to get through it. And what was really nice, on the lifeboat, – erm – the crew had a bottle of champagne which I think they were saving for a special occasion and they did actually open it and – er – drink the health of the new baby. And then they also engraved her name and date of birth on the lifeboat's bell so that it's always remembered!

The lifeboatmen were encouraging my sister to name the baby after the lifeboat, 'cos lifeboats always have a name – and this one was called Mora Edith Macdonald. And so they wanted my sister to call the baby Mora – but she'd already got a name planned. But she did use Mora as a middle name. So my niece has the name Hazel Beth Mora Banner, – er – she has two middle names. One of the lifeboatmen joked – he said it was a good job she didn't give birth on the ferry because she'd have had to call the baby Caledonian McBrayne – that's the name of the ferry company. Actually the story – erm – it was featured in the local newspapers after the birth – erm – so there was a photo, somebody had a camera on the boat and took photos straight away. So the story appeared with that photo in all the local papers.

T 12.9 See p99

T 12.10

'My Way'

And now, the end is near
And so I face the final curtain
My friend, I'll say it clear
I'll state my case, of which I'm certain
I've lived a life that's full
I've travelled each and every highway
And more, much more than this,
I did it my way.

Regrets, I've had a few
But then again, too few to mention

I did what I had to do
and saw it through without exemption,
I planned each charted course,
each careful step along the byway
And more, much more than this,
I did it my way.

Yes, there were times,
I'm sure you knew,
When I bit off
more than I could chew
But through it all,
when there was doubt
I ate it up and spit it out
I faced it all and I stood tall
and did it my way.

I've loved, I've laughed and cried
I've had my fill, my share of losing
And now, as tears subside,
I find it all so amusing
To think I did all that
And may I say, not in a shy way,
Oh, no, oh, no, not me, I did it my way.

For what is a man, what has he got?
If not himself, then he has naught.
To say the things he truly feels
and not the words of one who kneels,
The record shows I took the blows
and did it my way
Yes, it was my way.

T 12.11

1 A Excuse me, can you tell me where the post office is?
    B I'm sorry, I'm a stranger here myself.
2 A Ouch! That's my foot!
    B Oh, I'm sorry. I wasn't looking where I was going.
3 A Excuse me, what's that creature called?
    B It's a Diplodocus.
    A Pardon?
    B A Diplodocus. D-I-P-L-O-D-O-C-U-S.
    A Thank you very much.
4 A I failed my driving test for the sixth time!
    B I'm so sorry.
5 A Excuse me! We need to get past. My little boy isn't feeling well.
6 A Do you want your hearing aid, Grandma?
    B Pardon?
    A I said: Do you want your hearing aid?
    B What?
    A DO YOU WANT YOUR HEARING AID?!
    B I'm sorry, I can't hear you. I need my hearing aid.

Grammar Reference

UNIT 1

Introduction to auxiliary verbs

There are three classes of verbs in English.

1 The auxiliary verbs *do*, *be*, and *have*
   These are used to form tenses, and to show forms such as questions and negatives.

2 Modal auxiliary verbs
   Must, can, should, might, will, and *would* are examples of modal auxiliary verbs. They 'help' other verbs, but unlike *do, be*, and *have*, they have their own meanings. For example, *must* expresses obligation and *can* expresses ability. (See Units 4, 5, 8, and 9.)

3 Full verbs
   These are all the other verbs in the language, for example, *play, run, help, think, want, go*, etc.
   Do, be, and *have* can also be used as full verbs with their own meanings.

   do
   *I **do** my washing on Saturdays.*
   *She **does** a lot of business in Eastern Europe.*
   *What **do** you **do**?* = What's your job? (The first *do* is an auxiliary; the second is a full verb.)

   be
   *We **are** in class at the moment.*
   *They **were** at home yesterday.*
   *I want **to be** a teacher.*

   have
   *He **has** a lot of problems.*
   *They **have** three children.*

A note on *have* and *have got*
There are two forms of the verb *have*: *have* as a full verb with *do/does/did* for questions, negatives, and short answers and *have got* where *have* is an auxiliary.

▶▶ **Workbook p8**   More information on *have/have got*

▶ 1.1 Tenses and auxiliary verbs

When *do*, *be*, and *have* are used as auxiliary verbs, they make different verb forms.

do

In the Present Simple and the Past Simple there is no auxiliary verb, so *do*, *does*, and *did* are used to make questions and negatives (except with *be / have got*).
*Where **do** you work?*
*She **doesn't** like her job.*
*What **did** you buy?*
*We **didn't** buy anything.*

be

1 *Be* + verb + *-ing* is used to make continuous verb forms. Continuous verb forms describe activities in progress and temporary activities.
   *He's **washing** his hair.* (Present Continuous)
   *They **were going** to work.* (Past Continuous)
   *I've **been learning** English for two years.* (Present Perfect Continuous)
   *I'd like **to be lying** on the beach right now.* (Continuous infinitive)

2 *Be* + past participle is used to form the passive.
   *Paper **is made** from wood.* (Present Simple passive)
   *My car **was stolen** yesterday.* (Past Simple passive)
   *The house **has been** redecorated.* (Present Perfect passive)
   *This homework needs **to be done** tonight.* (Passive infinitive)

   There is an introduction to the passive on p137.

have

Have + past participle is used to make perfect verb forms.
*He **has worked** in seven different countries.* (Present Perfect)
*She was crying because she **had had** some bad news.* (Past Perfect)
*I'd like **to have met** Napoleon.* (Perfect infinitive)

Perfect means 'before,' so Present Perfect means 'before now.' (See Units 7 and 10.) Past Perfect means 'before a time in the past.' (See Unit 3.)

▶ 1.2 Negatives and auxiliary verbs

To make a negative, add *-n't* to the auxiliary verb. If there is no auxiliary verb, use *don't/doesn't/didn't*.

Positive	Negative
He's working.	*He **isn't** working.*
I was thinking.	*I **wasn't** thinking.*
We've seen the play.	*We **haven't** seen the play.*
She works in a bank.	*She **doesn't** work in a bank.*
They like skiing.	*They **don't** like skiing.*
He went on holiday.	*He **didn't** go on holiday.*

It is possible to contract the auxiliaries *be* and *have* and use the uncontracted *not*.
*He's **not** playing today.* (= He *isn't* playing today.)
*We're **not** going to Italy after all.* (= We *aren't* going to Italy …)
*I've **not** read that book yet.* (= I *haven't* read the book yet.)
But
*I'm **not** working.*   NOT   ~~I amn't working~~.

1.3 Questions and auxiliary verbs

1 To make a question, invert the subject and the auxiliary verb. If there is no auxiliary verb, use *do/does/did*.

	Question
She's wearing jeans.	*What **is she** wearing?*
You aren't working.	*Why **aren't you** working?*
You were born in Paris.	*Where **were you** born?*
Peter's been to China.	***Has Peter** been to China?*
We have been studying.	***Have you** been studying?*
I know you.	***Do I** know you?*
He wants ice-cream.	*What **does he** want?*
They didn't go out.	*Why **didn't they** go out?*

2 There is usually no *do/does/did* in subject questions. Compare:

Who wants ice-cream?	*What flavour ice-cream **do** you want?*
What happened to your eye?	*What **did** you do to your eye?*
Who broke the window?	*How **did** you break the window?*

1.4 Short answers and auxiliary verbs

Short answers are very common in spoken English. If you just say *Yes* or *No*, it can sound rude. We use short answers after *Yes / No* questions. To make a short answer, repeat the auxiliary verb. In the Present and Past Simple, use *do/does/did*.

	Short answer
Are you coming with us?	*Yes, **I am**.*
Have you had breakfast?	*No, **I haven't**.*
Kate likes walking.	*No, **she doesn't**. She hates it.*
Mary didn't phone.	*Yes, **she did**. You were out.*
Don't forget to write.	*No, **I won't**.*

UNIT 2

2.1 Present Simple

Form

Positive and negative

I We You They	work. don't work.
He She It	works. doesn't work.

Question

Where	do	I we you they	live?
	does	he she it	

Do you live in Bristol?
Does he have a car?

Short answer
*Yes, **we do**.*
*No, **he doesn't**.*

Use

The Present Simple is used to express:

1 an action that happens again and again (a habit).
   *I **go** to work by car.*
   *She **drinks** ten cups of coffee a day.*
   *I **wash** my hair twice a week.*

2 a fact that is always true.
   *Ronaldo **comes** from Brazil.*
   *Some birds **fly** south in winter.*
   *My daughter **has** brown eyes.*

3 a fact that is true for a long time (a state).
   *He **works** in a bank.*
   *I **live** in a flat near the centre of town.*
   *I **prefer** coffee to tea.*

Spelling of verb + -s

1 Most verbs add *-s* to the base form of the verb.
   wants   eats   helps   drives

2 Add *-es* to verbs that end in *-ss*, *-sh*, *-ch*, *-x*, and *-o*.
   kisses   washes   watches   fixes   goes

3 Verbs that end in a consonant + *-y* change the *-y* to *-ies*.
   carries   flies   worries   tries

   But verbs that end in a vowel + *-y* only add *-s*.
   buys   says   plays   enjoys

▶▶ **Workbook p14**   Pronunciation of *-s* at the end of a word

Adverbs of frequency

1 We often use adverbs of frequency with the Present Simple.

0% ——————————— 50% ——————————— 100%
never   rarely   not often   sometimes   often   usually   always

2 They go before the main verb, but after the verb *be*. Compare:

*I **usually** start school at 9.00.*	*They're **usually** in a hurry in the morning.*
*I don't **often** go to bed late.*	*I'm not **often** late for school.*
*She **never** eats meat.*	*He's **never** late.*
*I **rarely** see Peter these days.*	*We're **rarely** at home at the weekends.*

3 *Sometimes* and *usually* can also go at the beginning or the end.
Sometimes *we play cards.*   *We play cards* **sometimes**.
Usually *I go shopping with friends.*   *I go shopping with friends* **usually**.

Never, always, rarely, and *seldom* cannot move in this way.
NOT   ~~Never I go to the movies.~~
      ~~Always I have tea in the morning.~~

4 *Every day*, etc., goes at the end.
He phones me **every night**.

 2.2 Present Continuous

Form

Positive and negative

I	'm 'm not	
He/She/It	's isn't	eating.
We/You/They	're aren't	

Question

What	am is are	I he/she/it we/you/they	doing?

Short answer

Are you going by train?	Yes, I am. No, I'm not.

Use

The Present Continuous is used to express:

1 an activity that is happening now.
   Don't turn the TV off. I'm watching it.
   You can't speak to Lisa. She's having a bath.

2 an activity or situation that is true now, but is not necessarily happening at the moment of speaking.
   Don't take that book. Jane's reading it.
   I'm doing a French evening class this year.

3 a temporary activity.
   Peter is a student, but he's working as a waiter during the holidays.
   I'm living with friends until I find a place of my own.

4 a planned future arrangement.
   I'm having lunch with Glenda tomorrow.
   We're meeting at 1.00 outside the restaurant.

Spelling of verb + *-ing*

1 Most verbs add *-ing* to the base form of the verb.
   going   wearing   visiting   eating

2 Verbs that end in one *-e* lose the *-e*.
   smoking   coming   hoping   writing
   Verbs that end in *-ee* don't drop an *-e*.
   agreeing   seeing

❶ *lie   lying*

3 Verbs of one syllable, with one vowel and one consonant, double the consonant.
   stopping   getting   running   planning   jogging
   If the final consonant is *-y* or *-w*, it is not doubled.
   playing   showing

▶ 2.3 State verbs

1 There are certain groups of verbs that are usually only used in the Present Simple. This is because their meanings are related to states or conditions that are facts and not activities. This is a feature of the use of the Present Simple. The groups of verbs are:

Verbs of thinking and opinions

believe	think	understand	suppose	expect
agree	doubt	know	remember	forget
mean	imagine	realize	deserve	prefer

*I **believe** you.*
***Do** you **understand**?*
*I **know** his face, but I **forget** his name.*

Verbs of emotions and feelings

| like | love | hate | care | hope | wish | want | admit |

*I **like** black coffee.*
***Do** you **want** to go out?*
*I **don't care**.*

Verbs of having and being

| belong | own | have | possess | contain | cost | seem | appear |
| need | depend on | weigh | come from | resemble |

*This book **belongs** to Jane.*
*How much **does** it **cost**?*
*He **has** a lot of money.*

Verbs of the senses

| look | hear | taste | smell | feel |

*The food **smells** good.*

We often use *can* when the subject is a person.
***Can** you smell something burning?*
*I **can** hear someone crying.*

2 Some of these verbs can be used in the Present Continuous, but with a change of meaning. In the continuous, the verb expresses an activity, not a state. Compare:

*I **think** you're right.*	*We're **thinking** of going to the cinema.*
(opinion)	(mental activity)
*He **has** a lot of money.*	*She's **having** a bad day.*
(possession)	(activity)
*I **see** what you mean.*	*Are you **seeing** Nigel tomorrow?*
(understand)	(activity)
*The soup **tastes** awful.*	*I'm **tasting** the soup to see if it needs salt.*
(state)	(activity)

Introduction to the passive

The passive is dealt with in Units 2, 3, and 7.

Form

to be + past participle
The tense of the verb *to be* changes to give different tenses in the passive. Compare:
*A party **is being held** by the Patels next week.* (Present Continuous passive)
*My neighbour **is invited** to their party every year.* (Present Simple passive)
*He **was invited** last year, I wasn't.* (Present Perfect passive)
*I'd love **to be invited** to their party.* (Passive infinitive)

Use

1 Passive sentences move the focus from the subject to the object of active sentences.
   *Alfred Hitchcock **directed** Psycho in 1960.*
   *Psycho, one of the classic thrillers of all time, **was directed** by Alfred Hitchcock.*

   The passive is not just another way of expressing the same sentence in the active. We choose the active or the passive depending on what we are more interested in. In the first sentence, we are more interested in Alfred Hitchcock; in the second sentence, *Psycho* has moved to the beginning of the sentence because we are more interested in the film.

2 *By* and the agent are often omitted in passive sentences if the agent:
   – is not known.
     *My apartment **was robbed** last night.*
   – is not important.
     *This bridge **was built** in 1886.*
   – is obvious.
     *I **was fined** £100 for speeding.*

3 The passive is associated with an impersonal, formal style. It is often used in notices and announcements.
   *Customers **are requested** to refrain from smoking.*
   *It **has been noticed** that reference books **have been removed** from the library.*

4 In informal language, we often use *you*, *we*, and *they* to refer to people in general or to no person in particular. In this way, we can avoid using the passive.
   ***You can buy** stamps in lots of shops, not just the post offices.*
   ***They're building** a new department store in the city centre.*
   ***We speak** English in this shop.*

❶ Be careful! Many past participles are used as adjectives.
   *I'm very **interested** in modern art.*
   *We were extremely **worried** about you.*
   *I'm **exhausted**! I've been working hard all day.*

2.4 Present Simple and Present Continuous passive

Form

Present Simple Passive   *am/is/are* + past participle
Present Continuous Passive   *am/is/are being* + past participle

It	is is being	mended.
They	are are being	

Use

The uses are the same in the passive as in the active.
*My car **is serviced** every six months.* (habit)
*Computers **are used** in all areas of life and work.* (fact that is always true)
*Sorry about the mess. The house **is being redecorated** at the moment.* (activity happening now)

Introduction to past tenses

We use different past tenses to focus on different moments and periods of time in the past.
Look at the diagram. Read the sentences.
When Andrea arrived at work at 9.00 a.m. …

8.30	9.00	9.30	10.00

Her secretary opened the post.
Her secretary was opening the post.
Her secretary had opened the post.

 3.1 Past Simple

Form

The form of the Past Simple is the same for all persons.

Positive

I He/She/It We You They	finished left arrived	yesterday. at 3 o'clock. three weeks ago.

Negative

I She They (etc.)	didn't	finish leave	yesterday. at 3 o'clock.

Question

When	did	you he they (etc.)	finish the report? get married?

Short answer

Did you enjoy the meal?	Yes, we did. No, we didn't.

Use

The Past Simple is used to express:

1 a finished action in the past.
   *We **met** in 2000.*
   *I **went** to Manchester last week.*
   *John **left** two minutes ago.*

2 actions that follow each other in a story.
   *Mary **walked** into the room and **stopped**. She **listened** carefully. She **heard** a noise coming from behind the curtain. She **threw** the curtain open, and then she **saw** …*

3 a past situation or habit.
*When I **was** a child, we **lived** in a small house by the sea. Every day I **walked** for miles on the beach with my dog.*
This use is often expressed with *used to*.
*We **used to** live in a small house … I **used to** walk for miles …*

Spelling of verb + -ed

1 Most verbs add *-ed* to the base form of the verb.
worked   wanted   helped   washed

2 When the verb ends in *-e*, add *-d*.
liked   used   hated   cared

3 If the verb has only one syllable, with one vowel + one consonant, double the consonant before adding *-ed*.
stopped   planned   robbed
But we write *cooked*, *seated*, and *moaned* because there are two vowels.

4 The consonant is not doubled if it is *-y* or *-w*.
played   showed

5 In most two-syllable verbs, the end consonant is doubled if the stress is on the second syllable.
pre'ferred   ad'mitted
But we write *'entered* and *'visited* because the stress is on the first syllable.

6 Verbs that end in a consonant + *-y* change the *-y* to *-ied*.
carried   hurried   buried
But we write *enjoyed*, because it ends in a vowel + *-y*.

There are many common irregular verbs.

 **Irregular verbs p157**

Past Simple and time expressions
Look at the time expressions that are common with the Past Simple.

I met her	last night.
	two days ago.
	yesterday morning.
	in 2001.
	in summer.
	when I was young.

3.2 Past Continuous

Form

Positive and negative

I He She It	was wasn't	working.
We You They	were weren't	

Question

What	was	I she he it	doing?
	were	we you they	

Were you looking for me?
Were they waiting outside?

Short answer
Yes, I was./No I wasn't.
Yes, they were./No, they weren't.

Use

We often use the Past Continuous in sentences with the Past Simple. The Past Continuous refers to longer, background activities, while the Past Simple refers to shorter, completed actions.

The children were playing in the garden …
… when their grandparents arrived.

The Past Continuous is used:

1 to express activities in progress before, and probably after, a particular time in the past.
*At 7 o'clock this morning I **was having** my breakfast.*
*I walked past your house last night. There was an awful lot of noise. What **were** you **doing**?*

2 for descriptions.
*Jan looked beautiful. She **was wearing** a green cotton dress. Her eyes **were shining** in the light of the candles that **were burning** nearby.*

3 to express an interrupted past activity.
*When the phone rang, I **was having** a shower.*
*While we **were playing** tennis, it started to rain.*

4 to express an incomplete activity in the past in order to contrast with the Past Simple that expresses a completed activity.
*I **was reading** a book during the flight.* (I didn't finish it.)
*I **watched** a film during the flight.* (the whole film)

Note
The Past Simple is usually used to express a repeated past habit or situation. But the Past Continuous can be used if the repeated habit becomes a longer setting for something. Compare:
*I **went out with** Jack for ten years.*
*I first met Harry while I **was going out with** Jack.*

 **Workbook p20**   More information on *while*, *during*, and *for*

3.3 Past Simple or Past Continuous?

1 Sometimes we can use the Past Simple or the Past Continuous. The Past Simple focuses on past actions as simple facts. The Past Continuous focuses on the duration of past situations and activities. Compare:
A *I didn't see you at the party last night.*
B *No. I **stayed** at home and **watched** football.*

A *I didn't see you at the party last night.*
B *No, I **was watching** football at home.*

2 Questions in the Past Simple and Past Continuous refer to different time periods: the Past Continuous asks about activities before; the Past Simple asks about what happened after.
*When the war broke out, Peter **was studying** medicine at medical school. He **decided** that it was safer to go home to his parents and postpone his studies.*
*What **was** Peter **doing** when the war broke out?*   *He **was studying**.*
*What **did** Peter **do** when the war broke out?*   *He **went** home to his parents.*

3.4 Past Perfect

Perfect means 'before,' so Past Perfect refers to an action in the past that was completed before another action in the past.

Form

The form of the Past Perfect is the same for all persons.

Positive and negative

I You We (etc.)	'd (had) hadn't	seen him before. finished work at 6 o'clock.

Question

Where had	you she they (etc.)	been before?

Short answer

Had he already left?	Yes, he had. No, he hadn't.

Use

1 The Past Perfect is used to make clear that one action in the past happened *before* another action in the past.
*When I got home, I found that someone **had broken** into my apartment and **had stolen** my DVD player, so I called the police.*

Action 1: Someone broke into my apartment and stole my DVD player.
Action 2: I got home and called the police.

*I didn't want to go to the theatre with my friends because I'**d seen** the play before.*

Action 1: I saw the play.
Action 2: My friends went to the theatre to see the play.

2 Notice the difference between the following sentences:
*When I got to the party, Peter **went** home.*
(= First I arrived, then Peter left.)
*When I got to the party, Peter **had gone** home.*
(= First Peter left, then I arrived.)

3.5 Past tenses in the passive

Form

Past Simple Passive	*was/were* + past participle
Past Continuous Passive	*was/were being* + past participle
Past Perfect Passive	*had been* + past participle

Use

The uses are the same in the passive as in the active.
*The bridge **was built** in 1876.* (finished action in the past)
*The bomb **was being defused** when it exploded.* (interrupted past activity)
*The letter didn't arrive because it **had been sent** to my old address.* (one action before another action in the past)

UNIT 4

Introduction to modal verbs

The modal verbs are *can, could, may, might, must, will, would, should, ought to.* They are known as modal auxiliary verbs because they 'help' another verb. (See also Units 1, 5, 8, and 9.)
*I **can** swim.*
*Do you think I **should** go?*

Form

1 There is no *-s* in the third person singular.
*She **can** ski.   He **must** be tired.   It **might** rain.*

2 There is no *do/does/don't/doesn't* in the question or negative.
*What **should** I do?   **Can** I help you?   You **mustn't** steal!*
*He **can't** dance.   I **won't** be a minute.*

3 Modal auxiliary verbs are followed by the infinitive without *to*. The exception is *ought to*.
*You **must** go.   I'**ll help** you.   You **ought to** see a doctor.*

4 They have no infinitives and no *-ing* forms. Other expressions are used instead.
*I'd love to **be able to** ski.*
*I hate **having to** get up on cold, winter mornings.*

5 They don't usually have past forms. Instead, we can use them with perfect infinitives:
*You **should have told** me that you can't swim. You **might have** drowned!*
or we use other expressions:
*I **had to** work hard in school.*

Note
Could is used with a past meaning to talk about a general ability.
*I **could** swim when I was six.* (= general ability)

To talk about ability on one specific occasion, we use *was able to/managed to*.
*The prisoner **was able to/managed to** escape by climbing on to the roof of the prison.*   NOT ~~could escape~~

Use

1 Modal verbs express our attitudes, opinions, and judgements of events. Compare:
'Who's that knocking on the door?'
'It's John.' (This is a fact.)

'Who's that knocking on the door?'
*'It **could/may/might/must/should/can't/'ll** be John.'* (These all express our attitude or opinion.)

2 Each modal verb has at least two meanings. One use of all of them is to express possibility or probability. (See Unit 9 p147.)
*I **must** post this letter!* (= obligation)
*You **must** be tired!* (= deduction, probability)
***Could** you help me?* (= request)
*We **could** go to Spain for our holiday.* (= possibility)
*You **may** go home now.* (= permission)
*'Where's Anna?'   'I'm not sure. She **may** be at work.'* (= possibility)

Modal verbs of obligation and permission

 **4.1** *have (got) to*

Form

Positive and negative

I/You/We/They	have to / don't have to	work hard.
He/She	has to / doesn't have to	

Question

Do	I you (etc.)	have to work hard?

Use

Have to is not a modal verb.

1   *Have to* expresses strong obligation. It expresses a general obligation based on a law or rule, or based on the authority of another person. It is impersonal.
    Children **have to** go to school until they are 16. (a law)
    Mum says you **have to** clean your room before you go out. (mother's order)

2   *Have got to* is common in British English but it is more informal than *have to*.
    I**'ve got to** go now. See you!
    Don't go to bed late. We**'ve got to** get up early tomorrow.
    'Go and tidy your room.' '**Have I got to?**' 'Yes, you **have!**'

3   *Have to* expresses a general repeated obligation.
    I always **have to** tell my parents where I'm going.
    Have got to expresses an obligation on one particular occasion.
    I**'ve got to** get up early tomorrow to catch a train.

can and *be allowed to*

Form

Affirmative and negative

I/You/We/They	can/can't are allowed to aren't allowed to	park here.
He/She	can/can't is allowed to isn't allowed to	

Question

Can	I/you/we etc.		
Am	I		
Are	you	allowed to	park here?
Is	he		

Use

Can is a modal verb.

Can and *be allowed to* express permission. *Can* is more informal and usually spoken.
You **can** borrow my bike, but you **can't** have the car. I need it.
They **can't** come in here with those muddy shoes!
You**'re allowed to** get married when you're 16.
Are we **allowed to** use a dictionary for this test?
He **isn't allowed to** park here.

 **4.2** *should*, *ought to*, and *must*

Form

Should, *ought to*, and *must* are modal verbs.

I/You/We/They He/She/ It	should/shouldn't ought to/ought not to must	work hard.

Use

1   *Should* and *ought to* express mild obligation, suggestions, or advice. They express what, in the speaker's opinion, is the right or best thing to do. We often use them with *I think/don't think …* .
    You're always asking me for money. I think you **should** spend less.
    You **shouldn't** sit so close to the television! It's bad for your eyes.
    You **ought to** be more careful with your money.

2   *Should I/she/we … ?* is possible. We often use *Do you think … ?*
    Should I try to eat less?
    Do you think **I should** see a doctor?

3   *Must*, like *have to*, expresses strong obligation. *Must* expresses an obligation that involves the speaker's opinion. It is personal.
    I **must** get my hair cut. (This is me talking to me.)
    You **must** go and visit your grandmother. (A parent talking to a child.)

4   *Must* is also associated with a formal, written style.
    All visitors **must** show proper ID. (Sign in the lobby of an office building)
    Books **must** be returned on or before the due date. (Instructions in a library)

have to and *must*, *don't have to* and *mustn't*

1   *Have to* and *must* are sometimes interchangeable.
    I **must** be home by midnight.   I **have to** be home by midnight.
    But *have to* is used more often than *must*. If you are unsure which to use, it is probably safer to use *have to*.

2   *Must I … ?* is possible, but question forms with *have to* are more common.
    Do I **have to** do what you say, or can I do what I want?

3   *Have to* has all forms; *must* does not.
    I **had to** work until midnight last night. (Past)
    You'll **have to** study hard when you go to college. (Future)
    She's a millionaire. She's never **had to** do any work. (Present Perfect)
    I hate **having to** get up on cold, winter mornings. (-ing form)
    If you were a nurse, you would **have to** wear a uniform. (Infinitive)

4   *Don't have to* and *mustn't* are completely different.
    Don't have to expresses absence of obligation – you can but it isn't necessary.
    Some people iron their socks, but you **don't have to**. I think it's a waste of time.
    When you go into a shop, you **don't have to** buy something. You can just look.
    Mustn't expresses negative obligation – it is very important not to do something.
    You **mustn't** steal other people's things. It's wrong.
    You **mustn't** drive if you've been drinking. You could kill someone!

▶▶ **Workbook p28**   Further practice of *must* and *have to*

▶ 4.3 Making requests: *can, could, will,* and *would*

1 There are many ways of making requests in English.

Can Could Will Would	you	help me, please? pass the salt, please?

Would you mind helping me, please?

Can Could	I	speak to you, please? ask you a question?

Do you mind if I open the window?
Would you mind if I opened the window?

Can, could, will, and *would* are all modal verbs.

2 *Could* is a little more formal; *can* is a little more familiar. *Could I ... ?* and *Could you ... ?* are very useful because they can be used in many different situations.

3 Here are some ways of responding to requests:
   A *Excuse me! Could you help me?*
   B *Sure.*
      Of course.
      Well, I'm afraid I'm a little busy right now.
   A *Would you mind if I opened the window?*
   B *No, not at all.*
      No, that's fine.
      Well, I'm a little cold, actually.

▶ 4.4 Making offers: *will* and *shall/should*

1 *Will* and *shall/should* are used to express offers. They are both modal verbs.

2 The contracted form of *will* is used to express an intention, decision, or offer made at the moment of speaking.
   Come over after work. I'll cook dinner for you.
   'It's Jane's birthday today.' 'Is it? I'll buy her some flowers.'
   Give him your suitcase. He'll carry it for you.
   Don't worry about catching the bus. Dave'll give you a lift.
   Give it back or we'll call the police!

   In many languages, this idea is often expressed by a present tense, but in English this is wrong.
   I'll give you my number.   NOT   ~~I give you my number.~~
   I'll carry your suitcase.   NOT   ~~I carry your suitcase.~~

   Other uses of *will* are dealt with in Unit 5.

3 *Shall / Should ...?* is used in questions with the first person, *I* and *we*. It expresses an offer, a suggestion, or a request for advice.
   'Shall I carry your bag for you?' 'That's very kind. Thank you.'
   'Shall we go out for a meal tonight?' 'Mmm. I'd love to.'
   'What shall we do? We haven't got any money.' 'We could ask Dad.'

   We use **should** to make an informal suggestion.
   What should we have for dinner?
   What should we do tonight?

UNIT 5

Introduction to future forms

There is no future tense in English as there is in many European languages. However, English has several forms that can refer to the future. Three of these are *will, going to,* and the Present Continuous.
I'll see you later. (will)
We're going to see a film tonight. Do you want to come? (going to)
I'm seeing the doctor tomorrow evening. (Present Continuous)

The difference between them is *not* about near or distant future, or about certainty. The speaker chooses a future form depending on how the speaker sees the future event. Is it a plan, a decision, an intention, an offer, a prediction, or an arrangement? This is the important question to ask when choosing a future form. There is more about this in **Use** below.

▶ 5.1 *will/going to* and the Present Continuous

Form

Positive and negative

I He They	'll won't	help you. watch TV tonight.
I'm/I'm not She's/She isn't We're/We aren't	going to	
I'm/I'm not He's/He isn't You're/You aren't	catching the 10 o'clock train.	

Question

What time	will you are you going to	arrive?
	are you meeting the manager?	

Note
We avoid saying *going to come* or *going to go.*
We're coming tomorrow.
When are you going home?

Use

Plans, decisions, and intentions (*will* and *going to*)
will

Will is used as a modal auxiliary verb to express a decision, intention, or offer made at the moment of speaking. We saw this use in Unit 4. (See 4.4.) Remember that you can't use the present tense for this use.
I'll have the steak, please.   NOT   ~~I have the steak.~~
I'll see you tomorrow. Bye!   NOT   ~~I see you tomorrow.~~
Give me a call sometime. We'll go out for coffee.
'Jeff, there's someone at the door!' 'OK, I'll get it.'

going to

Going to is used to express a future plan, decision, or intention made before the moment of speaking.

*When I grow up, **I'm going to be** a doctor.*
*Jane and Peter **are going to get married** after they graduate.*
***We're going to paint** this room blue.*

Facts and predictions (*will* and *going to*)

will

The most common use of *will* is as an auxiliary verb to show future time. It expresses a future fact or prediction. It is called the pure future or the Future Simple.

***We'll be** away for two weeks.*
*Those flowers **won't grow** under the tree. It's too dark.*
*Our love **will last** forever.*
***You'll be** sick if you eat all those sweets!*

Will for a prediction can be based more on an opinion than a fact.

*I don't think Laura **will do** very well in her exam. She doesn't do any work.*
*I am convinced that inflation **will fall** to three per cent next year.*

going to

Going to can also express a prediction, especially when it is based on a present fact. There is evidence now that something is certain to happen.

*She's **going to have** a baby. (We can see she's pregnant.)*
*Our team **is going to win** the match. (It's four–nil, and there are only five minutes left to play.)*
*It **isn't going to rain** today. (Look at that beautiful blue sky.)*

Note

Sometimes there is no difference between *will* and *going to*.

This government	will ruin is going to ruin	the country with its stupid economic policies.

Arrangements (Present Continuous)

The Present Continuous can be used to express a future arrangement between people. It usually refers to the near future.

***We're going** out with Jeremy tonight.*
***I'm having** my hair cut tomorrow.*
*What **are** we **having** for lunch?*

Think of the things you might put in your diary to remind you of what you are doing over the next few days and weeks. These are the kinds of events that are often expressed by the Present Continuous for the future. The verbs express some kind of activity or movement.

***I'm meeting** Peter tonight.*
*The Taylors **are coming** for dinner.*
***I'm seeing** the doctor in the morning.*

Remember that you can't use the present tense for this use.

***We're going** to a party on Saturday night.*
NOT ~~We go to a party on Saturday night.~~
***We're catching** the 10 o'clock train.*
NOT ~~We catch the 10 o'clock train.~~
*What **are** you **doing** this evening?*
NOT ~~What do you do this evening?~~

Sometimes there is no difference between an agreed arrangement (Present Continuous) and an intention (*going to*).

We're going to get We're getting	married in the spring.

Introduction to *like*

Like can be a verb or a preposition.
Like as a verb can be followed by *-ing* or *to*, sometimes with a change in meaning.

*I **like** going out at the weekend. (general enjoyment)*
*I **like** to sit in a hot bath and read. (habits and preferences)*

Like as a verb has a person as the subject:

*I **like** modern art.*
*I don't **like** the way he looks at me.*
*Do you **like** fish?*
*Would you **like** a drink?*

Like as a preposition has an object after it:

*She's wearing a hat **like** mine.*
*He's nothing **like** his father.*
*That sounds **like** the postman.*
*You're behaving **like** children.*
*This new girlfriend of his – what's she **like**?*

6.1 *What ... like?*

What is/are/was/were ... like? is used to ask about the permanent nature of people and things. It asks for a description or an impression or a comparison.

***What's** the health service **like** in your country?*
***What are** the new students **like**?*

❶ Be careful!

1   With a description or an impression, we do not use *like* in the answer.

| *What's London **like**?* | *It's quite big, and it's very interesting.*
NOT ~~It's like quite big ...~~ |
| *What's Amanda **like**?* | *She's tall, attractive, and very funny.*
NOT ~~She's like tall ...~~ |

2   With a comparison, we can use *like* in the answer. Here, *like* means *similar to / the same as*.

| *What's London **like**?* | *It's **like** New York, but without the tall buildings. (= It's similar to ...)* |
| *What's Amanda's daughter **like**?* | *She's just **like** Amanda.
(= She's the same as ...)* |

▶▶ **Workbook p39**   *Like* and *as*

6.2 *How ... ?*

1   *How ... ?* is used to ask about the present condition of something that can change.

| ***How's** work these days?* | *It's better than last year.* |
| ***How** was the traffic this morning?* | *It was worse than usual.* |

To ask about the weather, we can use both questions.

How's the weather What's the weather like	where you are?

2   *How ... ?* is also used to ask about people's health and happiness. Compare:

How's Peter?   *He's fine.*
What's Peter like?   *He's a nice guy. He's quite tall, has dark hair ...*

3   *How ... ?* is also used to ask about people's reactions and feelings.

***How's** your meal?*
***How's** your new job?*

 **6.3** *How … ? or What … like?*

Sometimes we can use *What … like?* or *How … ?*, but they aren't the same. *What … like?* asks for an objective description. *How … ?* asks for personal feelings. Compare:
How's the party?   *It's great!*
What's the party like?   *It's very noisy, but there's lots to eat and drink.*

6.4 Verb + *-ing* or infinitive

▶▶ **Verb patterns p158**

6.5 Relative clauses

1 Relative clauses are used to tell us which person or thing we are talking about. They make it possible to give more information about the person or thing being spoken about.
   The boy has gone to the beach. (Which boy?)
   *The boy **who lives next door** has gone to the beach.*
   The book is very good. (Which book?)
   *The book **that I bought yesterday** is very good.*
   This is a photo of the hotel. (Which hotel?)
   *This is a photo of the hotel **where we stayed**.*

2 We use *who* to refer to people (and we can also use *that*).
   *The book is about a girl **who** marries a millionaire.*

   We use *that* to refer to things (and we can also use *which*).
   *What was the name of the horse **that** won the race?*

3 When *who* or *that* is the object of a relative clause, it can be left out.
   *The person **you need to talk to** is on holiday.*
   *The book **I bought yesterday** is very good.*

   But when *who* or *that* is the subject of a relative clause, it must be included.
   *I like people **who are kind and considerate**.*
   *I want a computer **that is easy to use**.*

4 *Which* can be used to refer to the whole previous sentence or idea.
   *I passed my driving test on my first attempt, **which surprised everyone**.*
   *Jane can't come to the party, **which is a shame**.*

5 We use *whose* to refer to someone's possessions.
   *That's the woman **whose dog ran away**.*
   *That's the man **whose wife won the lottery**.*

6 We can use *where* to refer to places.
   *The hotel **where we stayed** was right on the beach.*
   *We went back to the place **where we first met**.*

6.6 Participles

Participles after a noun define and identify in the same way as relative clauses.
*That woman **driving** the red Porsche is my aunt.*
*The men **seen** outside were probably the thieves.*

Introduction to the Present Perfect

The same form (*have* + past participle) exists in many European languages, but the uses in English are different. In English, the Present Perfect is essentially a present tense, but it also expresses the effect of past actions and activities on the present.

PAST   PRESENT PERFECT   PRESENT

Present Perfect means 'before now'. The Present Perfect does not express when an action happened. If we say the exact time, we have to use the Past Simple.
*In my life, I **have travelled** to all seven continents.*
*I **travelled** around Africa **in 1998**.*

7.1 The Present Perfect

Form
Positive and negative

I We You They	've haven't	
He She	's hasn't	lived in Rome.

Question

How long have	I we you	
How long has	she he	known Peter?

Short answer

Have you always lived in Budapest?	Yes, I have. No, I haven't.

Use

The Present Perfect expresses:

1 an action that began in the past and still continues (unfinished past).
   *We**'ve lived** in the same house for 25 years.*
   *Peter**'s worked** as a teacher since 2000.*
   *How long **have** you **known** each other?*
   *They**'ve been** married for 20 years.*

   Note
   Many languages express this idea with a present tense, but in English this is wrong.
   *Peter **has been** a teacher for ten years.*   NOT   ~~Peter is a teacher for ten years.~~

   These time expressions are common with this use.

for	two years a month a few minutes half an hour ages	since	1970 the end of the class August 8 o'clock Christmas

   We use *for* with a period of time and *since* with a point in time.

2 an experience that happened at some time in one's life. The action is in the past and finished, but the effects of the action are still felt. When the action happened is not important.

*I've **been** to the United States.* (I still remember.)
*She's **written** poetry and children's stories.* (in her writing career)
***Have** you ever **had** an operation?* (at any time in your life up to now)
*How many times **has** he **been** married?* (in his life)

The adverbs *ever, never,* and *before* are common with this use.

***Have** you **ever** been to Australia?*
*I've **never** tried bungee jumping.*
*I haven't tried sushi **before**.*

Questions and answers about definite times are expressed in the Past Simple.

*When **did** you **go** to the United States?*
***Was** her poetry **published** while she was alive?*
*I **broke** my leg once, but I **didn't** have to stay in the hospital.*
*He **met** his second wife in the dry cleaner's.*

3 a past action that has a present result. The action is usually in the recent past.

*The taxi **hasn't arrived** yet.* (We're still waiting for it.)
*What **have** you **done** to your lip?* (It's bleeding.)

We often announce news in the Present Perfect because the speaker is emphasizing the event as a present fact.

***Have** you **heard**? The Prime Minister **has resigned**.*
*Susan's **had** her baby!*
*I've **ruined** the meal.*

Details about definite time will be in the Past Simple.

*She **resigned** because she lost a vote of no confidence.*
*She **had** a baby boy this morning. It **was** a difficult birth.*
*I **didn't watch** it carefully enough.*

The adverbs *yet, already,* and *just* are common with this use.

*I haven't done my homework **yet**.* (Negative)
*Has the postman been **yet**?* (Question)
*I've **already** done my homework.*
*She's **just** had some good news.*

❶ Be careful with *been* and *gone*.
*He's **been** to the United States.* (experience – he isn't there now)
*She's **gone** to the United States.* (present result – she's there now)

▶▶ **Workbook p45**   Further practice of *been* and *gone*

7.2 Present Perfect or Past Simple?

1 The Present Perfect is for unfinished actions. The Past Simple is for completed actions. Compare:

Present Perfect	**Past Simple**
I've lived in Texas for six years.	*I lived in Texas for six years.*
(I still live there.)	(Now I live somewhere else.)
I've written several books.	*Shakespeare wrote 30 plays.*
(I can still write some more.)	(He can't write any more.)

2 We can see that the Present Perfect refers to indefinite time and the Past Simple refers to definite time by looking at the time expressions used with the different tenses.

Present Perfect – indefinite		**Past Simple – definite**	
I've done it	for a long time.		yesterday.
	since July.		last week.
	before.		two days ago.
	recently.	I did it	at 8 o'clock.
I've already done it.			in 1987.
I haven't done it yet.			when I was young.
			for a long time.

❶ Be careful with *this morning/afternoon,* etc.
***Have** you **seen** Amy this morning?*   (It's still morning.)
***Did** you **see** Amy this morning?*   (It's the afternoon or evening.)

 ## 7.3 Present Perfect Simple passive

Form

has/have been + past participle

It	has been	
They	have been	sold.

Use

The uses are the same in the passive as in the active.
*Two million cars **have been produced** so far this year.* (unfinished past)
***Has** she ever **been made redundant**?* (past experience)
*'Have you heard? Two hundred homes **have been washed** away by a tidal wave!'* (present importance)

7.4 Phrasal verbs

There are four types of phrasal verbs. Types 1, 2, and 3 can be literal or idiomatic. Type 4 are nearly always idiomatic.

Type 1
Verb + particle (no object)
a *He put on his coat and **went out**.*
b *I didn't put enough wood on the fire and it **went out**.*

In a, the verb and particle are used literally. In b, they are used idiomatically. *Go out* means stop burning.

Examples with literal meaning:
***Sit down**.*
*She **stood up** and **walked out**.*
*Please **go away**.*
*She **walked** right **past** the store without noticing it.*

Examples with idiomatic meaning:
*The marriage didn't **work out**.* (= succeed)
*Our plans **fell through**.* (= fail)

Type 2
Verb + particle + object (separable)
a *I **put up** the picture.*
b *I **put up** my sister for the night.*

In a, the verb and particle are used literally. In b, they are used idiomatically. *Put up* means give someone food and a place to sleep, usually for the night or a few days.
Type 2 phrasal verbs are separable. The object (noun or pronoun) can come between the verb and the particle.

*I **put up** the picture.*   *I **put up** my sister.*
*I **put** the picture **up**.*   *I **put** my sister **up**.*

If the object is a pronoun, it *always* comes between the verb and the particle.

*I put **it** up.*   NOT   ~~I put up it.~~
*I put **her** up.*   NOT   ~~I put up her.~~

Examples with a literal meaning:
*The waiter **took away** the plates.*
*Don't **throw** it **away**.*
*They're **pulling** that old building **down**.*

Examples with an idiomatic meaning:
*I **put off** the meeting.* (= postpone)
*Don't **let** me **down**.* (= disappoint)

Type 3

Verb + particle + object (inseparable)

a *She **came across** the room.*
b *She **came across** an old friend while she was out shopping.*

In a, the verb and particle are used literally. In b, they are used idiomatically. *Come across* means find by accident.
Type 3 phrasal verbs are inseparable. The object (noun or pronoun) always comes after the particle.

NOT ~~She came an old friend across.~~ or ~~She came her across.~~

Examples with a literal meaning:
*I'm **looking for** Jane.*
*They **ran across** the park.*
*We **drove past** them.*

Examples with an idiomatic meaning:
*I'll **look after** it for you.* (= care for)
*She **takes after** her father.* (= resemble in features, build, character, or disposition)
*He never **got over** the death of his wife.* (= recover from)

Type 4

Verb + particle + particle

*I **get along** very well **with** my boss.*
*I'm **looking forward to** it.*
*How can you **put up with** that noise?*

Type 4 phrasal verbs are nearly always idiomatic. The object cannot change position. It cannot come before the particles or between the particles.

NOT ~~I'm looking forward it to.~~

Introduction to conditionals

There are many different ways of making sentences with *if*. It is important to understand the difference between sentences that express real possibilities, and those that express unreal situations.

Real possibilities

*If it **rains**, we'll stay home.*
(*if* + Present Simple + *will*)
*If you've **finished** your work, you **can** go home.*
(*if* + Present Perfect + modal auxiliary verb)
*If you're **feeling** ill, **go** home and **get** into bed.*
(*if* + Present Continuous + imperative)

Unreal situations

*You **would understand** me better if you **came** from my country.*
(*would* + *if* + Past Simple)
*If I **were** rich, I **wouldn't have** any problems.*
(*if* + *were* + *would*)
*If I **stopped** smoking, I **could run** faster.*
(*if* + Past Simple + modal auxiliary verb)

There are several patterns that you need to know to understand the variations. Note that a comma is usual when the *if* clause comes first.

▶ 8.1 First conditional

Form

if + Present Simple + *will*

Positive

If I find your wallet, I'll let you know.
We'll come and see you on Sunday if the weather's good.

Negative

You won't pass the test if you don't study.
If you lose your ticket, you won't be able to go.

Question

What will you do if you don't find a job?
If there isn't a hotel, where will you stay?

Note that we do not usually use *will* in the *if* clause.

NOT ~~If you will leave now, you'll catch the train.~~
        ~~If I'll go out tonight, I'll give you a call.~~

If can be replaced by *unless* (= *if ... not*) or *in case* (= because of the possibility ...).

***Unless** I hear from you, I'll come at 8.00.*
*I'll take my umbrella **in case** it rains.*

Use

1 First conditional sentences express a possible condition and its probable result in the future.

Condition (*if* clause)	Result (result clause)
If I find a jumper in your size,	*I'll buy it for you.*
If you can't do the homework,	*give me a call.*
If you can find my purse,	*I might buy you an ice-cream.*
If you've never been to Wales,	*you should try to go there one day.*

2 We can use the first conditional to express different functions (all of which express a possible condition and a probable result).

If you do that again, I'll kill you! (a threat)
Careful! If you touch that, you'll burn yourself! (a warning)
I'll post the letter if you like. (an offer)
If you lend me £100, I'll love you forever. (a promise)

8.2 Time clauses

Conjunctions of time (*when, as soon as, before, until, after*) are not usually followed by *will*. We use a present tense even though the time reference is future.

*I'll call you **when** I **get** home.*
***As soon as** dinner **is** ready, I'll give you a call.*
*Can I have a word with you **before** I **go**?*
*Wait **until** I **come** back.*

We can use the Present Perfect if it is important to show that the action in the time clause is finished.

***When** I've **read** the book, I'll lend it to you.*
*I'll go home **after** I've **done** the shopping.*

8.3 Zero conditional

Zero conditional sentences refer to 'all time,' not just the present or future. They express a situation that is always true. *If* means *when* or *whenever*.

If you spend over £50 at that supermarket, you get a five per cent discount.

8.4 Second conditional

Form

if + Past Simple + *would*

Positive
If I won some money, I'd go around the world.
My father would kill me if he could see me now.

Negative
I'd give up my job if I didn't like it.
If I saw a ghost, I wouldn't talk to it.

Question
What would you do if you saw someone shoplifting?
If you needed help, who would you ask?

Note that *was* can change to *were* in the condition clause.

| If I
If he | were rich, | I
he | wouldn't have to work. |
|---|---|---|---|

Use

1   We use the second conditional to express an unreal situation and its probable result. The situation or condition is improbable, impossible, imaginary, or contrary to known facts.
    If I were the president of my country, I'd increase taxes. (But it's not very likely that I will ever be the president.)
    If my mother was still alive, she'd be very proud. (But she's dead.)
    If Ted needed money, I'd lend it to him. (But he doesn't need it.)
2   Other modal verbs are possible in the result clause.
    *I **could** buy some new clothes if I had some money.*
    *If I saved a little every week, I **might** be able to save up for a car.*
    *If you wanted that job, you'**d have to** apply very soon.*
3   *If I were you, I'd ...* is used to give advice.
    ***If I were you, I'd** apologize to her.*
    *I'**d** take it easy for a while **if I were you.***

8.5 First or second conditional?

Both conditionals refer to the present and future. The difference is about probability, not time. It is usually clear which conditional to use. First conditional sentences are real and possible; second conditional sentences express situations that will probably never happen.

If I lose my job, I'll ... (My company is doing badly. There is a strong possibility of being made redundant.)
If I lost my job, I'd ... (I probably won't lose my job. I'm just speculating.)
If there is a nuclear war, we'll all ... (Said by a pessimist.)
If there was a nuclear war, ... (But I don't think it will happen.)

would

Notice the use of *would* in the following sentences:
*She'**d** look better with shorter hair.* (= If she cut her hair, she'd look better.)

would to express preference
*I'**d** love a cup of coffee.*
*Where **would** you like to sit?*
*I'**d** rather have coffee, please.*
*I'**d** rather not tell you, if that's all right.*
*What **would** you rather do, stay in or go out?*

would to express a request
***Would** you open the door for me?*
***Would** you mind lending me a hand?*

UNIT 9

Modal verbs

Modal verbs can express ability, obligation, permission, and request. They can also express the idea of probability or how certain a situation is. There is an introduction to modal auxiliary verbs on p139.

Modal verbs of probability

 ### 9.1 Expressing possibility/probability: the present/future

1 *Must* and *can't* express the logical conclusion of a situation: *must* = logically probable; *can't* = logically improbable. We don't have all the facts, so we are not absolutely sure, but we are pretty certain.
   *He **must** be exhausted. He **can't** even stand up.*
   *Sue **can't** have a ten-year-old daughter! Sue's only 24!*
   *He's in great shape, even though he **must** be at least 60!*
   *A walk in this weather! You **must** be joking!*
   *Is there no answer? They **must** be in bed. They **can't** be out this late!*

2 *Could* and *may/might* express possibility in the present or future. *May/Might* + *not* is the negative. *Couldn't* is rare in this use.
   *He **might** be lost.*
   *They **could** move to a different place.*
   *Dave and Beth aren't at home. They **could** be at the concert, I suppose.*
   *We **may** go to Greece for our vacation. We haven't decided yet.*
   *Take your umbrella. It **might** rain later.*
   *I **might** not be able to come tonight. I **might** have to work late.*

The continuous infinitive
Must/could/can't/might + *be* + *-ing* make the continuous form in the present.
*Peter **might be working** late.*
*They **can't be working** very hard.*
Compare:
*'John's grass is lovely. He **must cut** it regularly.'* (habit)
*'What's John doing in the garden?' 'He **might be cutting** the grass.'* (now)

 ### 9.2 Expressing possibility/probability: the past

The perfect infinitive
Must/could/can't/might + *have* + past participle express degrees of probability in the past.
*He **must have been** exhausted.*
*She **can't have told** him about us yet.*
*He **might have got** lost.*
*They **could have moved** house.*

The continuous infinitive
Must/could/can't/might + *have* + *been* + *-ing* make the continuous form in the past.
*She **must have been joking**.*
*They **can't have been trying** very hard.*
*He **could have been lying** to you.*

 ▶▶ **Workbook p57** Further practice of the continuous infinitive

9.3 Asking about possibilities

To ask about possibility/probability we usually use *Do you think …?* Question forms with modal verbs of probability are unusual.
*'**Do you think** she's married?'*   *'She can't be.'*
*'Where **do you think** he's from?'*   *'He might be Spanish or Portuguese.'*
*'**Do you think** they've arrived yet?'*   *'They may have. Or they might have got stuck in the traffic.'*

9.4 So do I! Neither do I!

When we agree or disagree using *So …/Neither … I*, we repeat the auxiliary verbs. If there is no auxiliary, use *do/does/did*. Be careful with sentence stress.

AGREEING

I like ice-cream.	So do I.
I'm wearing jeans.	So am I.
I can swim.	So can I.
I went out.	So did I.

I don't like working.	Neither do I.
I can't drive.	Neither can I.
I haven't been to Paris	Neither have I.

DISAGREEING

I don't like Mary.	I do.
We're going now.	We aren't.
I can speak Polish.	I can't.
I haven't been skiing.	I have.

I like blue cheese.	I don't.
I saw Pat yesterday.	I didn't.
I'm going to have some coffee.	I'm not.

9.5 *too* and *either/neither*

We express that we have the same ideas as somebody else by using *too* and *either/neither*. With *too* and *either* we repeat the auxiliary verbs or, if there is no auxiliary, use *do/does/did*.

I like ice-cream.	*I do, too. / Me too.*
I have always studied hard.	*I have, too. / Me too.*
I don't like working.	*I don't, either. / Me neither.*
I can't play a musical instrument.	*I can't, either. / Me neither.*

Continuous forms

Remember, the following ideas are expressed by all continuous forms:

1 activity in progress.
  Be quiet! I'm thinking.
  I was having a shower when the phone rang.
  I've been working since 9 o'clock this morning.

2 temporary activity.
  We're staying with friends until we find a place of our own.
  We've been living with them for six weeks.

3 possibly incomplete activity.
  I'm writing a report. I have to finish it by tomorrow.
  Who's been eating my sandwich?

▶▶ **Workbook p63** Further practice of simple and continuous forms

10.1 Present Perfect Continuous

Form

Positive and negative

I We You They	've haven't	been working.
He She It	's hasn't	

Question

How long	have	I you we	been working?
	has	she it	

Use

We use the Present Perfect Continuous to express:

1 an activity that began in the past and is continuing now.
  I've been studying English for three years.
  How long have you been working here?

Sometimes there is no difference between the simple and the continuous.

I've played I've been playing	the piano since I was a boy.

If the continuous is possible, English has a preference for using it.

The continuous can sometimes express a temporary activity, and the simple a permanent state.
I've been living in this house for the past few months. (temporary)
I've lived here all my life. (permanent)

Remember that state verbs rarely take the continuous form (see 2.3 p136).
I've had this book for ages.
I've always loved sunny days.

2 a past activity that has caused a present result.
  I've been working all day. (I'm tired now.)
  Have you been crying? (Your eyes are red.)
  Roger's been cutting the grass. (I can smell it.)

The past activity might be finished or it might not. The context usually makes this clear.
Look out of the window! It's been snowing! (It has stopped snowing now.)
I've been writing this book for two years. (It still isn't finished.)
I'm covered in paint because I've been decorating the bathroom. (It might be finished or it might not. We don't know.)

10.2 Present Perfect Simple or Continuous?

1 The simple expresses a completed action.
  I've painted the kitchen, and now I'm doing the bathroom.

The continuous expresses an activity over a period and things that happened during the activity.
I've got paint in my hair because I've been decorating.

Because the simple expresses a completed action, we use it if the sentence gives a number or quantity. Here, the continuous isn't possible.
I've been reading all day. I've read ten chapters.
She's been eating ever since she arrived. She's eaten ten biscuits already.

2 Some verbs don't have the idea of a long time, for example, *find, start, buy, die, lose, break, stop.* These verbs are more usually found in the simple.

Some verbs have the idea of a long time, for example, *wait, work, play, try, learn, rain.* These verbs are often found in the continuous.
I've cut my finger. (One short action.)
I've been cutting firewood. (Perhaps over several hours.)

10.3 Time expressions

Here are some time expressions often found with certain tenses.

Past Simple
I lived in Chicago for six years.
I saw Jack two days ago.
They met during the war.
She got married while she was at university.

Present Perfect
We've been married for ten years.
They've been living here since June.
She hasn't been working since their baby was born.

Future
We're going on vacation for a few days.
The class ends in 20 minutes.
I'll be home in a half an hour.

Prepositions with dates, months, years, etc.

in	September 1965 summer the holidays the 1920s the 20th century	on	Monday Monday morning 8 August Christmas Day holiday	at	7 o'clock the end of May Christmas the age of ten dinner-time

Question words

Look at the questions. Notice that *What*, *Which*, and *Whose* can combine with a noun and *How* can combine with an adjective or an adverb.

What kind of music do you like?
What size shoe do you wear?
What colour are your eyes?
Which pen do you want?
Which way is it to the station?
Whose book is this?
How much do you weigh?
How many brothers and sisters do you have?
How many times have you been on a plane?
How much homework do you get every night?
How tall are you?
How often do you go to the dentist?
How long does it take you to get to school?

▶ 11.1 Indirect questions

1 Indirect questions have the same word order as the positive and there is no *do/does/did*.

   | Tom lives | in California.

   Do you know where | Tom lives |?
   NOT   ~~Do you know where does Tom live?~~

2 We often make direct questions into indirect questions to make them sound 'softer' or more polite.

   Direct question
   What time do the banks close?

   Indirect question
   Could you tell me
   Do you know
   Do you happen to know | *what time the banks close?*
   Have you any idea
   Do you remember
   Would you mind telling me |

   If there is no question word, use *if* or *whether*.
   I don't know **if** *I'm coming or not.*
   I wonder **whether** *it's going to rain.*

   Here are some more expressions that introduce indirect questions:
   I don't know
   I wonder
   I can't remember
   I've no idea | *how long the journey takes.*
   I'd like to know
   I'm not sure

▶ 11.2 Question tags

Form

1 Question tags are very common in spoken English. The most common patterns are:

   positive sentence – negative tag
   You're Jenny, **aren't** *you?*

   or negative sentence – positive tag
   It **isn't** *a very nice day,* **is** *it?*

2 We repeat the auxiliary verb in the tag. If there is no auxiliary, use *do/does/did*.
   You **haven't** *been here before,* **have** *you?*
   You **can** *speak French,* **can't** *you?*
   We **should** *take the dog out,* **shouldn't** *we?*
   Banks close at four, **don't** *they?*
   She eats meat, **doesn't** *she?*
   You went to bed late, **didn't** *you?*

   Note
   For negative question tags with *I'm …*, use *aren't*.
   I'm late, **aren't** *I?*   NOT   ~~I'm late, am't I?~~
   But,
   I'm not late, am I?   NOT   ~~I'm not late, aren't I?~~

3 Notice the meaning of *Yes* and *No* in answer to question tags.
   'You're coming, aren't you?'   'Yes.' (= I **am** coming.)
                                     'No.' (= I'm **not** coming.)

Use

We use question tags to keep a conversation going by involving listeners and inviting them to participate.
The meaning of a question tag depends on how you say it.
A question tag with rising intonation is like a real question – it is asking for confirmation. It means 'I'm not sure, so I'm checking'. The speaker thinks he/she knows the answer, but isn't absolutely certain.

Your name's Abigail, isn't it?

You're in advertising, aren't you?

You work in the city, don't you?

A question tag with falling intonation isn't really a question at all – it is a way of making conversation. It means 'Talk to me'. The speaker expects people to agree with him/her.

Beautiful day, isn't it?

It's wonderful weather for swimming, isn't it?

That was a great concert, wasn't it?

You haven't been here before, have you?

Note
We can also use question tags with negative sentences to make a polite request for information or help.

You couldn't lend me your car this evening, could you?

12.1 Tense changes in reported statements

1 It is usual for the verb in the reported clause to move 'one tense back' if the reporting verb is in the past tense (e.g., *said, told*).

Present ——————➤ Past
Present Perfect ——————➤ Past Perfect
Past ——————➤ Past Perfect

'I**'m going**.'   *He said he **was going**.*
'She**'s passed** her test.'   *He told me she **had passed** her test.*
'My father **died** when I was six.'   *She said her father **had died** when she was six.*

The verb also moves 'one tense back' when we are reporting thoughts and feelings.

*I thought she **was** married, but she isn't.*
*I didn't know he **was** a teacher. I thought he **worked** in a bank.*
*I forgot you **were coming**. Never mind. Come in.*
*I hoped you **would** call.*

2 There is no tense change if:

– the reporting verb is in the present tense (e.g. *says, asks*).
'The train **will be** late.'   *He says the train **will be** late.*
'I **come** from Spain.'   *She says she **comes** from Spain.*

– the reported speech is about something that is still true.
'Rain forests **are being destroyed**.'
*She told him that rain forests **are being destroyed**.*
'I **hate** football.'
*I told him I **hate** football.*

Some modal verbs change.

can ——————➤ could
will ——————➤ would
may ——————➤ might

'She **can** type well.'   *He told me she **could** type well.*
'I**'ll** help you.'   *She said she**'d** help me.*
'I **may** come.'   *She said she **might** come.*

Other modal verbs don't change.
'You **should** go to bed.'   *He told me I **should** go to bed.*
'It **might** rain.'   *She said she thought it **might** rain.*

Must stays as *must*, or changes to *had to*.
'I **must** go!'   *He said he **must/had to** go.*

 12.2 Reporting verbs

There are many reporting verbs.

We rarely use *say* with an indirect object (i.e., the person spoken to).
She said she was going.   NOT   ~~She said to me she was going.~~

Tell is always used with an indirect object in reported speech.

She told	me the doctor us her husband	the news.

We can use *that* after *say* and *tell*.
*He told her (**that**) he would be home late.*
*She said (**that**) sales were down from last year.*

Many verbs are more descriptive than *say* and *tell*, for example, *explain, interrupt, demand, insist, admit, complain, warn.*

| He | explained
complained
admitted | that he would be home late. |
| | | that sales were down that year. |

Sometimes we report the idea, rather than the actual words.
'I'll lend you some money.'   *He offered to lend me some money.*
'I won't help you.'   *She refused to help me.*

 **12.3 Reported questions**

1 The word order in reported questions is different in reported speech. There is no inversion of subject and auxiliary verb and there is no *do/does/did*. This is similar to indirect questions (see p149).
'Why have you come here?'   *I asked her why she had come here.*
'What time is it?'   *He wants to know what time it is.*
'Where do you live?'   *She asked me where I lived.*

Note
We do not use a question mark in a reported question.
We do not use *say* in reported questions.
He said, 'How old are you?'   *He asked me how old I am.*

2 If there is no question word, use *if* or *whether*.

She wants to know	if whether	she should wear a dress.

 12.4 Reported commands, requests, etc.

1 For reported commands, requests, offers, and advice, we use verb + person + *to* + infinitive.
*They **told us to** go away.*
*They **asked me to** look after their cat.*
*He **urged the teachers to** go back to work.*
*She **persuaded me to** have my hair cut.*
*I **advised the President to** leave immediately.*

❗ *Say* is not possible. Use *ask, told*, etc.

2 For negative commands, use *not* before *to*.
*He told me **not to** tell anyone.*
*The police warned people **not to** go out.*

3 We use *tell* for reported statements and reported commands, but the form is different.

Reported statements
He told me that he was going.
They told us that they were going abroad.
She told them what had been happening.

Reported commands
He told me to keep still.
The police told people to move on.
My parents told me to clean up my room.

We use *ask* for reported commands and reported questions, but the form is different.

Reported commands
I was asked to attend the interview.
He asked me to open my suitcase.
She asked me not to leave.

Reported questions
He asked me what I did for a living.
I asked her how much the rent was.
She asked me why I had come.

▶▶ **Workbook p77**   Further practice of *ask* and *tell*

Pairwork activities

 UNIT 1 *p9*

PRACTICE
An amazing thing happened!

Student A
Ask and answer questions to complete the information about Kaori Sato.

> *Where was Kaori Sato born?*

> *In Osaka. How many films has she made?*

> *Over forty. How long … ?*

KAORI SATO
United Nations Goodwill Ambassador

Kaori Sato was born in __Osaka, Japan__ (*Where?*), in 1956. She is a famous film star and has made over forty films.

She has been a UN Goodwill Ambassador for _____ (*How long?*). Her special interest is children's health and education. She goes to Africa _____ (*How often?*), and she visits schools and hospitals. She has raised _____ (*How much money?*) from people in Japan. As a Goodwill Ambassador, she is paid just $1 a year.

Her father was a famous _____ (*What/do?*). Kaori went to university in Tokyo, then studied _____ (*What?*) at the Tokyo Theatre School. She has also written seven best-selling books.

She is married, and has _____ (*How many?*) children. They are both at university, studying languages.

 UNIT 3 *p25*

PRACTICE
Getting information

Student A
Ask and answer questions to complete the story.

> *Where did Wanda and Roy go on holiday?*

> *They went to Florida. What did they do every day?*

> *They went swimming and lay in the sun. Where … ?*

THE TALE OF TWO WAVES
A TRUE STORY

Last summer, Wanda and Roy went on holiday to _____Florida_____ (*Where?*). Every day, they went swimming and lay in the sun.

One morning, they were _____ (*Where?*), swimming in the sea, when a huge wave knocked Wanda's expensive Italian sunglasses into the water. Wanda was very upset because _____ (*Why?*).

The next day, they were sunbathing on the same beach and Wanda was wearing _____ (*What?*), when suddenly there was another huge wave, which totally covered Wanda. She was _____ (*How … feel?*), but then she looked down and to her amazement, she saw the expensive sunglasses that she had lost the day before.

PRACTICE

Getting information

Student B

Ask and answer questions to complete the information about Kaori Sato.

> *Where was Kaori Sato born?*

> *In Osaka. How many films has she made?*

> *Over forty. How long … ?*

KAORI SATO
United Nations Goodwill Ambassador

Kaori Sato was born in Osaka, Japan, in 1956. She is a famous film star and has made <u>over forty</u> (*How many?*) films.

She has been a UN Goodwill Ambassador for 20 years. Her special interest is _____ (*What?*). She goes to Africa every year, and she visits _____ (*What?*). She has raised $25 million from people in Japan. As a Goodwill Ambassador, she is paid _____ (*How much?*).

Her father was a famous painter. Kaori went to university in _____ (*Where?*), then studied drama at the Tokyo Theatre School. She has also written _____ (*How many?*) best-selling books.

She is married, and has two children. They are both at university, studying _____ (*What?*).

PRACTICE

An amazing thing happened!

Student B

Ask and answer questions to complete the story.

> *Where did Wanda and Roy go on holiday?*

> *They went to Florida. What did they do every day?*

> *They went swimming and lay in the sun. Where … ?*

THE TALE OF TWO WAVES
A TRUE STORY

Last summer, Wanda and Roy went on holiday to Florida. Every day, they <u>went swimming and lay in the sun</u> (*What … do?*).

One morning, they were at the beach near their hotel, swimming in the sea, when a huge wave _____ (*What … do?*). Wanda was very upset because Roy had given her the sunglasses for her birthday.

The next day, they were sunbathing _____ (*Where?*) and Wanda was wearing a new, cheap pair of sunglasses, when suddenly there was another huge wave, which _____ (*What … do?*). She was furious, but then she looked down and to her amazement, she saw _____ (*What?*).

VOCABULARY
Talking about you

1 Work with a partner. List the following information.
- the name of a restaurant where you had a memorable meal
- the name of a city, town, or village that you have visited and that you would like to visit again
- the name of a relative, friend, or colleague who is important to you

Choose names of people and places that your partner does not know.

2 Exchange lists with your partner.
Ask and answer questions to find out about
the places and people your partner listed.

> Where was the restaurant?

> What was the food like?

3 Report back to the class about one of the names your partner wrote.

READING AND SPEAKING
Roleplay

1 Work with a partner.

Student A
You are a journalist. Interview your partner about his/her dream job from exercise 1 on p58. Ask these questions.
- What do you do?
- How did you get the job?
- What do you like most about it?
- What's an average day like?
- Have you made any sacrifices to do this job?
- What would you like to do next?
- What advice would you give to someone who wanted to do your job?

Student B
You have your dream job from exercise 1 on p58. Your partner is a journalist. Answer his/her questions.

2 Change roles.

I NEED HELP!
Lucy and Pam's letters

Here are Lucy and Pam's letters to 'Susie's Problem Page'.

Dear Susie,

I am 16 years old and totally depressed. I'm in love with Leon Rossi, the film star. I think about him night and day. I just sit in my room and watch videos of his films over and over again. I've written hundreds of letters to him and sent emails to his fan club, but all I get back are autographed photos. I dream that one day I'll meet him and that he'll feel the same way about me. My friends think I'm crazy, so I don't see them any more. I can't concentrate on my homework, and I have exams next month. I've tried to talk to my mum and dad, but they're both solicitors and much too busy to listen to me.

Please, please help me! I'm desperate. I'm thinking of running away to Hollywood to meet him.

Yours in misery,

Lucy

Dear Susie,

I'm almost too tired to write, but I have no one to turn to. I've been married for three years and everything was just fine until a year ago when Brian, my husband, lost his job. He became depressed, and because he has nothing to do, he just goes over to his mother's house and spends all day with her. He says he's worried about her because she lives alone.

I'm a nurse at a hospital. I'm exhausted after work, but when I get home I have to cook and clean. Brian refuses to cook or do housework – he says it's boring and gets angry with me if I ask him to do anything around the house. His whole personality has changed – we don't communicate any more. We're always short of money and I'm worried that he might have a gambling problem. I found hundreds of lottery tickets in a drawer yesterday, but I haven't said anything about it.

What can I do? I still love him. We were hoping to start a family soon, but now I'm not so sure this is a good idea.

Yours sincerely, *Pam*

PRACTICE
Who's who in the family?

1   Work in small groups. Look at photos 1–5. They are all of Simon and his family. In each photo, who do you think is Simon? Who do you think the others are? Why?

> This must / could / can't be Simon because …

> But this must / could / can't be Simon's wife …

PRACTICE
Finding out about Madonna

Student A
Ask and answer questions to complete the information about Madonna.

> *When was Madonna born?*

> *On 16 August, 1958. Where was she born?*

> *In Bay City, Michigan. What ... ?*

Madonna was born Louise Veronica Ciccone on __16th August, 1958__ (*When?*), in Bay City, Michigan. She was the oldest of eight children. Her mother died of _____ (*What?*) when she was six years old. She was brought up by _____ (*Who ... by?*), who was an engineer. He remarried, and Madonna's stepmother was called Joan.

She started singing and dancing when she was _____ (*How old?*), participating in school shows and being a cheerleader. She also had piano and ballet lessons.

She went to the University of Michigan, where she studied _____ (*What?*), but she put aside her studies after two years and went to New York, because _____ (*Why?*).

She had no money, so she worked in shops and as a model. She decided to start singing, and found work as a backing vocalist. She wrote songs, and performed at local discos. She signed a contract with _____ (*Who ... with?*) in 1982, and immediately her career took off. She had her first number one hit in 1984 with *Like a Virgin*. In 1985 she appeared as the lead in the film *Desperately Seeking Susan*.

Around this time she married _____ (*Who?*). Unfortunately the marriage only lasted for four years.

In 1992 she founded her own record company called *Maverick*. In 1996 she starred in the film _____ (*Which?*), and she was awarded the *Golden Globe* for Best Actress. In the same year she had her first child, Lourdes Maria. The father was _____ (*Who?*). She currently lives in London with _____ (*Who ... with?*), with whom she had a second child, a boy called Rocco.

She has had eleven number one hits – more than any other female artist.

PRACTICE
Finding out about Madonna

Student B
Ask and answer questions to complete the information about Madonna.

> *When was Madonna born?*

> *On 16 August 1958. Where was she born?*

> *In Bay City, Michigan. What ... ?*

Madonna was born Louise Veronica Ciccone on 16 August, 1958, in ___Bay City, Michigan___ (*Where?*). She was the oldest of eight children. Her mother died of cancer when she was _____ (*How old?*). She was brought up by her father, who was an engineer. He remarried, and Madonna's stepmother was called _____ (*What ... name of ... ?*).

She started singing and dancing when she was eight, participating in school shows and being a cheerleader. She also had piano and ballet lessons.

She went to the University of _____ (*Which ... to?*), where she studied dance, but she put aside her studies after two years and went to _____ (*Where ... to?*), because she had dreams of becoming a star.

She had no money, so she worked in shops and as a model. She decided _____ (*What ... do?*), and found work as a backing vocalist. She wrote songs, and performed at local discos. She signed a contract with Warner Brothers in 1982, and immediately her career took off. She had her first number one hit in _____ (*When?*) with *Like a Virgin*. In 1985 she appeared as the lead in the film *Desperately Seeking Susan*.

Around this time she married Sean Penn. Unfortunately the marriage only lasted for _____ years (*How long?*).

In 1992 she founded her own record company called *Maverick*. In 1996 she starred in the film *Evita*, and she was awarded _____ (*What?*). In the same year she had her first child, Lourdes Maria. The father was her personal trainer, Carlos Leon. She currently lives in _____ (*Where?*) with her English husband, Guy Ritchie, with whom she had a second child, a boy called Rocco.

She has had _____ (*How many?*) number one hits – more than any other female artist.

PRACTICE
Conversations

1 Work with a partner. Choose one of the conversations below and add question tags.

  1 A You broke that vase.
     B Yes, I did. I dropped it. I'm sorry.
     A You'll replace it.
     B Yes, of course I will. How much did it cost?
     A £300.
     B £300?! It wasn't *that* much.
     A Yes, it was.

  2 A Have you paid the electricity bill yet?
     B No, *you* paid it.
     A No, I haven't paid it. I thought you paid it.
     B Me? But you *always* pay it.
     A No, I don't. I always pay the phone bill.
     B Oh, yes, sorry.

  3 A We love each other.
     B Erm, I think so.
     A We don't ever want to be apart.
     B Well ...
     A And we'll get married and have lots of children.
     B What? You haven't bought me a ring.
     A Yes, I have. Diamonds are forever.
     B Oh, dear!

  4 A Helen didn't win the lottery.
     B Yes, she did. She won £2 million!
     A She isn't going to give it all away.
     B As a matter of fact, she is.
     A Wow. Not many people would do that.
     B Well, *I* certainly wouldn't.

  5 A I think we're lost. Let's look at the map.
     B Uh-oh.
     A What do you mean, 'Uh-oh'? You didn't forget to bring the map.
     B Sorry.
     A How are we going to get back to the campsite without a map?
     B Well, we could ask a police officer.
     A There aren't many police officers on this mountain!

2 Act out your conversation for the class.

Irregular verbs

Base form	Past Simple	Past participle
be	was/were	been
beat	beat	beaten
become	became	become
begin	began	begun
bend	bent	bent
bite	bit	bitten
blow	blew	blown
break	broke	broken
bring	brought	brought
build	built	built
buy	bought	bought
can	could	been able
catch	caught	caught
choose	chose	chosen
come	came	come
cost	cost	cost
cut	cut	cut
dig	dug	dug
do	did	done
draw	drew	drawn
dream	dreamed/dreamt	dreamed/dreamt
drink	drank	drunk
drive	drove	driven
eat	ate	eaten
fall	fell	fallen
feed	fed	fed
feel	felt	felt
fight	fought	fought
find	found	found
fit	fit	fit
fly	flew	flown
forget	forgot	forgotten
forgive	forgave	forgiven
freeze	froze	frozen
get	got	got
give	gave	given
go	went	been/gone
grow	grew	grown
hang	hanged/hung	hanged/hung
have	had	had
hear	heard	heard
hide	hid	hidden
hit	hit	hit
hold	held	held
hurt	hurt	hurt
keep	kept	kept
kneel	knelt	knelt
know	knew	known
lay	laid	laid
lead	led	led
learn	learned/learnt	learned/learnt

Base form	Past Simple	Past participle
leave	left	left
lend	lent	lent
let	let	let
lie	lay	lain
light	lighted/lit	lighted/lit
lose	lost	lost
make	made	made
mean	meant	meant
meet	met	met
must	had to	had to
pay	paid	paid
put	put	put
read /ri:d/	read /red/	read /red/
ride	rode	ridden
ring	rang	rung
rise	rose	risen
run	ran	run
say	said	said
see	saw	seen
sell	sold	sold
send	sent	sent
set	set	set
shake	shook	shaken
shine	shone	shone
shoot	shot	shot
show	showed	shown
shut	shut	shut
sing	sang	sung
sink	sank	sunk
sit	sat	sat
sleep	slept	slept
slide	slid	slid
speak	spoke	spoken
spend	spent	spent
spoil	spoiled/spoilt	spoiled/spoilt
spread	spread	spread
stand	stood	stood
steal	stole	stolen
stick	stuck	stuck
swim	swam	swum
take	took	taken
teach	taught	taught
tear	tore	torn
tell	told	told
think	thought	thought
throw	threw	thrown
understand	understood	understood
wake	woke	woken
wear	wore	worn
win	won	won
write	wrote	written

Verb patterns

Verbs + -ing

adore can't stand don't mind enjoy finish look forward to	doing swimming cooking

Note
We often use the verb *go* + *-ing* for sports and activities.
> I **go swimming** every day.
> I **go shopping** on weekends.

Verbs + to + infinitive

agree choose dare decide expect forget help hope learn manage need offer promise refuse seem want would hate would like would love would prefer	to do to come to cook

Notes
1 *Help* and *dare* can be used without *to*.
> We **helped clean up** the kitchen.
> They didn't **dare disagree** with him.
2 *Have to* for obligation.
> I **have to wear** a uniform.
3 *Used to* for past habits.
> I **used to smoke**, but I quit last year.

Verbs + sb + to + infinitive

advise allow ask beg encourage expect help invite need order remind tell want warn would like	me him them someone	to do to go to come

Note
Help can be used without *to*.
> I **helped** him **do** the dishes.

Verbs + sb + infinitive (no to)

help let make	her us	do

Notes
1 *To* is used with *make* in the passive.
> We were **made to work** hard.
2 *Let* cannot be used in the passive. *Allowed to* is used instead.
> She was **allowed to leave**.

Verbs + -ing or to + infinitive
(with little or no change in meaning)

begin continue hate like love prefer start	doing to do

Verbs + -ing or to + infinitive
(with a change in meaning)

remember stop try	doing to do

Notes
1 I **remember posting** the letter.
> (= I have a memory now of a past action: posting the letter.)

   I **remembered to post** the letter.
> (= I reminded myself to post the letter. I didn't forget.)

2 I **stopped drinking** coffee.
> (= I gave up the habit.)

   I **stopped to drink** a coffee.
> (= I stopped doing something else in order to have a cup of coffee.)

3 I **tried to** sleep.
> (= I wanted to sleep, but it was difficult.)

   I **tried counting** sheep and **drinking** a glass of warm milk.
> (= These were possible ways of getting to sleep.)

Phonetic symbols

Consonants				
1	/p/	as in	**pen**	/pen/
2	/b/	as in	**big**	/bɪg/
3	/t/	as in	**tea**	/ti:/
4	/d/	as in	**do**	/du:/
5	/k/	as in	**cat**	/kæt/
6	/g/	as in	**go**	/gəʊ/
7	/f/	as in	**four**	/fɔ:/
8	/v/	as in	**very**	/'veri/
9	/s/	as in	**son**	/sʌn/
10	/z/	as in	**zoo**	/zu:/
11	/l/	as in	**live**	/lɪv/
12	/m/	as in	**my**	/maɪ/
13	/n/	as in	**near**	/nɪə/
14	/h/	as in	**happy**	/'hæpi/
15	/r/	as in	**red**	/red/
16	/j/	as in	**yes**	/jes/
17	/w/	as in	**want**	/wɒnt/
18	/θ/	as in	**thanks**	/θæŋks/
19	/ð/	as in	**the**	/ðə/
20	/ʃ/	as in	**she**	/ʃi:/
21	/ʒ/	as in	**television**	/'telɪvɪʒn/
22	/tʃ/	as in	**child**	/tʃaɪld/
23	/dʒ/	as in	**German**	/'dʒɜ:mən/
24	/ŋ/	as in	**English**	/'ɪŋglɪʃ/

Vowels				
25	/i:/	as in	**see**	/si:/
26	/ɪ/	as in	**his**	/hɪz/
27	/i/	as in	**twenty**	/'twenti/
28	/e/	as in	**ten**	/ten/
29	/æ/	as in	**stamp**	/stæmp/
30	/ɑ:/	as in	**father**	/'fɑ:ðə/
31	/ɒ/	as in	**hot**	/hɒt/
32	/ɔ:/	as in	**morning**	/'mɔ:nɪŋ/
33	/ʊ/	as in	**football**	/'fʊtbɔ:l/
34	/u:/	as in	**you**	/ju:/
35	/ʌ/	as in	**sun**	/sʌn/
36	/ɜ:/	as in	**learn**	/lɜ:n/
37	/ə/	as in	**letter**	/'letə/

Diphthongs (two vowels together)				
38	/eɪ/	as in	**name**	/neɪm/
39	/əʊ/	as in	**no**	/nəʊ/
40	/aɪ/	as in	**my**	/maɪ/
41	/aʊ/	as in	**how**	/haʊ/
42	/ɔɪ/	as in	**boy**	/bɔɪ/
43	/ɪə/	as in	**hear**	/hɪə/
44	/eə/	as in	**where**	/weə/
45	/ʊə/	as in	**tour**	/tʊə/

OXFORD
UNIVERSITY PRESS

Great Clarendon Street, Oxford OX2 6DP

Oxford University Press is a department of the University of Oxford. It furthers the University's objective of excellence in research, scholarship, and education by publishing worldwide in

Oxford New York

Auckland Cape Town Dar es Salaam Hong Kong
Karachi Kuala Lumpur Madrid Melbourne
Mexico City Nairobi New Delhi Shanghai Taipei
Toronto

With offices in

Argentina Austria Brazil Chile Czech Republic
France Greece Guatemala Hungary Italy Japan
South Korea Poland Portugal Singapore
Switzerland Thailand Turkey Ukraine Vietnam

OXFORD and OXFORD ENGLISH are registered trade marks of Oxford University Press in the UK and in certain other countries

© Oxford University Press 2003

The moral rights of the author have been asserted
Database right Oxford University Press (maker)

First published 2003
2009 2008 2007
10 9 8 7 6

No unauthorized photocopying

All rights reserved. No part of this publication may be reproduced, stored in a retrieval system, or transmitted, in any form or by any means, without the prior permission in writing of Oxford University Press, or as expressly permitted by law, or under terms agreed with the appropriate reprographics rights organization. Enquiries concerning reproduction outside the scope of the above should be sent to the ELT Rights Department, Oxford University Press, at the address above

You must not circulate this book in any other binding or cover and you must impose this same condition on any acquirer

Any websites referred to in this publication are in the public domain and their addresses are provided by Oxford University Press for information only. Oxford University Press disclaims any responsibility for the content

ISBN-13: 978-0-19-438750-7 International edition

ISBN-13: 978-0-19-439002-6 German edition

Bestelinummer 136027

Printed in China

ACKNOWLEDGEMENTS

The authors and publisher are grateful to those who have given permission to reproduce the following extracts and adaptations of copyright material: p16 'College grad loves life as $60,000-a-year paperboy' by Philip Smith, The National Enquirer 23 January 2001. Reproduced by permission of American Media Inc. p18 Information about The Clown Doctor. Reproduced by permission of Theodora Children's Trust. p68 Amnesty International information and Logo © Amnesty International Publications, 1 Easton Street, London WC1X 0DW ww.amnesty.org . Reproduced by permission. p68 Information about WWF. Reproduced by permission of WWF-UK. p82 Information about Dennis Woodruff. Reproduced by permission. p84 Information about Andrea Levitt. Reproduced by permission. p98 Information about Jane Banner. Reproduced by permission. p99 'Twelve Songs IX' from Collected Poems by WH Auden. Reproduced by permission of

Faber and Faber Ltd. p100 My Way. Original Words by Gilles Thibaut. English Translation by Paul Anka. Music by Claude François and Jacques Revaux © 1967 Editions Jeune Musique SARL and Warner/ Chappell Music, France. (50%) Warner/Chappell Music Ltd., London W6 8BS. (50%) Sony Music Ltd. Reproduced by permission of International Music Publications Ltd. and Sony Music Publishing (UK) Ltd. All Rights Reserved.

Illustrations by: Jamel Akib/Illustration pp114/115, Francis Blake/Three in a Box p89; Marc Burckhardt p22/23; Kasia Charko p106; Mark Duffin pp25, 32, 44; Hannah Firmin/ Illustration p110; Jacey/Debut Art p40; Karen Minot p9; Joerg Saupe/Illustration pp22, 49, 70, 78, 86; Carlotta Tormey p107; Harry Venning pp6, 14, 30, 38, 46, 54, 62; Katherine Walker pp 49, 60, 73, 138; Sam Wilson pp17, 65

Commissioned photography by: Dennis Kitchen Studio; Jodi Waxman/OUP pp8, 9, 12, 15, 32, 38, 39, 41, 46, 47, 48, 51, 55, 84, 85, 86, 88, 151, 152; Mark Mason; pp27 (books – 'For Whom the Bell Tolls' and 'A Farewell to Arms' book covers used by permission of the Random House Group Limited), 28 (books and DVDs – 'Captain Corelli's Mandolin' book cover used by permission of the Random House Group Limited; 'Harry Potter and the Philosopher's Stone' book cover used with kind permission from Bloomsbury Publishing and the illustrator, Thomas Taylor), 53 (labels); Chris King; pp75 (grown up father and daughter), 65, 79, 80, 96, 97, 101 (woman asking for directions), 103 (writing paper and pencil)

We would also like to thank the following for permission to reproduce photographs: Agence France Presse pp11 (Olympic flame), 34 (Muslim women); AgeFotostock pp69 (P.Coll/Maria and Paul), 77 (P.Coll/Rose); AKG London p92 Auguste Rodin, (The Thinker, bronze sculpture, 1889); Amnesty International p68 (logo); The Anthony Blake Photo Library p153 (pizza restaurant); Artcars/www.artcaragency.com p83 (H.Blank/ Dennis Woodruff); BAA Aviation Photo Library p53 (airport sign); The Bridgeman Art Library p26 (Pablo Picasso, *Guernica*, 1937, Museo Nacional Centro de Arte Reina Sofia, Madrid, © Succession Picasso/DACS 2003); Bubbles Photo Library p108 (J.Woodcock/exams), (J.Powell/café); © Daily Record, Glasgow p98 (group photo); Claudia Carlson p12; Corbis pp6 (K.Weatherly/ Olympic flag), 7 (Bettmann/John Lennon, 14 (M.Barrymore/two women drinking coffee), (D.Modricker/ bowling), 29 (C.Penn/sitting on steps), 34 (C.Bissell/ business lunch), (P.Ward/large family meal), 37 (P.Schermeister), 42 (L.Kennedy/Ice Hotel), (S.Warren/ The Burj Al-Arab), (S.Balfour/Gallo Images/Baobab Rivers Lodge), 43 (D.S.Robbins/hotel bedroom), 45 (M.McQueen/ferry), 52 (B.Krist/NY street scene), 56 (R.Holmes/hurricane), (M.Brennan/ boxers), 59 (D.Jones/ trapeze artist), 61 (R.Hutchings/ retired man), 63 (R.Juno/ lemons), 69 (R.Ressmeyer/ animal rescue), 81 (S.Maze), 90 (D.S.Robbins/ bristlecone pine), 91 (Bettmann/Uncle Sam), 100 (Bettmann), 153 (F.Seguin/ footballers); Corel p109; Getty Images pp6-7 (D.Scott/ aeroplane), 10 (H.Kingsnorth/internet café), 13 (B.Ayres), 14 (Antonio Mo/three young people laughing), 20 (A.Myers/ snowboarding), (D.Epperson/fishing), (W.R.Sallaz/ basketball), (P.Grumann/football), (C.Bissell/aerobics), (J.Kelly/mountain biking), (S.McClymont/joggers), (A.Marsland/Yoga), 21 (B.Ayres/Mary), (J.F.Causse/ Jenny), (G.Lepp/ Thomas), 24 (M.Malyszko), 28 (S.Mason/ four people at table), 29 (Piecework Productions/two women talking in street), (S.Cohen/man with glasses talking), 31 (A.Sacks/supermarket), (P.Cade/man and car), 32–33 (J.Wang /Thailand), 34 (K.Usami/business card exchange), 36 (A.Weinbrecht/people at table in Japan), (M.Miyatake/sushi), 43 (R.McVay /Karen Saunders), 45 (V.C.L./Tipp Howell/man in hotel),

53, 74 (A.Pistolesi/London taxi), 55 (A.Incrocci/ Geneva), 61 (R.McVay/man on phone), 62 (R.Davies/ people in rain), 64 (J.Lamb/black woman), (D.Boissavy/boy), (E.Holub/older man), 72 (C.M.Rogers/Carl), (T.Anderson/Andy), 74 (A. Pistolesi), 77 (D.Healey/ Louisa), 86 (P.Gridley/ Toronto), 91 (Z.Kaluzny/old women), 94–5 (D.Oliver), 99 (F.Seifert), 101 (R.Lockyer/ man), 116 (J.Cummins), 153 (S.Egan/hillside village), (Creaps/ women on sofa); Getty Images/Foodpix p47 (Burke/Triolo Productions/food); Getty Images/Sport p20 (D.McNamara/volleyball); Hulton Archive/Getty Images pp26 (Picasso portrait), 27 (Hemingway); Index Stock pp10–11 (J.Halaska/medical researcher), 11 (NASA/Space Shuttle), 14 (C.Freelance/two young boys hugging), 30 (D.Frazier), 50 (Great American Stock/ large Pepperoni pizza), 51 (SW Production/ pizza delivery), 53 (H.Kaiser/NY skyline), 59 (S.Dunwell Photography Inc/ironworker), 61 (B.Lai/woman on phone), 69 (M.Cate/soup kitchen), 70 (M. Giolas), 72 (J.Fly/snow scene), 83 (M.Diamond/Hollywood), 90 (L.Stone/dog), (K.Su/Great Wall of China); Andrew Itkoff p58 (hurricane hunter): Katz Pictures p68 (A.Patrick/ World Food Programme); Larry Luxner/ Luxner News Inc. p11 (Tourists at Macchu Picchu); Midweststock p11 (K.Sink/farm); National Enquirer p16; Courtesy of The Nobel Foundation p117 (painting of Alfred Nobel by Emil Österman); PA Photos pp50 (EPA/giant pizza Naples), 56 (EPA/ police), (D.Jones/car workers), 67 (J.Giles/family), (PA/couple and cheque), (S.Rousseau/couple and car), 87 (EPA), 155 (W.Conran/ Madonna), 156 (W.Conran/ Madonna); PhotoDisc pp51 (C Squared Studios/pizza in letter O), 64 (A.Morgan/ young man), 93 (R.McVay), 119 (J.Hollingworth); Photofusion pp52 (R.Roberts/London Eye), 64 (P.Baldesare/white woman); Photonica (M.Steinbacher/person in rock formation), 29 (Johner/ couple at a table); Courtesy of Pizza Hut Inc. p50 (Wirepix/pizza in space); Powerstock Superstock pp25 (couple), 151 (couple), 152 (couple); Reuters p56 (Nobel Prize), 91 (disaster); Robert Harding Picture Library pp89; 90–91 (earth); Roberstock.com p91 (L.Smith/ plane); Sally & Richard Greenhill pp45 (underground), 154 (Simon and baby), (Simon and siblings), 155 (couple with two children), (four adults), (large group); Science Photo Library p101 (T.McHugh/Diplodocus); Science & Society Picture Library p6 (Science Museum/glasses); Scotland in Focus p98 (R.G.Elliott/landscape); Still Digital p20 (Still Moving Picture Company/golf); Still Pictures p69 (R.Giling/ Lineair/African child), (M.Harvey/ rhino); By kind permission of Theodora Children's Trust, www.theodora.org pp18, 19; WWF/ www.panda.org p68 (logo); www.artcaragency.com p83 (H.Blank/Dennis Woodruff); Zefa pp33 (R.James /grandmother), 101 (P.Leonard/grandmother), 153 (Visual Media/ G.Rossenbach/town fountain); Janie Zohrer; p74 (young father and daughter)

Although every effort has been made to trace and contact copyright holders before publication, this has not been possible in some cases. We apologize for any apparent infringement of copyright and if notified, the publisher will be pleased to rectify any errors or omissions at the earliest opportunity.